FLINT HILLS COWBOYS

Flint Hills Cowboys

TALES FROM THE TALLGRASS PRAIRIE

JIM HOY

UNIVERSITY PRESS OF KANSAS

© 2006 by the University Press of Kansas
All rights reserved

Published by the University Press of Kansas (Lawrence, Kansas 66045), which was organized by the Kansas Board of Regents and is operated and funded by Emporia State University, Fort Hays State University, Kansas State University, Pittsburg State University, the University of Kansas, and Wichita State University

Library of Congress Cataloging-in-Publication Data

Hoy, James F.
  Flint Hills cowboys : tales from the tallgrass prairie / Jim Hoy.
     p.   cm.
  Includes bibliographical references and index.
  ISBN 978-0-7006-1456-1 (cloth : alk. paper)
  ISBN 978-0-7006-1758-6 (pbk. : alk. paper)
  1. Cowboys—Flint Hills (Kan. and Okla.)—History.
2. Cowboy—Flint Hills (Kan. and Okla.)—Social life and customs. 3. Ranch life—Flint Hills (Kan. and Okla.—History. 4. Flint Hills (Kan. and Okla.)—History. 5. Flint Hills (Kan. and Okla.)—Social life and customs. I. Title.
  F687.F55H69 2006
    978.1'88—dc22   2005035961

British Library Cataloguing-in-Publication Data is available.

Printed in the United States of America

10 9 8 7 6 5 4 3 2 1

The paper used in this publication is recycled and contains 30 percent postconsumer waste. It is acid free and meets the minimum requirements of the American National Standard for Permanence of Paper for Printed Library Materials Z39.48-1984.

FOR HENRY, LUCY, & JOSIE

Contents

I am getting into the range region . . . I am really West.

Vachel Lindsay, 1912, upon entering the Flint Hills of Chase County
after leaving Emporia on his walking trip across America

To a stockman from West Texas, where a cow has to
be a detective to find the next spear of grass,
the Flint Hills are simply unbelievable. He can hardly
imagine that there is that much grass in the world.

C.L. Sonnichsen, Cowboys and Cattle Kings

Acknowledgments

There are far too many people to list who have contributed to this book in one way or another. I appreciate especially the men and women of the Flint Hills who have shared their stories, many of whose names will appear in the text. I am grateful to Amanda Weaverling for constructing a map showing some of the sites mentioned, as well as to Virgil Dean of the Kansas State Historical Society for permission to print a revised and expanded Chapter 24, which earlier appeared in *Tallgrass Essays: Papers for the Symposium in Honor of Dr. Ramon Powers*. This book benefited greatly from the advice and suggestions of my wife, Cathy, and daughter, Farrell, as well as from those of University Press of Kansas staff members Hilary Lowe, Susan Schott, and Susan McRory. Finally, I would undoubtedly have spent another dozen years gathering stories and putting off writing without the periodic reminders of Nancy Jackson, who deserves thanks for both her patience and her prodding.

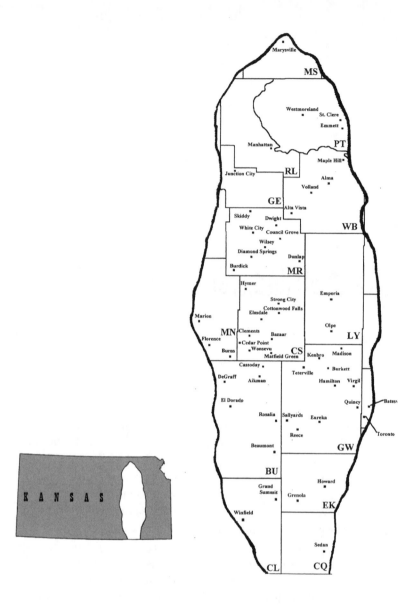

Marysville

MS

Westmoreland

St. Clere

Emmett

Manhattan

PT

Maple Hill

RL

Alma

Junction City

Volland

GE

Alta Vista

Skiddy

Dwight

White City

Council Grove

WB

Wilsey

Diamond Springs

Dunlap

Burdick

MR

Hymer

Emporia

Strong City

Cottonwood Falls

Elmdale

Olpe

Marion

MN

Clements

Bazaar

LY

Florence

Cedar Point

Burns

Wonsevu

CS

Matfield Green

Kenbro

Madison

Cassoday

Burkett

DeGraff

Aikman

Teterville

Hamilton

Virgil

El Dorado

Quincy

Bates

Rosalia

Sallyards

Eureka

Reece

Toronto

Beaumont

GW

BU

Howard

Grand Summit

Grenola

Winfield

EK

Sedan

CL

CQ

KANSAS

The Flint Hills-Bluestem Grazing Region of Kansas

Into the Hills: An Introduction

When I was growing up, my dad would sometimes say, "Let's drive down into the Hills and see so-and-so," or "Let's drive up in the Valley and see so-and-so." Now where in the world would anyone drive *down* into hills or *up* into a valley? The latter actually makes a little more sense, because the Valley was to the north of us (although what it was a valley of I don't know; it was not noticeably lower than the surrounding area and no river was close by). But the Flint Hills were formed by erosion, not upheaval, so if you live to the west of the Hills proper, as we did, you *do* drive down into them. Head east of Cassoday past the old Watkins Flats Pasture, and just beyond the old Coffelt place you'll drop down into the rugged terrain, the terraces and table-lands, of the Harsh Hill Pasture.

Another anomaly: Most of the rock in the Flint Hills is limestone, not flint. Even the flint is, to be technical, chert. But as a name, the Chert Hills just doesn't have the right ring to it, and the attempt a century ago to call them the Bluestem-Limestone Hills didn't catch on, either. Limestone might be the dominant rock, but it is the flint strata under the Hills, along with the surface rocks with hearts of flint encased by limestone, that give the Hills their character. The Hills themselves, along with less rugged areas bounding them on the east and west, are sometimes referred to as the Bluestem Grazing Region, or just the Bluestem.

The Flint Hills are America's last tallgrass prairie, an enclave of green set in the midst of the varicolored farmland of eastern Kansas. This country that spawned me is the best grazing land in the world, the home of the Big Beef Steer, to borrow the celebratory phrase of Rolla Clymer, longtime editor of the *Eldorado Times*, who was known for the purple prose of his laudatory editorials on the Hills. This is cowboy country. In my mind's eye I see the big old Texas steers of my youth, the open-range roads, the cattle guards, the railroad stockyards. I hear the click of horseshoes on flint rock and see the sparks from their hooves while riding home across nighttime pastures after loading cattle onto trains. And I also see the cattle pens, the flatbed pickups pulling gooseneck trailers, the potbelly semis that haul today's yearling cattle. I see grass-covered hilltops sloping down to limestone rimrocks. I see giant sycamores along clear-running streams and lone cottonwoods by the springs farther up the draws. There are deer along those streams, and coyotes and badgers sharing the grassland with mice, snakes, horny toads, gophers, and grasshoppers. Hawks and buzzards and an occasional eagle circle over the meadowlarks, prairie sparrows, plover, killdeer, and prairie chicken nesting in the grass. The grass. Above all, the grass: big bluestem, little bluestem, switch grass, and Indian grass; sideoats grama, eastern gamma, buffalo. Even more than the rock, grass—green gold—is the distinguishing feature, the life's blood, of the Flint Hills.

The Flint Hills had their origin in the Permian period over 250 million years ago when all of Kansas and the Central Plains were covered by a succession of huge inland seas, the drying up of which (to oversimplify the geologic process) created the Great Plains. The slope of the plains is gradual and occasionally interrupted, but insistent. Thus, you could theoretically run out of gas on top of Mount Sunflower in Wallace County (highest point in Kansas, with an altitude just over 4,000 feet) and coast southeast 380 miles as the crow flies, all the way to Coffeyville, some 3,200 feet lower.

Typical Flint Hills landscape. Pottawatomie County. (Kansas State Historical Society)

All the vales and swales that intervene would add a few speeding-ups and slowing-downs to the trip, but the real roller-coaster ride would come when you hit the Flint Hills somewhere between Burden and Grenola.

Those inland seas left behind not only a rich fossil history in the Flint Hills, but also large pools of oil. The El Dorado Pool was dramatically ushered in by famed Stapleton Number One in 1915, at the time the largest oil strike in the country; the Golden Fingers oil pools of Greenwood County were discovered about a decade later. At one time at least four refineries were running day and night in Butler County: two in El Dorado and one each in Potwin and Augusta. The bustling oil-boom towns of Butler and Greenwood counties, Midian and Oil Hill near El Dorado and Teterville, Thrall, Kenbro, and Burkett northwest of Eureka, are ghost towns today.

The limestone and flint have saved the Flint Hills from the plow. As an Osage chief once remarked, "The white man will have a hard time putting that iron thing in the ground here." That didn't keep settlers from trying, however. When my Grandmother Hoy's family, the Breidensteins, first came to Kansas, her father, August, bought a farm east of Rosalia. As my great-aunt Lilly (eldest and only unmarried Breidenstein sister) used to tell the story, the land agent was extolling the virtues of the property when her father pointed to a hillside half a mile away and wondered about the white objects he saw there.

"Why that s.o.b.!" the agent said indignantly, "I told him to get those sheep off of this place!"

Grandpa Breidenstein bought the farm, but those "sheep" are still there today. He soon moved the family from the rocky Flint Hills proper to the more gentle rolling prairie near DeGraff, then finally to Cassoday, where he farmed in the valley of the Walnut River.

On 12 September 1806 the first official American explorer to cross the Flint Hills, Zebulon Pike, stood on a hill above where Camp Creek runs into the Verdigris River in Chase County and while recording this scene in his journal unintentionally gave the Flint Hills their name: "Passed very ruff flint hills. My feet blistered and very sore. I stood on a hill and in one view below me saw buffalo, elk, deer, cabrie [pronghorn antelope], and panthers."

According to a Cowley County legend, Pike was far from the first non–American Indian to enter the Flint Hills. In 1537 Hernando de Soto, on his search for the Fountain of Youth, beat him by 269 years. Unfortunately, the story doesn't fit too well with the facts. (Not that facts have ever gotten in the way of a good legend.) De Soto, who was appointed governor of Cuba in 1538, didn't even reach the mainland of North America until 1539, and he got only as far as central Arkansas, or maybe eastern Oklahoma, before dying in 1542. Seems to me that a man who had discovered the Fountain of Youth five years earlier would not have died in his early forties. Not to mention that it was Ponce de Leon who was looking for the fountain; de Soto, like most Spaniards of his era, was seeking gold. De Soto's Fountain of Youth, by the way, still bubbles in Cowley County a few miles southwest of Winfield, where it is better known today as Geuda Springs.

Evidence of human activity in the Flint Hills goes back thousands of years. Clovis points, which date to some 13,000 years ago, have been found along the streams that flow through the Hills. In the early nineteenth century the southern Flint Hills were part of the hunting grounds of the Osage tribe, and the northern Hills were part of the territory controlled by the Kaw (or Kansa, the "people of the south wind" for whom the state is named).

Except for four years of graduate school in Columbia, Missouri, I have lived in the Flint Hills region all my life. My boyhood was spent at Cassoday, Cow Capital of Kansas, and since 1970 I have taught English at Emporia State University. Although I was trained as a medievalist, most of my research and part of my teaching since the mid-1970s have been on ranching and cowboy folklife with a special interest in the Flint Hills. Happily, I have been able to combine my scholarly life with my personal life, to merge writing with riding.

The riding started early. By the time I was six years old, I was helping my father drive cattle for Frank Klasser, who lived near Flint Ridge a dozen or so miles southeast of Cassoday. Klasser was a pastureman, a distinctive Flint Hills occupation. In other words, he pastured other people's cattle on his ranch, receiving them in the spring of the year and shipping them all out by the fall. This custom grazing of transient cattle (i.e., cattle raised somewhere else, then sent on to market or the feedlot after a summer on Flint Hills grass) is one of three hallmarks of Flint Hills ranching. A second major feature of Flint Hills folklife is the annual spring burn-off of the dead grass from the previous year, a colorful ritual that was carried over by ranchers from the Kaw practice of wrapping rawhide thongs around a large ball of dead grass, setting it afire, then dragging it horseback at full run across the prairie. The final feature is a mix of farming and ranching. Whereas in most of the ranching West the average annual rainfall ranges from fifteen inches down to single digits, the Flint Hills get over thirty inches, easily enough to raise crops in the fertile, rock-free bottomlands of the streams that cross the Hills. There's a song in the musical *Oklahoma!* that goes something like the farmer and the cowboy can be friends. In the Flint Hills the farmer and the cowboy can be, and often are, the same person, a farmer-stockman who might well drive a tractor one day and ride a horse the next, raising both cattle and crops.

Creepfeeder and windmill in Butler County.

The pastureman (some of whom are women), sometimes referred to as a custom grazier, is a go-between who serves and deals
with both pasture owners and cattle owners. The pastureman may
or may not be a rancher with land and cattle of his own, but in the
parlance of the Flint Hills he "runs cattle" and "looks after grass."
Sometimes, like Frank Klasser, he owns pastures and takes in other
people's cattle rather than buying or raising his own. Sometimes he
is contracted by a cattle owner or a pasture owner to care for cattle
at so much per head. Sometimes he leases grass from a landowner,
then "fills" it with steers or heifers from a cattle owner, making
his money from the difference between the lease and the sublease
prices. Often landowner and cattle owner never meet. Sometimes
even the landowner or the cattle owner and a pastureman don't
meet. A landowner's heirs sometimes, in essence, inherit a pastureman along with a pasture, and sometimes a pastureman with a
good reputation will get hired by telephone from a cattleman he
has never met in person. Sometimes pasturing deals are sealed with
a handshake; sometimes there are signed contracts.

The late Phill Pinkston, one of four brothers (now all dead) who ran cattle for some half a century, once told me that he and his brothers (Gib, Windy, and Slim) looked after 10,000 steers each year scattered throughout 40,000 acres in four counties (Lyon, Chase, Butler, and Greenwood). During grazing season, Phill said, they tried to be in each pasture at least once a week. About the only day they took off was the Fourth of July to go to Countryman's Rodeo. Betty Pinkston, widow of Phill, handled the paperwork on this operation, dealing with as many as thirty-eight different cattle owners and thirty-two different pasture owners. Sometimes, she said, in the first year or two with a new owner there would be formal contracts, and often after that the arrangements would be made with a handshake or over the phone. Dusty Anderson of Skiddy, on the edge of Morris and Geary counties, once ran an operation that spanned nine counties. He did it partly by airplane (a technique other pasturemen have also employed, although rarely), partly by having cowboys he could subcontract some of the work to, and partly by being constantly on the go throughout pasture season. It was not unusual, he told me, to wear out two or three horses a day. He kept spare horses in pastures where he had cattle, and when he needed a fresh mount he would catch one and turn his jaded horse loose to be caught and used another day. Chris Locke, who looks after pastures in Butler and Greenwood counties, told me that he easily puts over a hundred thousand miles a year on his pickup trucks.

In this triumvirate of landowner, cattle owner, and pastureman, each has specific duties. The landowner is responsible for paying taxes and paying for major capital improvements, such as new fences, stock pens, or ponds. The cattle owner must provide transportation for his livestock to and from the pasture, pay for any special feeding needs or veterinary expenses, and pay the pasture bill when the cattle are shipped at the end of the season. The pastureman is responsible each spring for repairing fences and water gaps (a troublesome spot where the fence line crosses a stream or draw and is often washed out after a big rain) and for burning pasture. After he receives the cattle, he is responsible for looking after them and providing routine medical care (such as "doctoring," i.e., treating animals for pinkeye or foot rot) during the grazing season, for providing adequate salt and access to good water, and for providing a crew to gather the cattle at shipping time. Traditionally, the pasture-man was responsible for the "count." In other words, if he received 2,000 cattle in the spring, he had to produce enough live cattle or the bones or the brands cut from the hides of dead ones to equal the 2,000 placed in his care. If he could not, then he had to pay for each animal, at the average value per head minus the pasture bill, that had strayed or been stolen and thus could not be accounted for at shipping time.

Because of the central importance of the cattle industry here, I divide Flint Hills cultural history into three eras, each one associated with the way cattle are transported into the Hills. The earliest of these segments, the Trail Drive Era, effectively began in 1854 when Kansas Territory was opened for settlement, although there had been oxen grazing in the Flint Hills at various times since the Santa Fe Trail opened in 1821. During the great overland cattle drives from 1867 to the mid-1880s, many Texas longhorns grazed on Flint Hills grass before being sent on to market by train from cow towns such as Abilene, Ellsworth, and Wichita.

The Trail Drive Era began to give way to the Railroad Era in the later 1870s, but it was not until 1887 that the Atchison, Topeka, and Santa Fe railroad ran a spur south a dozen miles from Strong City and thus transformed the Chase County hamlet of Bazaar into the major cattle shipping point on the entire line, a distinction it would hold until 1923, when the line was extended south through Matfield Green and Cassoday, the honor then transferring to the latter town. Although a few herds were still being trailed overland as the Gay Nineties began (and, in fact, some cattle would be trailed into Flint Hills pastures as late as the 1930s), the Trail Drive Era had effectively come to an end by 1890.

After World War II, flatbed semi-trailers began to be used for the long-distance hauls that brought cattle from their home pastures in Texas to their summer quarters in the Hills, but it was the introduction sometime around 1960 of the triple-decker "pot belly" trailer, combined with the desire of the railroads to get out of the often nettlesome cattle shipping business, that firmly established the third period of Flint Hills history, the Trucking Era. By the late 1950s and early 1960s, trucks were taking on more and more of the shipping business, and by the mid-1970s most of the stockyards in the Flint Hills were not only abandoned, but torn down. Today there are railroad stockyards in various stages of disrepair still standing at Matfield Green, Diamond Springs, and Sallyards, but most of them, including the giants among railroad shipping pens at Bazaar and Cassoday, at Grand Summit and Volland, at Hamilton and Root Station, at Virgil and Batesville, have been torn down, the heavy creosote-soaked lumber and posts salvaged or burned.

Two major changes in Flint Hills cattle handling roughly coincided with the transition from trains to trucks. One was the move toward younger cattle, and the other was double stocking. During the 1960s and 1970s, as the public preference for more tender beef was increasing, yearling cattle became more and more common in the Hills, replacing the three- and four-year-olds that had dominated during most of the Railroad Era. At about the same time experiments in double stocking proved successful enough so that as of the twenty-first century, the majority of summer cattle in the Flint Hills are double stocked.

In the Railroad Era a big, aged steer would be allowed four to five acres over the six-month grazing season (normally from mid-April to mid-October). Thus a pasture of a thousand acres would be stocked with from 200 to 250 steers. Yearlings, however, have smaller appetites than older cattle, so that same pasture, at three acres per yearling, could handle 333 steers. With double stocking, twice as many cattle are placed on that thousand-acre pasture, but are taken off after 90 days rather than staying on for the full six months. The grass, which would be clipped short during the abbreviated grazing season, will recover with a late summer rain or two and grow tall enough to be burned the following spring. This system, if scrupulously adhered to, has several advantages, among them that the cattle will be on the pasture when the grass is the most palatable and the most nutritious. This is also the time of year when rainfall is most abundant, which means the greatest growth of grass, all of which result in good weight gains on the cattle. One of the potential disadvantages of double stocking is the threat of an exceptionally dry May and June, which could result in damage to the grass. Also, in good weather when the grass in late July or early August is still abundant, there is the temptation, sometimes exacerbated by a weak market, to leave the cattle on the pasture for an extra week or two, again with damage to the grass. Although I was skeptical of double stocking when I first heard of the practice in the early 1970s, I now believe that, if the schedule is strictly adhered to, the system can be a good one.

With cattle and ranchers come cowboys, and the Flint Hills have produced good cowboys, both the ranch and the rodeo variety. Cowboys are good storytellers, and their work gives them plenty of good material for stories. Along about 1980 I developed a course in Flint Hills folklife, a class in which we mix classroom instruction with field trips to the farms, ranches, and small towns of the Flint Hills. We learn about some of the interesting people who are part of Flint Hills history: Charles Curtis, who was reared by his grandmother on the Kaw Reservation in Morris County and became vice president of the United States, the highest political office in U.S. government ever achieved by anyone of American Indian ancestry; Perry Lowery, "The Ragtime Kid," son of ex-slaves and a world-renowned cornet player from Greenwood County, who received a gold cornet from the king of England; Judge Granville Aikman of Butler County, who impaneled the first all-woman jury in America; Doctor John Brinkley, medical pioneer and jury-certified quack, who opened a branch of his virility-restoring clinic (transplanting goat-testicle tissue into impotent men) in Butler County. We visit local museums in Flint Hills counties, we read century-old newspapers from Flint Hills towns, and we meet with men and women who have spent much or all of their lives in the Flint Hills. Over the years I have also taped interviews with many of these men and women. In the early 1990s Tom Eddy and I began taking students into the Flint Hills in covered wagons for a weekend summer school class. The Flint Hills Overland Wagon Train supplies the wagons and the food, Tom handles the ethno-botany, and I give the participants a crash course in the history and folklore of the Hills. Developing these classes, conducting research (both field and library), interviewing, and learning from my students have provided the impetus, the background, and much of the material for this book. Much also comes from my own experience in working cattle, breaking horses, rodeoing, knowing the people, and otherwise living life in the Flint Hills.

The Flint Hills have their quirks and peculiarities, their drawbacks, and even their detractors, but they are my home country. My roots here are as deep as those of bluestem grass in black-soil bottomland. I cling to this country as tenaciously as wildflowers cling to rocky hillsides. I feed on the stories of the Hills and the characters who tell them as the cattle feed on the grasses.

Thus this book derives both from a quarter of a century of teaching and research and from a lifetime of experience. My intent is to convey both information about and a feeling—my feeling—for the Flint Hills. As a result, the book is part memoir, part history, part ethnography. Founded in scholarship, it is intended to be informally informative, not scholarly. In most instances I have tried to write the stories as I heard them or as I would tell them, and even in those pieces with a more formal tone I occasionally insert some memory or experience of my own. I hope that the stories and the descriptions in this book will add to the enjoyment and understanding of the Bluestem Grazing Region, for I think one can best know an area from the lives of the ordinary people who live there, from the tools and work methods they use to cope with their environment, and from the stories they think important enough to pass down.

The primary focus of *Flint Hills Cowboys* is the cattle culture of the Flint Hills. Other authors could write about the farming culture or the oil culture or the small towns of the Flint Hills. But I was reared among cattle and horses, ranchers and cowboys, pasture work and rodeos, and these are the Hills that I know and these are the stories I have heard.

This paean to the Flint Hills is my thanks to the land that has nurtured my life and nourished my soul.

Part one

Flint Hills Cowboys

E.C. Roberts, Strong City. (Chase County Historical Society)

One

Granville and John

I never knew the Badger brothers, but I sure wish I had. These two old bachelors lived near Elk on the western edge of Chase County, and the country around there is still full of stories about them. John was six years old, Granville eight when their parents moved from Wind Fall, Indiana, to Chase County in 1882. Granville was ninety when he died in 1964, outliving his younger brother by seven years. I'm not sure how Granville died, but John had a heart attack while working on a windmill at their home place and was found on the ground at the base. More than one man has pointed out that windmill tower to me, a sense of awe still in his voice half a century later, for John and his brother are legendary. Part of that legend is that they were only ten and twelve when their father died after just five years in the Flint Hills, and they took over watching after the cattle he was pasturing. Another version says they were sixteen and eighteen, still plenty young to become the breadwinners for their mother and three sisters and begin dealing with Texas cattlemen and Flint Hills landowners. But the following year, 1893, they handled leases, patched fences, burned pastures, received cattle, looked after them during the summer, and shipped them in the fall. And they continued looking after other people's cattle for the rest of their lives.

The late Jim Cauthorn, a kind and gentle man who lived on the old Wiley Ranch (now Five Oaks Ranch, the home of John and Annie Browning Wilson), was their neighbor in their later years. Of the various stories he told me about them, one of my favorites is about how he hated to find himself behind them on the road, for the brothers drove very slowly and Jim considered it disrespectful to pass them. (Attitudes have definitely changed!) Any frustration he felt about poking along, though, was soon dissipated by watching the reactions of the two old men as they meandered along the curves of Middle Creek Road, looking here, pointing there, talking to each other, heads nodding and shaking animatedly. "It was just like they'd never been on that road before in their lives, everything looked so fresh and new to them," Jim said. What a tribute to the beauty of the Flint Hills and to the temperaments of these men.

Both men were good with cattle and horses, although it was John who worked full time in the pastures while Granville kept up the home place, in addition to helping out during receiving and shipping season. During the winter they would make rawhide quirts, cutting strips of salted, stretched, and cured calf hide, which they braided around handles of turkey leg bones. According to Granville and John, a man might as well be undressed as to ride without a quirt. They made scores of quirts over the years, giving many of them away to neighborhood youngsters—I've been shown some of them by men now in their sixties and seventies.

Every morning John would mount his horse before dawn and head northeast across country to Diamond Creek near Hymer, where he rode pastures for Charley Lipps, a wealthy Texan with extensive holdings in the Flint Hills. At night he would ride back home, a routine he repeated daily during pasture season. The late Glen Pickett, long-time executive secretary of the Kansas Livestock Association, was reared at Hymer and told me how he and some of his friends would hang around the stockyards after school, hoping to be asked to help drive the steers to grass. These aged steers tended to be very thin, some so weak they could hardly stand. On

John and Granville Badger as young men. (Chase County Historical Society)

weekends, Pickett said, he and his friends would sometimes ride out into the pastures and rope a weak and wobbly steer just for practice, then turn him loose. He quit when one day the skinny steer he had roped, invigorated by the Kansas sun and the rich new bluestem grass he had been eating, turned out to be full of life. Just like Windy Bill's saddle in the old cowboy folksong, young Glen saw his dad's new rope "go driftin' down the draw." Glen told me, "I was worried sick about telling him, but he didn't punish me. Not physically, that is. He just said, 'What are you going to tell John Badger when he wants to know why his steer is dragging a rope around?'"

Except for going into town, the Badger brothers rode horseback everywhere they went. After loading cattle late at night at Hymer, on Diamond Creek, John and Granville would head out across pastures to their home on Middle Creek. I've been told that they knew the country so well that even on a moonless night under a cloudy sky, they could ride across a thousand-acre pasture and always hit the gate on the far side. Bill Shumate told me about a time in the early 1950s when he was fixing fence as John came riding by on his way home. (John would often, I've heard, manage to be riding by Shumate's, or some other neighbor's house, just about supper time and rarely turned down an invitation to come in and eat. Apparently he didn't share Granville's alleged culinary enthusiasm for crackers and grapes and sardines.) Bill and John visited a while, then Bill told John, "Why don't you jump your horse in the back of the pickup with mine, and I'll haul you home?" This was long before stock trailers had come into use on farms and ranches, and even pickups with stockracks were just coming into vogue.

"Oh, no," John said, "My horse wouldn't do that."

"Nonsense," Bill told him, "that horse was shipped up from the Texas ranch. I'll bet he's been hauled all over the Panhandle." Bill opened the tailgate, and John's horse jumped right in. But all the way to the Badger house, he told me, John rode slouched down in the seat with his hat held up in front of his face in embarrassment, afraid that someone would see him riding in a pickup, hauling his horse instead of riding it as ordained by God and Nature.

One reason Charley Lipps employed the Badger brothers was because they saved him money, not just in wages but in the way they worked—long hours and scrimping on supplies. They were as parsimonious with their boss's millions as with their own nickels and dimes. If a fence could be patched with skinny posts and rusted wire, so much the better. Perhaps my favorite Badger story is about the time the brothers were working some cattle in the Hymer stockyards and the cattle owner drove up in a new Cadillac. He stepped out of the car with his expensive Boss-of-the-Plains Stetson hat on his head and a pair of shiny custom-made boots on his feet. He strapped some big-roweled silver-mounted spurs on the heels, then buckled on a pair of fancy chaps with his brand embossed on the belt and walked out into the pen toward a horse that was tied to the fence.

"I don't think you can ride that horse," John said quietly.

"Why not?" was the reply. "I own him, don't I? He's my horse, isn't he?" And he got on, stuck those big rowels into the horse's sides, and immediately flew through the air when the horse broke in two. As he lay flat on the ground, gasping for air, John Badger ambled up to him, stuck a boot toe in his ribs, and said, "See there, you son-of-a-bitch, I told you you couldn't ride him."

Now I have my doubts about the total veracity of this story, especially since John reputedly didn't cuss. The strongest word anyone ever heard either him or Granville use was to call something a "peckerwood." As in the time they were pulling a windmill one spring to put in new leathers before pasture season began. Wrapped around the pipe just above water level were several blacksnakes, immobilized by the cold. As the sunshine warmed the snakes, they unwrapped themselves from the pipe lying on the ground and began moving back toward the well. John felt something tapping on his leg as he was putting the cylinder back together, and he looked down to see a big old blacksnake butting against him. He casually tossed the snake aside with the handle of the pipe wrench, saying "Get out of here, you peckerwood."

So I don't know whether or not this fifty-dollar-a-month hired hand actually called a millionaire rancher a son-of-a-bitch, but no other incident I've ever heard of is more illustrative of the independent spirit of the cowboy. Besides, whatever the nature of the interchange, the Badger brothers were too valuable to be fired.

A few years ago Howard Collett gave me a pair of batwing chaps he'd bought at the auction that followed the death of Granville Badger. I have them hanging in my tack room, and whenever I get

Granville and John Badger in the 1950s. (Chase County Historical Society)

to feeling a little too worthy for my own good, I go take a look at them and remind myself of a real Flint Hills cowboy.

Much of the time period during which I've been collecting oral histories from the Flint Hills has overlapped with the contemporary upsurge in cowboy poetry that began in 1985 with the first Cowboy Poetry Gathering in Elko, Nevada, which sparked a revival of versifying by cowboys (and would-be cowboys) throughout the West. The movement that began in Elko brought to light a tradition of cowboy poetry in the Flint Hills. When a year later I first encountered Lou Hart's poem, "Springtime at Crockers," I was reminded of the poems my dad recited—"The Ride of Jennie McNeal," "Sheridan's Ride," and "Charlotte the Frozen Girl"—as we rode pastures. Then in 1990 I helped organize a cowboy poetry gathering, which was held at the middle school in Strong City. Some of the younger poets (Jerry Wright, Tom McBeth) had probably been inspired by Elko to write about the cowboy life, while

John Markley had actually been writing about his veterinarian experiences before Elko. What was really gratifying was to hear the life experiences that had been put into verse by a couple of old-time cowboys, Wilbur Countryman and Jack Hurlburt. All these influences encouraged me to write some verse of my own about interesting Flint Hills characters such as the Badger brothers and, in the next chapter, Elmer Cooper.

In the Days of Granville and John

Oh the days of Granville and John are past
Never to come again,
And we won't see the likes of times like theirs
In the current affairs of men.

Now Granville and John were bachelor brothers
Who lived high up Middle Creek,
Where the grass grows tall and the steers get fat
And the streams run clear and deep.

Their daddy had helped to fence the Flint Hills
At the end of the open range
When cattle that once trod the Old Chisholm Trail
Now arrived on the Santa Fe trains,

Shipped up from Texas or New Mexico
Or the swamps of Louisiane,
Lean, four-year-old steers as tall as a horse,
But no wider than your hand.

Tail up the sick ones out of the cars,
Get them out in the pasture and sun,
By the Fourth of July they'll be fat as a pup
On the grass of the Hundred and One.

Now John rode the pastures and looked out for strays
While Granville hauled salt and kept house
And cooked in a skillet of cold bacon grease
All filled with the tracks of a mouse.

"Nothing at all to worry about,"
He'd say in a slow kind of way,
"Just turn on the fire and let her get warm
And those tracks will soon go away."

No, fine dining was not what you'd get at their house
And to them their work was their fun,
With no call to spend much of the hundred a month
They were paid by the One-Oh-One.

For what better life than a cowboy's life,
Plain, without any frills?
And what better life for a single man
Than a horse and a song in the Hills?

Squeeze chutes were unknown to Granville and John;
They worked with a horse and a rope.
It was a pleasure to see them drag calves to the fire,
Or ride along home at a lope.

Shipping time was when Granville and John
Were at their peak and their prime.
They could gather a herd of the spookiest steers
And never leave one behind.

They could ride across pastures on the darkest of nights
And always come out at the gate,
And if you helped ship, I'll tell you for sure,
You sure didn't get to sleep late.

On shipping mornings they'd gather a crew
And start for the pasture at three,
Then sit on their horses an hour, or two,
'Til there was enough light to see.

Now why they didn't just wait at the barn
Or stay a bit longer in bed
Is a question you might as well not even ask;
They'd be jogging too far ahead.

They'd round up the cattle on top of a hill
And cut out five loads of the best,
Then head 'em for Hymer with John in the lead
While Granville counted the rest.

Their horses weren't fancy; their saddles were plain,
But they always got the job done.
And owner or buyer, you got a fair count
In the days of Granville and John.

Now the trains no longer haul cattle to grass
And the stockyards have all been torn down,
Replaced by goosenecks and portable pens
That would have made Granville frown.

For how can you train a horse to watch cows
If he rides in a trailer all day?
And how can you have any worth to your life
If you use a machine to load hay?

If your work is your life, then what better life
Than to ride the Flint Hills in the dawn?
And what better time to have lived in the Hills
Than the days of Granville and John.

But the days of Granville and John have passed
Never to come again,
And seldom today will anyone see
The likes of these good men.

Two

Elmer Cooper

lmer Cooper was the kind of fellow that people told good stories about, and like a lot of the Flint Hills old-timers I've known, Elmer told a good story himself. In 1980, I drove into the wide-open country of eastern Chase County to interview Elmer, about half a dozen years before he died at age ninety-one. He was in his mid-eighties at the time, pretty well stoved up and hobbling around in his house several miles south of Saffordville. Again like a lot of old-timers I've heard, he couldn't say three words without cussing, but he was a good storyteller and his mind was tack sharp as he recalled horses and cowboys he had known.

"Vic Kirk, now he was a tough one," Elmer told me. "I saw him at one of these pasture rodeos and the horse broke away from the snubber when Vic was only half on. He had the rein in one hand, the other on the saddle horn, and his foot in the stirrup when the

Unidentified wild cow milker, Countryman's Rodeo, 1950s.

bronc broke loose and started bucking. But he pulled himself up into the saddle and won."

Elmer didn't say much about his own riding, but I know from talking to others that he had a reputation of sticking to the bad ones. His eldest son, Puncher, inherited some of his dad's ability. Puncher either won or placed high in the saddle bronc riding at the first national high school rodeo, and as a small kid I remember him making some good rides at the Flint Hills Rodeo in Strong City. Puncher told me that when he was young and single he took a job on a New Mexico ranch. When winter came, they put him out at a line camp all by himself to look after the cattle there. Every month a truck would come by the line shack and throw out a big sack of groceries, never even slowing down, much less stopping. The reason for this, Puncher said, was that the driver might have infected Puncher with a cold, and if he had gotten sick there was no way for him to call for help or get to a doctor. It was the loneliest four months of his life, and when spring came he drew his pay and headed back to the Flint Hills where he has raised good quarter horses on his ranch north of Saffordville for as long as I can remember.

I remember seeing Pete Cooper, another of Elmer's sons, ride saddle broncs at Countryman's Rodeo. He was a colorful fellow with a big handlebar mustache, a neckerchief, and Blucher boots, and he always wore a white shirt. Not too long ago Tom Miller told me about the time Pete took a job on a big ranch down in the Osage Hills of Oklahoma. He was just a teenager at the time, and when he first arrived on the ranch the hands there, in typical cowboy fashion, decided to put the kid through a humorous initiation. Now each cowboy on the ranch was provided a string of seven horses, the top one a good, well broke cow horse. The next two were decent mounts with plenty of miles under the saddle, well on their way to becoming good cow horses. The next three were young horses, green broke and usually bronky. The seventh, however, was wild—an outlaw recently run in from the blackjack oak country of the Osage Reservation, four or five years old, and untouched by human hands. "Never saw a human being since they were weaned," was the way Tom put it.

On Pete's first morning the other hands told him about the horse situation and that he could start out on his top horse so he could kind of get a feel for the job and get acquainted with the pastures before he had to ride one of the less well trained horses. The horse they had run into the corral, however, was his seventh. When Pete's rope went around his neck, the horse turned inside out, kicking and lunging and rearing and squealing. Pete finally got him snubbed up close enough on the snubbing post to get his saddle strapped on. When he swung into the saddle, the horse really came apart, making the preliminary ruckus seem tame. The horse leaped high, he sunfished, he bucked blind and splintered corral poles. Pete eventually got the horse's head pulled up out from between his front legs, circled him around the corral a couple of times, then pulled him to a stop. As the dust finally cleared and the outlaw stood panting and quivering, the other cowboys told Pete it was just a joke, that this was the worst horse in his string, not the best. "Why, hell," said Pete, "this horse is just like all the ones I ride at home. Open the gate and let's get to work."

But back to Elmer, and his riding ability:

Some horses pitch, and some just hop,
and some will flat out buck.
It helps to know which one does which,
not just rely on luck.

Now Elmer Cooper was an honest man;
he could ride anything with a hide.
If he said, "Why, anybody can ride him,"
you could get right on and ride,

But you better take a good strong hold,
deep down in your old saddle tree,
If Elmer shook his head and drawled,
"Well, he never has thrown me."

Not many horses ever did.

When he was around eleven or twelve years old, Elmer's father took him along on a horse-buying trip to Miami, Oklahoma. After making the purchase, Ide put his young son in charge of driving the herd back to Cedar Point while he went on down to Tulsa on other business. Elmer headed home with the horses, camping out along the way. He never got lost, he told me, because whenever he got a little uncertain of his direction, he'd stop at a farm house and ask which way it was to Chase County. "They'd point," Elmer said, "and I'd head that way."

More than six decades later, long after he'd moved to the Saffordville country, if Elmer had a steer or a cow that he wanted to sell at the Emporia livestock auction, he wouldn't borrow a neighbor's truck or his son's pickup and trailer to haul the critter. Instead he'd mount his horse and head the steer east, driving him across

pastures, down lanes, and along back roads until he got to the sale
barn on the west side of town. No wonder the country is full of
Elmer Cooper stories.

Elmer Cooper was an old-time hand,
He could drive cattle and read a dim brand,
Ride any horse that ever grew hair,
Fix water gaps and do windmill repair.
But age will get anybody down
And one day Elmer came to town,
Hobbling around on a leg that was sore,
To buy some oats at the old feed store.

"Why, Elmer," one of the young bucks said,
"We were beginning to think that you were dead
And the coyotes had carried your bones away.
How's things in the Flint Hills, anyway?"
"Oh, ever'thing's fine but this blamed right leg,"
Elmer said as he sat on an old nail keg.
"I surely don't know what's wrong with it, lad,
But I can hardly move, it hurts so bad."

"Why that's no mystery," said the feed-store man
As he spit some tobacco juice in a can.
"Sounds to me like the rheumatiz;
It's just old age, that's all it is."
"No," he drawled, "I don't think so.
My right leg hurts clean down to my toe,
And ever' time I walk it shoots pain to my hip—
But my left leg's just as old, and it don't hurt a bit."

Three

Black Cowboys in the Flint Hills

A few years back I did some research on black cowboys during the open-range period, the results of which certainly don't square with the image presented by the popular media. According to the movie version of reality on the Great Plains, an occasional black would sometimes hire on as cook for a roundup or a trail-driving crew; otherwise the cinema prairie, except for some Indian or Mexican villains, was as monochromatic as the driven snow. In real life, however, African Americans did everything there was to do in the West. Many of them were indeed cooks, but many others were regular ranch cowboys. There were black trail bosses, mustangers, horse breakers, rodeo performers, jockeys, horseshoers, outlaws, cavalrymen, herders, drovers, and ranchers.

Kansas, present at the creation of the Great American Cowboy, has had some experience with black cowboys, most of them as unsung as their counterparts in the rest of the plains region. The earliest black cowboys came into Kansas with the trail drives. George Glenn, for instance, helped Bob Johnson drive cattle to Abilene in 1870. While there his boss (and former master) died, thereby commencing a string of circumstances that immortalized Glenn among the old-time Texas trail drivers. In September, two months after Johnson's death, Glenn had the body disinterred and loaded onto a Studebaker wagon. He then set out for Columbus, Texas, a trip of forty-two days, sleeping each night in the horse-drawn wagon beside the casket while transporting Johnson's body back home for burial beside his wife.

Another black trail driver, Al Jones, made eight trips with cattle to Kansas, seven of them as a trail boss for Kenedy and King of King Ranch fame in South Texas. Glenn's accomplishment is more sensational, but I have a feeling, considering the racism of the time, that Jones's was more difficult.

Of the few black cowboys in Kansas that I know much at all about, most were active in the Flint Hills in the late nineteenth and early twentieth centuries. Bill Pickett, for example, bulldogged a steer with his teeth at the Burdick Field Day rodeo in 1915. Pickett appeared there, I am told, at the invitation of Bob Woods, a black roper and bronc rider who lived just west of Strong City and whose skill with horses and cattle won him the respect of his fellow Flint Hills cowhands (as a group probably not that much more culturally enlightened than their drover forebears). Woods apparently had a wit as sharp as it was quick. One spring while burning pasture, a young coworker remarked, rather insensitively: "That pasture's about as black as you are, Bob." To which Woods replied: "Might be, but in a couple of weeks it'll be as green as you are." I haven't been able to learn much more about Woods, but I have gathered some stories about a couple of other black hands—Bill Brewer and Gene Lowery.

William Martin Brewer arrived at Hamilton in Greenwood County behind a herd of horses in 1869 or 1870, a teenager from Kentucky (he was born 25 February 1854) with "slave marks" (whip scars) on his back. Between the time of his arrival and his death on 14 November 1938, Bill Brewer lived a life of one adventure after another, according to the stories that Bill Browning (a physician and member of the well-known ranching family near Madison) has collected and generously shared with me.

Perhaps the horses Bill Brewer helped drive into Hamilton were delivered to a rancher named Johnson, for he gave Bill his first job, which was to help another cowboy hunt for unbranded cattle and burn Johnson's brand on them, no matter whose herd they were running in. The Flint Hills were open range at that time, and this method of livestock acquisition is said to have made Johnson rich.

For whatever reason (perhaps his conscience, for later on Bill was well known for his sense of fair play), Bill quit Johnson a year or two later and went to work for a rancher named Jackson a few miles west of Madison, staying with him until Jackson's death in the 1890s. Jackson was a large man, too fat to ride a horse, so he went around his ranch in a buggy, taking with him a hired boy whose job it was to open and shut gates. The problem was that once the kid had the gate open, Jackson would drive through at a trot and never stop or look back, so the boy had to run hard to catch up, especially if the gate happened to be a difficult one to close. "We'll fix that," Brewer said when he learned of the kid's problem. The cure—it took only one lesson—was simple: Bill tied a long lariat rope to the back axle of the buggy and told the boy, "Just drop the loop on the post the next gate you go through."

In the later 1890s James Bradfield, who ranched on the Verdigris River near the Lyon-Greenwood county line, found Bill shining shoes at the Cattleman's Hotel in Eureka. Bradfield figured that Bill was too good a hand with livestock to waste his time with shoe polish, so he offered to build Bill a house on the ranch and provide him a living in his old age in return for his labor. The house was small but adequate, and the deal seemed a good one, especially to a black man in his mid-forties with no family. Bill lived to be eighty-four, surviving Bradfield, whose own heirs, unfortunately, went broke, so Bill spent his last years in the Heritage, the euphemistic name for the county poor farm in Emporia.

One of Bill's jobs with the Bradfields was to herd sheep. He was especially proud of his sheepdog and had a standing $100 bet that no one could hide a sheep that his dog couldn't find. Once in Madison a man climbed a utility pole with a lamb and tied it to the top. Bill's dog ran around and around, circling in on the pole and treeing the lamb like a bluetick on a raccoon.

There was no attempt to welsh on the bet, for Bill was a big man with an even bigger reputation as a fighter. At age sixty-eight he boxed to raise money for the Olpe school, but many of his fights were for his own protection, not for an exhibition benefit. Once, for example, two men threatened to throw him in the Verdigris River. They both went home wet. Another time two other men decided to throw him out of a dance (Bill played the bass fiddle and the bones for many country dances). Bill grabbed the first one by the seat of the pants and the nape of the neck and tossed him through the window. The second followed in like fashion almost before the broken glass had hit the ground. Bill also monitored other fights, and these in the days when Madison was as rough an oil-boom town as any in the West. One brawler pulled a knife on his opponent, but quickly tossed it aside when Bill told him, "Put that knife in your pocket or you'll eat it blade first."

There are many more Bill Brewer stories—stories about bootleg whiskey, his prowess as a cook (roast turkey, mountain oysters, and snapping turtle were three specialties), his success as a poker player (which is how he earned a living at the Heritage after he had to leave the Bradfield ranch), and his acceptance, such as it was, in an all-white community (he was the only black allowed in Madison during this time period; he would enter the house of a white person only upon extreme and repeated urging; and he was called "Nigger Bill" by almost everyone). But above all else Bill Brewer was a ranch hand. He could make a team of balky mules behave just by talking to (or sometimes yelling at) them, and he could ride any bucking horse in the area. As one old-timer put it, "I don't think anybody in this country would ever tell you they saw him thrown from a horse."

Back in the 1880s another black cowboy from Greenwood County, known only as Nigger John, had an equally good reputation as a bucking-horse rider. He also had a proclivity to boast about his abilities, a trait that can irritate the peers of any cowboy, black or white. Other cowboys in the area searched high and low for a horse that would stop his bragging. They found one that had never been ridden, an outlaw so mean that the rancher said he'd give the horse to anyone who could ride him. A day and time was set for the big contest, and people came to Eureka from all over the county to watch the action. They were not disappointed by what is still considered the rankest ride ever undertaken in Greenwood County. Nigger John stayed with the horse through every twist and turn, every duck and dive that the outlaw could throw at him. The horse bucked for over fifteen minutes, and when he finally stopped John was bleeding from the nose and both ears. The bleeding continued for two days, but the horse was tamed, his critics were silenced, and John was the proud owner of a fine new horse.

I doubt if any cowboy—black or white, from Kansas or anywhere else—was any better than Gene Lowery. Gene died too young at age forty-three on 5 February 1922, but he is still remembered and talked about by ranchers in eastern Butler and western Greenwood counties. The Lowery family came to Kansas from Ohio after the Civil War, part of the small settlement of former slaves on Spring Creek near Reece. Perry Lowery, Gene's uncle, became a world-renowned musician who was bandmaster for the Ringling Brothers Circus Sideshow Band (black musicians were not allowed to play under the Big Top), had his own brass band that toured the country in a Pullman railroad car, and was presented a gold cornet by King Edward VII of England. Gene himself played tuba in the family band before becoming a cowboy, working on ranches in the Eureka-Rosalia vicinity. At the time of his death Lowery was foreman for the Stanhope-Greg cattle syndicate. He was an expert reader of brands and had earned the confidence of cattlemen in Texas, Oklahoma, and New Mexico, as well as in Kansas. Sherman Cornett, who wrote his obituary for the *Eureka Herald*, stated that Lowery had undoubtedly "handled more cattle in the past 25 years than any other one man in the state of Kansas, and he has accounted for every hoof." That is, he either produced a live beef or the brand from a dead one at shipping time—no strays escaped his search and no rustlers successfully invaded his territory during that time.

Frank Cannon worked with Lowery on the Shotwell Ranch near Rosalia, according to his son Cliff, who told me some stories about and gave me some old photographs of Lowery. Frank Cannon remembered seeing Lowery ride a bronc at a 1906 or 1907 contest held in the Cassoday Pasture, the arena formed by buggies and wagons pulled into a circle. Gene's horse was a wild one, jumping completely over one buggy and going down in a heap on the outside of the arena. As any competent cowboy would (if circumstances allowed him to), Gene stepped out of the saddle as the horse went down, but then he stepped back on as the bronc got up, riding the rest of the buck out of him. It was a hell of a ride and Lowery

Gene Lowery.

should have won, but one of the judges goose-egged him. The reason given was that when the horse went down the rider was on the ground, but Frank Cannon always figured that Gene's color had a lot to do with it. The two cowboys worked together for years near Rosalia and Sallyards, and Cannon averred that Lowery was the best bronc rider he had ever seen and as good a cowboy as anyone he ever knew. High praise indeed from a man who spent his entire lifetime working cattle in the Flint Hills.

The late Hap Jackson, lifelong resident of western Greenwood County, remembered Lowery's funeral, paid for by cattlemen and the first ever to be held in the recently built Presbyterian church at Reece. The place was full to overflowing, mostly ranchers and their families. "Contrary to what some people expected," Hap told me, "lightning didn't strike the church." Gene is buried in the Reece cemetery, whereas the rest of his family and many other blacks from Reece are buried in the now-abandoned graveyard on the Lowery farmstead, donated to the community by Gene's father. The pallbearers were all Flint Hills cattlemen, mourners came from Texas and New Mexico, and the ranchers whose cattle Gene had looked after put together a fund to care for Gene's widow and children.

Hap also told me about a time during the oil boom at Sallyards when his father (Harry), uncle (Charley Lehman), and Gene unloaded some cattle at the stockyards then went into town to eat dinner. This was during the late teens when Sallyards, now totally gone except for one abandoned shotgun shack and a couple of cattle pens, boasted a cafe, a drugstore, a barbershop, two rooming houses, and three lumberyards (to supply wood for building oil derricks). Most of the population worked in the oil field, and those workers are not called roughnecks for nothing. The weekly dances at Sallyards, for instance, often lasted until three in the morning, the festivities routinely punctuated by the sound of gunshots. Anyway, when Gene, Harry, and Charley got to the cafe, Gene started for the rear entrance. "Where do you think you're going?" Harry asked. "To get something to eat," Gene said. As he turned to go, Charley suddenly wrapped his arms around him and carried him inside and plopped him down onto a counter stool between himself and Harry, which set off an immediate round of betting amongst the skinners, roustabouts, and roughnecks concerning whether or not Gene would be served. When the proprietor gruffly informed the cowboys that colored people weren't allowed to eat there, Charley informed him right back, "He eats where we eat," then pulled a .38 revolver from his chaps pocket and slapped it on the counter. It was an expensive meal for those who had bet against Gene.

Obviously it was not (and is not) easy to be black and a working cowboy, despite the fact that in the original trail-driving days just after the Civil War perhaps 20 to 25 percent of the crew members were black. I think that obituary writer Sherman Cornett expressed the triumph of Gene Lowery (and of all his fellow black cowboys) best when he compared the homage paid Gene with that received by his world-famous musician uncle: "It seems a great thing to be honored by royalty in a foreign country, but to be honored by home people who know you for what you are every day in the week ... people who have overcome race prejudice ... seems even greater."

Four

Lou Hart and the Boys Who Work for Crockers

For years I have hoped to discover a Flint Hills folk song, some evidence that the special spirit of this tallgrass prairie had inspired its pioneer citizens to reflect upon local conditions or events by setting new lyrics to a familiar tune, a typical pattern in folk song creation on the Kansas plains, as elsewhere. The search has not turned up any songs, but it hasn't been entirely fruitless, either. In the summer of 1986, Lyle Burkhart, who had recently moved into the old Norton Creek Ranch east of Bazaar in Chase County, gave me a photocopy of a typescript poem he had found in the attic of the ranch house. The poem, entitled "Springtime at Crockers," describes work just after the turn of the century on the Crocker Ranch near Matfield Green in Chase County. The author was Lou Hart, a cowboy who worked for Ed and Arthur Crocker from 1906 to 1910 and probably wrote the poem during this time. If Hart was as handy with

a rope and horse as he was with pen and rhyme, then the Crocker
brothers had themselves the "top-hand" that he terms himself in
the note he added at the end of the poem. Here it is:

Springtime at Crockers

In the valley of the Southfork
Many many miles away,
That is where the Crocker Brothers
Have ranched for many a day.

Now these lines that I am writing
Are of punchers one and all,
Who will try to keep the fences
Up in shape from spring till fall.

In the spring when sun-warmed south winds
Green the pastures near and far,
Then the boys who work for Crockers
Meet the cattle at Bazaar.

To the pastures up old Southfork
Where the grass is getting green,
Many a herd of scrawley longhorns
Driven southward may be seen.

After days of toil and trouble
All the cattle have come in,
From the wild and frisky yearling
To the old cow poor and thin.

Johnnie rides the Butler County
Nate rides everything east side,
While the Farrington and Lincoln
Jennings is supposed to ride.

Elm Creek and Kemp and Rogler,
Though they are three miles apart,
With the Morrill in between them,
All are rode by Old Man Hart.

In the month of fair September
When the grass is turning brown,
Then the boys who work for Crockers
Bring the beef herds back to town.

In the first faint flush of morning
From the ranch the boys will start,
Ed and Arthur, Jack and Russell,
Cooper, Daddy, and Lou Hart.

They'll get Virgil in Matfield,
At the Farrington get Clay,
Mapes is taking the chuck wagon,
They will work the "U" today.

Ed and Arthur do the cutting
On their horses Si and Ben;
Which is best is often argued
After supper by the men.

"Cut ten loads of my best cattle,"
Was the message Popham wired;
If they do in time to load them,
Men and horses will be tired.

Now at noon the boys are hungry
It is eight hours since they eat,
Mapes will have them something special,
As a cook he can't be beat.

After dinner at the wagon,
Arthur says, as sure as fate,
"We will have to keep them drifting,
Or we surely will be late."

Down the trail past Seward Bakers
They will take them to Bazaar.
Maybe they will eat at Gaddies
When the last steer's in the car.

NOTE: Written by Lou Hart, who for years was a "top-hand" with Crocker Brothers cow-outfit in the Flint Hills of Chase and Butler Counties, Kansas.

Warning: some of the following paragraphs contain explicit literary language.

As a piece of literature, a kind of local-color realism, "Springtime at Crockers" isn't bad. ("Isn't bad," by the way, is, in Flint Hills colloquial, a compliment. Understatement and roundabout expression are common here. For instance, if you're walking in a corral and a cow on the prod heads your way, the warning you get is more likely to be "You might want to get out of the way," instead of "Watch out or you'll get hit!" Or instead of being ordered to "Shut the gate," you'll hear "You might want to close that gate.") Hart's prosody, apparently untutored, is adept. The quatrains, rhyming xaxa, are dominantly trochaic tetrameter, but an occasional three-beat line prevents the rhythm from becoming monotonous. Moreover, because the rhyming lines invariably end on a single stressed syllable, the poem combines the lightness of feminine verse with the solidity of masculine. In form the poem is essentially a narrative, but it does not tell a straightforward story in the way that, say, a ballad does. Rather, in mirroring the cycle of work in the Flint Hills, the poem takes on some of the characteristics of the epic: catalogs of cowboys (not ships), long cattle drives (instead of vast wanderings around the Mediterranean), implied heroic actions in the mundane work of the cowboy (rather than explicit descriptions of mighty clashes of warriors). Just as an epic is a compendium of knowledge of the culture that produces it, so this poem, with the single exception of pasture burning, comprises the entirety of ranch work in the Flint Hills at that time. In contrast to the epic, this poem is short and the scope local, to be sure, but then the world of the men who worked for Crockers, as for many others in the central Flint Hills at the turn of the twentieth century, in large degree began and ended at the shipping pens of Bazaar.

Although not strictly a folk poem, "Springtime at Crockers" does have folk elements. Originally it was undoubtedly intended to be recited, not published, and it did circulate orally for some fifty years before it was first printed in the 6 August 1958 edition of the *Chase County Leader-News*. I would call it a "memory poem," corresponding to the label "memory painting" that folklorist Jennie

Chinn, the executive director of the Kansas State Historical Society, applies to the paintings Marijana Grisnik made of Strawberry Hill, a Croatian neighborhood in Kansas City, Kansas. Memory art, whatever the medium, can be defined as deliberate esthetic works created by an academically untrained artist that reflect the folklife of a particular culture. Just as Grisnik's unschooled but evocative scenes of Strawberry Hill, which she was inspired to create when much of Strawberry Hill was destroyed by highway construction many years ago, have preserved the distinctive folklife of this neighborhood—weddings, funerals, daily chores, celebrations—so Lou Hart's verses accurately mirror and preserve the work of a cowboy in the Flint Hills at the turn of the twentieth century.

Hart exhibits poetic ability in his selective use of alliteration—line 9 for instance ("In the spring when sun-warmed south winds"), or line 14 ("Where the grass is getting green"), or line 33 ("First faint flush of morning"). His rhymes are effective and natural, only the words "eat" and "beat" in lines 50 and 52 appearing to be forced (by grammatical usage, not sound). In fact, however, the use of "eat" (and, for that matter, "et") as a past tense is not uncommon in the Flint Hills; I have heard both usages many times, particularly among older residents. The use of poetic diction that might otherwise tend toward cliché (e.g., "sun-warmed south winds" in line 9, or "the month of fair September" in line 29) is in each case meliorated by the literal truth of the causal relationship to the lines immediately following each image (the warm winds of spring do help to "Green the pastures near and far," just as the grass turns brown in the autumn).

The smooth flow of this poem when read aloud, along with its pictorial language and many allusions to local places and people, would make it easy to memorize, and indeed it is well known in the Bazaar–Matfield Green area. I have collected six different versions, two of them handwritten copies that show varying degrees of having been written from memory. The poem was apparently known well enough to have figured into the work of late Emporia artist Laurence Coffelt, a native of Cassoday who promoted himself as the "Artist of the Flint Hills." Among some pencil drawings that were preliminary sketches for later Coffelt oil paintings is one of some cowboys at the Bazaar depot with the caption: "The men who worked for Crockers." I have spoken to many people from Chase

County who remember having heard the poem or having seen a copy of it. Some of these memories were aided, I am sure, by the poem's publication (in slightly altered form) in the local paper.

Hart applies some deft touches of characterization. He obviously likes Ed and Arthur Crocker and has a high regard for their abilities as horsemen. On the other hand, he does not seem to have much respect for the ability of Jennings to take care of the cattle in the two pastures he "is supposed to ride"—or else Hart is poking good-natured fun at one of his fellow workers. A third alternative is that Hart simply needed more syllables to fill out the line of poetry. The commentary that accompanied the publication of the poem in the *Chase County Leader-News* supports the first interpretation. This article, based partly on a conversation among Mrs. Fred (Beverly) Howard (daughter of Ed Crocker), Mrs. Ernest McKenzie (who knew most of the men named in the poem), and Fred Siler (Santa Fe agent at Bazaar during the time the poem was written), contains the following sentence: "The poet even speaks out on a pet peeve with the telling of the territory covered by each hand and the failure apparently of one in carrying out his share of the duty." As another example of characterization, the reader gets the impression that Arthur Crocker's after-dinner admonition to the men, to keep the cattle "drifting / Or we surely will be late," is one they may well have heard, "as sure as fate," nearly every single shipping day. Finally, one senses both the ego and the self-deprecating irony of the poet in Hart's reference to himself both as a "top-hand" and as "Old Man Hart."

Perhaps the most striking example of Hart's poetic inspiration is his use of the word "scrawley" (line 15) to describe the long-horn cattle, a coinage that evokes the image of scrawny, bony steers stretched out (i.e., "sprawled") in long droves as they trek to their summer homes. That Hart intended "scrawley" instead of "scrawny" is supported by the fact that the only extant version of the poem using the latter word is the one published in the *Leader-News*. Even the two memorial transcriptions of the poem (most likely made within a few years after the poem was first written) use "scrawley," which suggests an aural awareness of an unusual usage. This usage was, naturally enough, misapprehended fifty years later by an editor who, with appropriate journalistic sensibility,

Detail of pencil sketch by Laurence Coffelt of "Springtime at Crockers."

substituted a reasonable correction for what must have seemed to him an obvious typographical error.

The mental image created by "scrawley" is an entirely accurate one, reflecting the nature of the aged Texas cattle customarily received into the Flint Hills for fattening on grass during this time period. Despite the reference to "wild and frisky" yearlings, these steers were often three to four years old or older. (In the 1950s I recall often hearing the term "Texas yearling" in reference to a two-year-old steer. Unweaned cattle nearly a year old were referred to as "calves" and sometimes sent with their mothers to Flint Hills pastures, their two-year-old counterparts sent as "yearlings" as their owners sought ways to exploit the pasture rates set for a cow-calf unit or for young stocker cattle.) The horn spans of these cattle were sometimes so broad that cowboys had to twist their heads in order to unload them through the four-foot-wide doors on a railroad stock car, which in the spring would hold up to forty-five head. Many were so thin and weak (from hunger or from shipping fever) that they had literally to be "tailed up," that is, have their tails twisted to get them standing so they could be pushed out of the cars. Others were dead when they arrived, their bodies dragged out and salvaged for skinning and hog feed. On the long drives to the pastures the weaker cattle played out and were dropped into pastures along the wayside to be driven on to rejoin the rest of their herd a few days or weeks later, assuming that they lived and regained their strength.

The railroad arrived at Bazaar in 1887, immediately transforming this small village into the major cattle shipping point of the central Flint Hills, a distinction it held for over thirty years. The expanse of grass that lay between Bazaar on the north, Rosalia on the south, Madison on the east, and Degraff on the west was not served by a railroad until the Santa Fe extended its tracks south through Matfield Green and Cassoday, on to Winfield, and into Oklahoma in 1923–1924. Until this time cattle that summered in the 1,500-plus square miles that radiated out from Cassoday and Matfield Green had to be driven up to thirty miles and more to and from railheads, thus combining characteristics of both the Trail Drive and Railroad Eras of cattle work in the Flint Hills.

Despite some surface differences the general pattern of cattle work in the Flint Hills at the time the poem was written (between 1906 and 1910) had changed little from the earlier era and is similar to that of today. Most of the cattle coming into the Flint Hills in the early years of the century would have been very much like the longhorns of the trail-driving days, but whereas these earlier cattle would have been loose-herded on what was essentially open range in the 1870s and 1880s, they were being kept behind fences by the time Lou Hart went to work for Crockers. Arthur Crocker himself had been a "herd boy," as they were sometimes called, during the summer on the headwaters of the Verdigris River some dozen miles east of Matfield Green. Today the stocker cattle summered on Flint Hills grass are younger and smaller than those at the turn of the century, and their meatier appearance reflects the improved breeding programs that have been practiced in the intervening years. Moreover, technology has greatly changed transportation not only for cattle but for horses as well. Whereas Lou Hart and his comrades would have done every bit of their work on horseback, today's cowboy, in the Flint Hills as elsewhere in cattle country, often checks cattle in a pickup, rides fence on an ATV, trailers his horse to roundups, and loads cattle from portable pens set up in the pasture. Still, despite changes in tools and equipment, the general cycle of pasturing transient cattle (i.e., non-native cattle brought in for a limited grazing season) in the Flint Hills has remained constant for nearly a century and a half.

This cycle begins in early spring with preparations for the receiving of summer cattle. Following the introduction of barbed wire into the Flint Hills, a major part of this preparation has included the repairing of fence and replacing of water gaps that have been washed out by spring rains. While major fence-mending occurs in early spring, riding fence is a never-ending chore if fences are to be kept "up in shape from spring till fall."

Pasture season traditionally begins in mid-April when the dominant grasses of the tallgrass prairie are beginning to green, especially if the previous year's dead grass has been burnt off in late March or early April and there has been sufficient rainfall and warm weather to promote the new growth. Pasture burning, incidentally, is the only part of the work cycle of the Flint Hills omitted by Hart in his poem, perhaps because it was not a major job at the time he wrote the poem. In those days massive general fires were set, instead of burning individual pastures piecemeal.

The process of receiving cattle in the spring more often than not did indeed entail the "days of toil and trouble" stated by Hart. Trainloads of cattle would be unloaded at Bazaar, at Hymer, at Degraff, at Batesville, at Junction City, at Sallyards, at Volland, at Root Station—at stockyards throughout the Flint Hills. As mentioned above, many of these cattle were thin and weak and required special attention if they were to be saved. Those that had their health, on the other hand, could be wild and skittish and difficult to drive. Others, after having been put in a pasture, would sometimes crawl through the fences or, in later years, walk the cattle guards and end up several pastures away from where they were supposed to be.

April is not the cruelest month in the Flint Hills (March, in the minds of many residents, with its unpredictable mix of sun, wind, rain, snow, and cold lays claim to that dubious honor), but mid-April can be cold and wet—sometimes even drizzle mixed with snow—weather as hard on cowboys as it is on cattle. Sometimes, too, cattle of several different brands owned by several different cattlemen and intended for several different caretakers would arrive on the same train, which could mean extra effort to prevent mix-ups as the animals were being let out of the pens and started toward their various summer pastures. Many (to the cowboy it must have seemed most) of the cattle trains arrived during the dead of night, which meant a trip to the yards to unload, then a brief resumption of interrupted sleep, often on the depot floor, and setting out for the pasture as soon as it was daylight. Sometimes so many cattle came in during the night that the pens couldn't hold them. Then cowboys would have to ride night herd, attempting in the dark to hold cattle made restless by the long train trip and by the unfamiliar country in which they found themselves. If, as occasionally happened, the cattle got mixed during the night, then much of the next morning was spent sorting brands before the drive to the pasture could begin.

Once unloaded, the cattle would be driven to a particular pasture for the summer, pasture set by contract between cattle owner and Flint Hills pastureman. Sometimes pasturemen were large landholders, such as the Crocker brothers; other times they might be middlemen who leased pastures from landowners and sublet them to cattle owners. In either case, as noted in the introduction, a pastureman had certain obligations: to receive cattle in the spring and deliver (or account for, if some had died) the same number in the fall, to supply salt and water, to maintain fences, to care for sick animals. Lou Hart and his fellow cowboys were hired by the Crockers to help in this process, to fix fence and drive cattle to pasture in the spring and, once the cattle were in place, to ride fence and look after them during grazing season until shipping time in the fall. Note that certain cowboys in the poem are assigned responsibility for specific pastures: Johnnie looks after the cattle in Butler County, Nate those on the eastern side of the Crocker holdings. Hart himself was responsible for riding three pastures—Elm Creek, Kemp, and Rogler—while Jennings may have done less than justice to his duties in the Farrington and the Lincoln. These five pastures, by the way, are known today by the same names as in Hart's time, although the eight-section Farrington pasture (which I used to look after when I rode for Wayne Rogler) has since been divided into two pastures. It is common, in fact, for pastures throughout the Flint Hills to retain the names of early-day owners even though they may have changed hands numerous times in the intervening years.

Full pasture season officially ends in mid-October, although many times cattle are shipped out earlier, especially if market conditions encourage an earlier sale. Up through mid-twentieth century, for example, grass-fat older steers were often shipped as early as July. Many present-day cattle owners practice what is termed "double-stocking," i.e., putting twice the usual number of cattle on a particular pasture for only half as long as normal, thus allowing the grass to rest in late summer from the intensive grazing that has occurred earlier. Hart's poem suggests that at the turn of the century the major shipping season was in late summer and early fall. Today, especially with double-stocking, pastures tend to be "cleaned out" in one shipping, but in Hart's time a pasture was shipped a few loads at a time, as the cattle got fat and as the owner (or commission man) determined that the market was right. Commission men who worked with many cattle owners and large numbers of cattle often selected those cattle, and the number of cattle, to be sold at any one particular market on any one particular market day in order to help maintain the best possible price for their customers. In this poem the cattle owner (Popham) has instructed the two pasturemen (Ed and Arthur Crocker) to select ten loads of fat cattle (branded with the letter U) for shipping, probably on Sunday so that the cattle would be in Kansas City in time for the Monday morning market.

In the poem the shipping crew includes the regular ranch hands, some additional cowboys to provide extra help, and a chuck wagon cook. The day begins early, the men having saddled up, eaten breakfast, and set out for the pasture by 4:00 a.m. By the "first faint flush of morning," the crew will be in the pasture to be shipped (in this case most likely one of the Butler County pastures, which lie south of the Farrington, where Clay Jennings will join the riders), and the men will be in the far corners when the unfolding of the morning provides light to see cattle well enough to push them toward a prearranged cutting ground. This spot, perhaps a corner of the pasture or perhaps a flat area on a hilltop, is where the herd will be gathered so that the two ranch owners, mounted on their cutting horses, can separate out the fat cattle to be shipped (about 250 head for ten loads) and start them toward Bazaar, some fifteen to eighteen miles away. Johnnie, who is responsible for this particular pasture, will undoubtedly count the remaining U cattle as they are released to graze until the next roundup, probably a couple of weeks later.

Chuck wagons were not common in the Flint Hills: the Crockers had one of the few, perhaps a result of their additional ranching activities in Texas and Arizona. Wayne Rogler, who was born in 1905 and reared north of Matfield Green on the family ranch that bordered the Crocker Ranch headquarters, recalled that in the mid-teens this particular chuck wagon was kept in a pasture about four miles west of town, its purpose that of a cupboard—to provide food for the Crocker hands so that they would not have to come all the way in to ranch headquarters in order to eat dinner. Rogler remembered one time when he was helping Arthur Crocker move some cattle and around noon they stopped at the wagon for something to eat. It was stocked, he told me, with canned goods—sardines, peaches, and tomatoes, the latter especially effective in quenching thirst. On shipping days, however, the chuck wagon was outfitted with a cook, a good one to Hart's mind, and in this poem the wagon was probably located somewhere west of Matfield Green, assuming that the cattle to be shipped had left the pasture by mid-morning.

A drive of something like eight or ten miles would await the men after dinner as they followed the trail along the ridges west of Matfield Green and then north into the Baker Pasture (the "Seward Baker's" of line 57, and the same pasture in which Knute Rockne's plane crashed in 1931), then on up toward Rock Creek and into Bazaar from the cattle lane on the northwest side of town. No wonder that Arthur Crocker urges the men to "keep them drifting," for once in the stockyards, the cattle have to be sorted into drafts (of probably fifteen to twenty head) and weighed before being loaded onto the railroad stock cars. At the end of the day, and of the poem, Lou Hart is looking forward to a nice hot meal cooked by Mrs. Frank Gaddie, who ran a boardinghouse that complemented her husband's livery barn in Bazaar.

Shipping drives such as this one, probably beginning in mid to late July, would continue at the rate of one or two a week throughout the fall until pasture season ended. Lou Hart, in describing the general nature of one such drive, along with references to other aspects of his work for the Crocker brothers, has thus provided an accurate overview of ranch work in the Flint Hills. But who was Lou Hart and who were the people about whom he wrote?

The Crocker Ranch

Fed by Thurman Creek and Little Cedar Creek, the Southfork (South Fork) River rises in Butler County near the Greenwood County line and runs north into Chase County past Matfield Green and Bazaar until it joins the Cottonwood River about four miles east of Cottonwood Falls. The rich bottomlands of the Southfork grow bountiful crops of alfalfa, corn, and grain sorghums, while the steeply rising uplands constitute some of the best native pasture to be found anywhere. It was into this region that ex–Union cavalry captain Erastus Bryant Crocker came in 1866, having set out on foot from Fort Leavenworth where he had recently received his discharge. According to local tradition, Crocker stopped at a house along Peyton Creek one evening to ask for lodging; the man who answered his knock was his brother Ashbel, with whom he had lost contact during the war. Erastus Crocker took up land along the Southfork, the core of the ranch that his sons Ed and Arthur would later develop into one of the largest, most progressive in the Flint Hills. At the peak of operation the Crocker Ranch controlled thousands of acres of Flint Hills grass and farmland in three counties—Chase, Butler, and Greenwood. The brothers also acquired ranches in Texas and at one time leased a ranch of some 100,000 acres of the White Mountain Apache Reservation in Arizona. They were among the first ranchers in the Flint Hills to install cattle guards on their land, and some of the early field testing of O.M. Franklin's experimental blackleg vaccine was conducted on their Matfield Green ranch. Unfortunately, financial reversals and bad markets forced them to liquidate many of their holdings in the early 1920s, and by the end of the decade their ranching glory days were essentially over.

In subsequent years Ed's son Mason managed to regain the core of the Chase County ranch, as well as sizeable holdings near Brady, Texas. Both generations of Crockers have enjoyed a good reputation among their neighbors in the Flint Hills. Cowboys liked to work there, partly because of fair wages, partly because they hired good cooks, and in no small part because the Crockers raised the kind of horses cowboys liked to ride. "If you provide them with good horses," Mason once told me, "you won't have any trouble getting good men to work for you." This philosophy, judging from Hart's poem, seems to have been standard Crocker Ranch practice from early on.

The Boys Who Worked for Crockers

Nate Russell was called the Irishman, and he was foreman on the Crocker Ranch for twenty-seven years, beginning in 1899, according to his daughter, Bertha (Mrs. Edward) Baker of Matfield Green. Mrs. Baker was born in 1911, a year or more after Hart wrote "Springtime at Crockers," but she recalls clearly the Crocker brothers and other men named in the poem. Her father is the Nate who looked after "everything east side" and the Russell referred to in line 35. The Russell family lived on Sharpes Creek, southeast of Bazaar and some ten or more miles from the Crocker Ranch. Nate Russell had inherited the farm from his father (who had moved back to Kansas from Sagauche, Colorado, in 1873 when Nate was four years old), but for much of the time he worked for Crockers he was a commuter. Mrs. Russell stayed on the farm with the children and, with the help of a hired man, ran the place, while Nate would come home on weekends, sometimes more often if he needed clean clothes or if he was needed for any special work at home. Bertha Baker recalls once as a child answering a knock on the door and seeing a strange man who asked to speak to her mother—she didn't recognize her father, who had shaved his mustache while at the Crockers'. Later, after her father quit the Crocker Ranch in 1926, Bertha would go to the field with him, each of them driving a team. She also rode pastures with him when he worked for Roy Beedle, a rancher from Bazaar. "Mother said that I spoiled him," Mrs. Baker told me. "He would unhook his team of horses at the barn and tell me, 'There they are, kid,' and I would take care of them. It was two years after I was married before he quit expecting me to come help him milk."

The account of Russell's death, published in the 21 May 1941 issue of the *Chase County Leader-News,* reveals that he was a cowboy to the end. He was killed in an accident involving the roping of a cow for Floyd Fisher, tenant on the neighboring Hilton farm. Mr. Fisher described the scene for me, telling me how Russell had roped the cow in a stone corral and how Fisher's sister, standing on the windmill tower the better to watch the action, had called to him: "Irishman, you'd better face your horse to the cow." Russell, whose mount was standing sideways to the cow, responded that the horse was big enough to handle a cow no matter which way he faced. Just as he spoke, the cow lunged, jerking the saddle to the side and causing the horse to buck. Distracted and caught off guard, the sixty-seven-year-old cowboy was thrown and his skull fractured by a blow from the kicking horse. According to Fisher the horse was not only big but mean tempered and cantankerous, so much so that one of Russell's sons-in-law, Windy Pinkston, had earlier threatened to ride him into one of the big pastures far from the house and shoot him before he hurt someone.

Chase Countians still remember Nate Russell as an excellent cowhand. In fact, when Dee Fink and Gene Peacock opened a restaurant, the Pioneer Club, a mile east of Strong City in the mid 1980s and lined its walls with old photographs of early-day Chase County cowboys and cattlemen, one of the first pictures they sought was of the Irishman.

Johnnie Blackmore is the Johnnie of line 21 and the Jack of line 35. He was born in 1886 in Louisburg, Kansas, according to his son, the late Mason Blackmore. When Johnnie was seven years old, his father made the run into the Cherokee Outlet, settling with his family on a claim near Shawnee. Sometime around the turn of the century, young Johnnie accompanied a cattle drive from Shawnee out west to Laverne, Oklahoma, where he sold his horse to his older brother Ern and rode back to Shawnee on a burro, living off wild plums and grapes the whole way. A few years later Johnnie again joined Ern, who had by this time moved to the Flint Hills at Cassoday. Johnnie signed on with the Crockers in 1906 (the same year as Lou Hart) to look after cattle in their Butler County pastures. He married Mamie Golden of Matfield Green in 1911, and for the next several years they lived with Dave Bennett on the Red Ranch east of Cassoday. He rode for Crockers for eighteen years straight, quitting in 1924. Mason once told me a story his father often told about a pair of pants. It seems that one day as he was riding horseback through Matfield Green, a storekeeper held up the pants and asked Johnnie what he'd give for them. "Twenty-five cents," Johnnie answered, "that's all I've got," and the storekeeper threw the pants to him. The next day Johnnie was riding pastures with a man named John Bailey and told him about his bargain pants. Bailey offered him six bits, a 200 percent profit, and Johnnie took it, whereupon Bailey insisted on immediate delivery. Johnnie had to finish riding that day in his underwear, then dig around the granary to find an old pair of ragged overalls in order to get to the house after work. But he learned a lesson that came in handy later. Nate Russell had tried for years to buy Johnnie's silver mounted saddle, which he consistently priced high—$145. One day Nate gave up trying to get a lower price and agreed to Johnnie's price, but Blackmore refused to accept payment until they were back at the barn: "I'm not going to ride bareback," he said. Johnnie Blackmore died on December 17, 1939.

Of the other hands listed, Clay and Virgil Jennings were father and son. Charlie Jennings, Virgil's grandfather, had a house west of the railroad tracks in Matfield Green where Virgil was apparently staying at the time this poem was written. I assume, since the men will stop by to get Clay at the Farrington pasture half a dozen miles southwest of town, that Clay is the Jennings referred to in line 24.

At the time the poem was written, Isaac "Ide" Cooper lived near the head of Sharpes Creek; earlier he had lived near Cedar Point in western Chase County. One of his sons, Elmer, a lifelong cowboy in Chase County who died at age ninety-one in 1986, once told me about riding with his father down in northwest Oklahoma when he was eleven or twelve years old. While the elder Cooper stayed behind to conduct other business, young Elmer by himself drove a herd of horses all the way back to Kansas.

The Daddy of line 36 was Charley Rudolph, an old man variously known as Daddy or Granddaddy Rudolph. He was a white-whiskered widower ("an old-timer when I was a kid," according to Wayne Rogler) who rode some fence for Crockers, carrying his staples in a saddle pocket he had made out of an old boot top and taking an occasional pull from the half-pint bottle he usually carried with him. The late Edward Tincum Baker (Bertha's husband) remembered him as "quite an old character. He'd just go out and ride as long as he wanted to and when he got tired, he'd just go in."

Baker also told me that Al Mapes, a bachelor, cooked on the Crocker chuck wagon for "a good many years.... It was the only chuck wagon that I can remember that ever operated in this country." He remembers, as well, that when Crockers were shipping from their pastures west and southwest of Matfield Green, they would station the chuck wagon west of his father's house (the Seward Baker of line 57), about halfway between Matfield Green and Bazaar, and Mapes would cook dinner there for the crew. Mapes also operated the chuck wagon for the Crockers when they drove cattle from Foraker, Oklahoma, to Matfield Green in the early 1930s. David Mercer recalls that Mapes, with his large mustache, had a forbidding appearance, one that frightened young David when his father, William Mercer, would hire Mapes to cook barbecue for the Fourth of July celebrations staged on the Mercer Ranch near Wonsevu. The Crocker chuck wagon, by the way, is on display at the Chase County Historical Museum in Cottonwood Falls.

Al Popham was a big operator from the Texas Panhandle who sent many cattle up into the Flint Hills, according to Wayne Rogler. Popham was one of the genuine pioneers of the cattle industry, having been sent by Lee and Scott, owners of the famous LS Ranch near Channing, to manage their Montana holdings in 1884, then brought back to serve as a foreman of the Texas ranch in 1889. In that job he incurred the wrath of neighboring cattlemen by not allowing them to drive their cattle across LS land in order to ship from the railroad pens at Tascosa: "The LS Ranch is a closed range," he said, "and I mean to keep it that way." Despite this adverse relationship with other ranchers, Popham had a good reputation as a stockman (he was, according to Rogler, one of the first to use cottonseed cake in the wintering of cattle) and greatly improved the LS ranch during the many years he worked there.

I am not sure when he quit the LS, but from 1903 through 1913 Al Popham is listed in the Amarillo City Directory as a stockman and as president of the Western Stock Yards Company, maintaining offices in the First National Bank building. The brand book from Pampa, county seat of Gray County (he also had brands registered in Carson, Hutchinson, and Armstrong counties), shows six brands registered to Popham in 1913. These included a diamond J, a bar over a U, a U over a bar, and a plain U (the brand mentioned in all the copies of the poem except one, which shows a U with a line under it—the U Bar). On 31 March 1917 Popham died in Kansas City following a long illness, and he was buried in Minneapolis, suggesting that he may have been a Minnesota resident before going to Texas in the early 1880s.

Frank Cannon, who began working for the Crockers a year or two after Hart's poem was written, told his son Cliff, who told me, about an incident in which Popham was cutting cattle on a good sorrel Crocker horse that was in Cannon's string. Instead of giving the horse his head, Popham rode with too tight a rein ("stayed on his head" was the phrase Cliff used) and at the same time complained about the poor quality of his mount, all of which irritated Frank no little bit, for he had trained the horse and knew he was a good one. So on Popham's next trip into the herd to cut a steer, Frank followed and when the horse started to move after the steer and Popham started to pull him up, Cannon whipped the sorrel on the rump with a bridle rein. The horse, responding to the training Cannon had given him, jumped after the steer and brought him out of the herd in short order—although nearly unseating Popham in the process. Whether Cannon was acting from irritation because his horse was being maligned, from some latent antagonism between cowboy and cattleman (or youth and age or Kansan and Texan), or out of the tradition of rough cowboy humor I am not sure.

Lou Hart

I am convinced that the life of any man or woman, no matter how mundane or obscure that life might seem, contains the seeds for a masterpiece of literature. Certainly Lou Hart's story has all the tragic elements of a Thomas Hardy novel: his father drowning a short time before Lou himself was born, his wife dying shortly after the birth of their fifth child, his attempt to be both father and mother to his children, his mother killed by a train as she was bringing Lou's children back from a visit, a second marriage that may have been more convenient than happy, poverty that drove him to cattle stealing and suicide at only thirty-eight years of age. Yet the picture that one derives, both from his poetry and from talking to those who knew him, is that Lou Hart was a friendly and happy man, a good cowboy, and a loving father.

Louis Hart, Sr., came to Kansas from Illinois in the late 1860s, a young veteran (in his early twenties) claiming land along the Whitewater River near Towanda in Butler County for his service in the Grand Army of the Republic. On the first of February, 1875, eight months before the birth of his son and namesake in October, the elder Hart drowned. As young Lou grew up, he picked up the skills of a cowboy—and when he was twenty years old, a wife, Zoe Angleton Hart. A brother, Clifford, had died as a baby, but his sister, Grace, married his wife's brother, William. Lou moved to a farm east of Cassoday sometime before 1906, the year he started work on the Crocker ranch. At that time he lived at Jack Springs on the Farrington (one of the pastures named in his poem), the first home that his daughter Olive Hart Riffey (born 1903) remembered. The following year the family moved to Matfield Green where in March 1908, Zoe Hart died shortly after the birth of their fifth child. Lou then moved into a tenant house on the Crocker Ranch where the wives of Ed and Arthur Crocker helped to watch over his children. His mother, Ellen Green Fisk, also helped, coming to Matfield Green to care for the new baby, Grace. In October 1908, Mrs. Fisk, who had taken Grace and young Olive to her home in Butler County for a time, was accidentally killed at the El Dorado depot, on her way to return with the children to Chase County. Olive had wandered onto the tracks, and her grandmother pushed her to safety but was then struck by the engine.

"Springtime at Crockers" was not likely to have been written before 1907, the year Hart moved off the Farrington. Perhaps it was written during that year, before the death of his wife in early 1908, for the tone of the poem is almost idyllic, reflecting a contentment on the part of the persona that seems to me would have been absent in the poet himself if he had been suffering the effects of a deep, recent personal loss. The poem most likely was written no later than 1910, the year Hart bought a farm some five miles south of El Dorado, county seat of Butler County. In March 1912, he married a widow, Alice Griffith Hess of Towanda, and moved to the Bare Ranch near Leon.

1913 was a year of drouth in the Flint Hills, the kind of summer that could drive cattle owners and pasturemen to desperate straits. Grass and water ran low and cattle did poorly, causing pasturemen to refuse to relinquish cattle when owners could not come up with pasture rent and causing cattle owners to sue pasturemen for not properly caring for the livestock placed in their charge. 1913, Olive Riffey recalls, was a hot, dry summer of shriveled crops and desperation for her father: "His hogs got cholera and I remember him burning them on a fire [in the barnyard]." And 1913 was the year that Lou Hart felt compelled to steal a load of cattle.

On Wednesday, the first day of October, according to the warrant for his arrest, Hart shipped a carload of Whit Turney's cattle (the number in the different news stories varies from twelve to twenty-nine head, but twenty-seven is the one most often cited) from the stockyards at Pontiac in eastern Butler County, billing them to the stockyards at St. Joseph, but selling them in Kansas City. The following Sunday, shortly after his return by train from Wichita where he had gone to meet his wife (who had been visiting relatives in Oklahoma), the sheriff from Greenwood County (Grant Smethers), accompanied by a deputy from Butler County (Newt Purcell), came to his house on the Bare Ranch. Hart was self-possessed, according to Smethers, talking about "crops, weather, farm conditions in general" in a disarming manner. Thus when he asked permission to go into the house to change his clothes, the officers readily agreed. After changing, Hart asked if he might talk to his wife, who did not realize that he had been placed under arrest. Going into a bedroom with her, he told her that he was in trouble and would have to go to Eureka for a few days. Then he took a .38 Colt out of a dresser drawer, saying he was going to take it with him, and seemed to put it in his pocket. Instead he shot himself in the heart, dying within minutes. Olive, too, was in the room.

The jury at the coroner's inquest ruled that Hart died of a self-inflicted gunshot wound, but they assigned no cause for the action. The author of the article in the Leon newspaper suggested, plausibly, that "financial difficulties were at the bottom of his troubles." The *Chase County Leader-News* expressed shock: "About three years ago the Hart family lived ... southwest of Bazaar, and Mr. Hart worked for the Crocker boys. The family was quite favorably known throughout the southern part of the county ... and the above dispatch coming from Leon, to which place the family moved after leaving Chase County came as a surprise to his friends and acquaintances." The Butler County editor of the *Walnut Valley Times*, who shared with the community a high regard for Hart, believed that his motivation could only have been temporary insanity. Below is his tribute, printed in full:

> The tragic death of Lou Hart was a distinct shock to Butler county people who had known him for many years. He was regarded as an upright, honest, straightforward man, and despite the circumstances culminating in his death we believe that Lou Hart would not commit a dishonorable act if in his right mind.

Lou Hart was reared here in Butler county. He had always borne a reputation for dealing squarely with his fellow-men. He was experienced in the cattle business. He knew, if in his right mind, that in this day and age it would be impossible to make away with another man's cattle and market them in the manner he is said to have done, without the act being discovered. He knew the system of keeping track of brands and purchases and sales and shipments. And would a man in his right mind attempt such a thing? He would not.

Lou Hart may have done the things with which he was charged. There is no way of knowing absolutely, but the people back of the prosecution certainly believed he did, and they acted as anyone else would under the circumstances. Lou Hart was caught in the toils this summer like many another dealer in cattle and farmer. He worried over it until—something snapped. Lou Hart then was a changed man and not responsible for his acts. He did something he should not have done. Once in, he knew not how to get out. Doubtless that preyed upon his mind and he resolved with shattered reasoning that the quickest way to end it all would be the best.

Fear of physical suffering would not lead a man like Lou Hart to commit suicide. There must have been an awakening when the officers came—a realization of what he had done and the disgrace of it all, together with the thought that his friends and the world never would understand. And then—the end. And Lou Hart has paid for any misstep he may have taken, knowingly or unknowingly. We have known him for a number or years and always regarded him as a good man. We shall always remember him as such, despite his untimely fate. Lou Hart's tragedy may indeed appear to have resulted from a lapse in reason, but there seems little doubt that economic desperation was the ultimate cause.

1913 was the year that Lou Hart wrote his final poem, "Ode to the Farmer." It survives in Hart's own pencil-written draft. The copy "somehow fell into my hands," Olive Riffey wrote when she sent a photocopy to me, "and I've always kept it." The poem was not put into stanzas, and its uneven metrics (especially of lines five through eleven), unpolished organization, and abrupt ending are all evidence of its unfinished status. Unquestionably the troubled tone of this poem, reflecting Hart's own economic woes, stands in marked contrast to the idyllic tone of the Crocker poem. Still there is humor amid the adversity here, a touch of irony that turns that potential lament into an affirmation.

Ode to the Farmer

The farmer is a happy guy,
He's up at four o'clock,
he builds the fires, he calls his wife,
Then goes to feed the stock.

He curries sleek the old bay mare
Cleans out the barn,
Milks the cows before the break of day

He wonders if his wood pile
Throughout the day will last
With fear of two big stoves
On all day at full blast.

While he eats his breakfast
His good wife lets him know
They are out of soap and coffee
And the flour is getting low.

The children still are sleeping,
He notes with silent joy,
And says "By George, things sure are changed
Since I was just a boy."

His father used to yell at him
"Hey, are you still in bed?
Come out of it you lazy cuss,
The east is getting red."

He stops awhile to listen
To hear their loud and healthy snores
Then hies him to the barn again
To finish up the chores.

While city folks are still in bed
And chilly is the morn
He's on his way to distant fields
For a load of kaffir corn.

His dog is always with him
And seems to say with his eye
"I'm glad I'm just a dog;
I'm sorry for that guy."

But nothing cares the farmer
Though winter winds do blow
In sun or rain, its just the same
He's always on the go.

His clothes are getting seedy
His hair is getting gray
His back is bent from chopping wood
Through many a weary day.
He won't complain, he doesn't growl
Though drought and flood and fire
To work him grievous mischief
Do seemingly conspire.

His children they all have good clothes
His wife, she wears the best
But the farmer's coat is faded
And he hasn't any vest.

The boys have got new duds
The girls all need new frocks
But the farmer hasn't got the change
To buy a pair of socks.

Yes, happy is the farmer
He's happy as the day,
For when there's nothing else to do
He's got the bills to pay.

His credit's good at all the stores
The merchants all are glad
No matter what the family buys
To charge it up to dad.

And when earthly things are ended
And Gabriel blows his trump
To get the others ready
The farmer will have to hump.

This humorously ironic lament of hard times, in light of subsequent events, has a sharpness, a poignance reflected in the understated comment of Mrs. Riffey: "I expect there was much truth in this poem." One might wonder about Hart's relationship with his second wife, and hers to her stepchildren, but there seems to me little doubt that the time Lou Hart spent cowboying for the Crocker brothers must have seemed a golden age to him, one he preserved for all of us in "Springtime at Crockers."

Part two

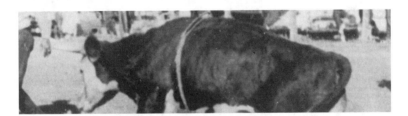

Cattle and Horses

Outlaw steer in Cassoday stockyards, 1938.

Five

Some Horses
(Title borrowed from Tom McGuane)

major drawback to being a cowboy is that you have to work with cows, and cows are (choose one or more of the following adjectives, or supply one of your own): obstinate, stupid, contrary, dim-witted, ornery, neurotic, aggravating animals. With not a cow in sight, you can leave a gate open just long enough to drive to the windmill and in the few minutes it takes to throw out a salt block, half a dozen head are liable to be a mile down the road. But try to gather and drive those same critters out that same gate, and they'll either break for the far side every time you get close to it or else mill in front of the wide-open gate for what seems like half the morning before a few brave and hardy steers take a few timorous steps out onto the road. Makes you wonder if there's some sort of invisible wall between the high poles. I've seen an Erwin E. Smith photograph that shows two Texas cowboys trying to dislodge a cow that has wedged herself, literally, between a rock and a hard place, nary a blade of grass in sight to have logically lured her onto that bare hillside and into her predicament. Getting stuck behind a bunch of poky cows, yelling yourself hoarse trying to get them to move just a little faster than the turtle that's speeding down the grassy lane in front of them, or else running your horse ragged trying to get some flighty heifers into a set of pens reminds me of a poem I heard at an early National Cowboy Symposium in Lubbock several years ago. I don't remember the name of the poet or the title of his verse, but he had definitely experienced some aggravating cattle in his day. The gist of his poem was a vegetarian giving a cowboy a hard time for his part in the meat industry. His response to this harangue was straightforward: "Lady, I don't even like the taste of beef; I just eat it for revenge."

Ah, but then there's the cow pony, that bringer of joy, that mitigator of bovine contrariness. The feel of a good cow horse between your knees, reins slack as she ducks and dodges half a step ahead of a steer you're pushing out of the herd, anticipating his every move. The wind whistling past your ears as your sure-footed rope horse races across a rocky pasture, closing the gap and giving you a clear shot at a foot-rot steer just before he hits the timber. A good horse makes up for a lot of cantankerous cattle, not to mention trailer tires gone flat, pickups that won't start, windmills that won't pump, washed-out water gaps, and the myriad other tribulations of a Flint Hills cowboy.

To a cowboy there's nothing better than a good horse, and nothing much worse than a bad one. The late Mason Crocker of Matfield Green once told me that he didn't have any trouble hiring good cowboys because he raised good horses and a cowboy, especially one without a family, would even work for lower wages if he was well mounted. And the Crocker roans were noted for their cowing ability.

Not all horses are created (or trained) equal. There are degrees of goodness and badness among them, as in most other things in life. Most often there is goodness and badness in the same animal. I've owned a couple of geldings in recent years, a gray and a grulla, that were good enough horses. They were both decent sized and smooth riding and gentle, and, although the gray wasn't as consistently unflappable as the mouse-colored one, pretty much anyone who knew even a little about horses could ride either one in safety. Each pony would follow a steer if you needed to rope one, and each could pull one into a trailer. You could work cattle in a pen, although neither one ever showed much desire to move with a cow unless he was reined.

That deficiency in natural cowiness was the problem. They would do whatever you asked of them, but neither one of them seemed to take any pleasure, any overt interest in his work. But they were good looking and they sold well. The mouse-colored horse is now enjoying a life of leisure in Michigan, and the gray has found his calling as a team roping horse, a good one. I never would have guessed he had it in him, but it took his new owner less than six months to win nearly ten grand off his back heeling steers. His full brother, by the way, is a saddle bronc in the Rumford Rodeo PRCA (Professional Rodeo Cowboys Association) bucking string. So both grays are doing well in the rodeo arena.

When you get down to it, almost every horse has a flaw or a shortcoming of some kind, but if he's reasonably good looking and reasonably gentle and reasonably capable at cow work, then there's not much room for complaining. Cold-jawed or hard-headed or rough-riding or hard-to-catch horses are a pain, although not much is more irksome than a horse that whinnies every time you get more than a dozen feet away from the other riders. Range-country wisdom holds that every cowboy will have one top horse in his lifetime, one that will make up for all the average (and worse) horses he's had to put up with. Actually, I think that truism is a little exaggerated on the negative side. Chances are, it seems to me, that you'll run across several good ones, horses that you look forward to riding, even if only a couple could be considered truly exceptional.

As I look back over the years, only one of my horses, the first, probably fits that truly exceptional category, a gelding called Tony that for many years was the best cutting horse in the central Flint Hills. I remember watching him win cutting contests at Strong City and at Wilbur Countryman's rodeo nearly every year during the late 1940s and well into the 1950s. But by that time he wasn't my horse anymore and hadn't been from the time I was only a couple of years old. I, naturally, don't remember any of this, but according to the family story, Dad had early on picked out this bluish mouse-colored colt for me. I think he was about a four- or five-year-old when

Dad sold him, so he must have been about two-and-a-half at the time of my birth, the middle of December, 1939. (Also according to family lore, Dad first took me horseback when I was only two weeks old; I assume it wasn't snowing. I don't know what Mother thought of this; she was leery of horses and as far as I know never once got on one.) Gwyn Liggett, a rancher from Rosalia who had been a top calf roper back in the 1920s and 1930s, came by one day, maybe just to visit or maybe to look over some of our horses. (My grandfather and his two sons ran two or three dozen good mares for raising riding horses and work mules.) Gwyn liked the looks of Tony and asked about him. Dad said he wasn't for sale, but Gwyn persisted, so Dad named a price high enough, he thought, to scare him off. I seem to recall hearing it was five hundred dollars, this at a time when you could buy a decent broke horse for fifty or seventy-five dollars and a really good pasture horse for a hundred. But instead of being spooked off, Gwyn whipped out his check-book, changed Tony's name to Smoky, and my first horse became a champion cutting horse.

I did have a good calf roping horse, if not of the same championship quality as Tony. When I was fifteen, a man from Whitewater sent over two five-year-old horses and gave me the mare for breaking the gelding. I called her Kitty (after Kitty Wells, the Queen of Country Music). People called her sorrel, but she wasn't red. Her color was a kind of very deep chocolate, but not brown. She looked something like the liver chestnut that Ben K. Green shows in his book on horse colors. This was just about the time I was wanting to rodeo, and Kitty turned out to be a good roping horse. She was eager but not chute crazy, and she was quick, although not racehorse fast. I suppose that my best memory with Kitty is winning second at the state high school rodeo, or else the string of three straight twelve-second times back in the days when elevens were rare and nobody roped calves in ten. (Now they tie them in seven. I doubt if I could have done that in my prime, even if I'd started on the ground with the calf already caught.)

The first horse of mine I remember was Trigger, an old horse well into his twenties that Dad bought from Frank Klasser, along with a kid saddle that I, my sister Rita (two years younger than I), Rita's girls, our kids, and now my granddaughter all rode. I was six or seven years old when Trigger had to be put down, but by that time

Loading Kitty to go to a rodeo in 1957.

he had done his job of training me to ride. Neither my sister nor I ever had a pony, Dad figuring rightly that an old broke cow horse was a better teacher for a kid than an ornery Shetland.

I'm using that same philosophy with my grandchildren. They ride Molly, the favorite of all my horses, who is in her mid-twenties now. Her bloodline goes back to Man o' War, and we raised her from a Leo mare (Cinnamon) I traded Jay Young out of for a big bay grade gelding (Hector). I took Cinnamon back to Jay's when she was about ten and bred her to his Windchester stud, with the happy result of Molly, a sorrel mare that pushes it to weigh a thousand pounds and stand fourteen hands. I've kidded Jay a lot about his stud throwing Shetlands, but Molly has a classic Quarter Horse build, natural cowing ability, and the biggest heart of any horse I ever rode. We didn't ride her all that much until she was six or seven, and she tended to be kind of high-strung in those younger years, really wanting to move out and tossing her head when you held her back—not a good habit for someone like me who likes a calm horse. Until she was in her late teens, she'd also pitch a little when you first got on if you'd let (or encourage) her.

I started riding her more about the time our son Josh was living at Cassoday and day-working wherever he could. I'd occasionally go along with him at shipping time, usually riding a tall red roan gelding we called Zennor (named, for some odd reason, after a town in Cornwall). Zennor was a decent enough horse. You could rope off him and work cattle, but his mouth was a little hard and he never showed much natural inclination to cow. Not like Molly. A Zennor story, and then back to her.

One time when our son Josh was working for Carl Grunder, I went down to help move some heifers southwest of Cassoday. The infamous Florida heifers. Not wild or crazy, but not quite sane. Josh worked quite a bit for Carl that summer, and those heifers were a source of constant frustration. Many of them had cropped ears and bobbed-off tails, probably the result of frostbite from being shipped to Kansas before spring had fully replaced winter. Josh blamed it on alligators. The day I was helping, we spent at least an hour just trying to get them out of the pasture. They'd go right up to the gate, but they wouldn't go through. They didn't run, but they'd scatter like chickens when pushed, and we'd have to go back and bring them up to the gate again, then repeat the process until finally a few ventured onto the road. Josh told me about getting one of them out of a neighbor's pasture through which a highline ran. He and Carl got her separated from the herd and started back to her own pasture, half a mile away. They only thing between them and the gate was an electric utility pole. Open spaces all around it, but the heifer ran headlong into the pole, bounced back two or three yards, then hit it again before they could get her shoved to the side and past the pole. On another day that I was helping, one of the heifers, rather than drive over easy ground to the gate, plunged into a seemingly shallow pond and stopped about halfway across. Zennor, who stood a little over fifteen hands, and I plunged in after her, he splashing along in chest-deep water and me hollering at the heifer. All of a sudden the horse stepped off a ledge, and in an instant he had totally disappeared, water completely over his ears—and I was up to my shoulders. I don't know if the horse hit the bottom or started swimming, but he bobbed up like a cork and we drove the heifer on out of the pond.

We eventually sold Zennor to Carl for use in his dude-ranch operation. He was a decent enough horse, but he never really took after cattle the way Molly did. I recall vividly the first time that happened. I was helping Vestrings that day, driving cattle toward their headquarters from a pasture east of the Cassoday–Rosalia road. Up until this particular day Molly hadn't shown any special proclivity toward cowiness. I was riding along at the back of the herd, which was moving easily. A yearling made a sudden turn out from the other cattle, and while I was still just thinking about reining her after him, Molly whirled on her hind legs, laid her ears back at the steer, and jumped him back into the herd, leaving me off balance and hanging to the right. From that moment on she was a cow horse.

Like a lot of good working horses (actually, a lot of horses period), Molly isn't easy to catch without oats. I can understand why she doesn't have much patience for being fussed over out in the pasture or in a corral (too much pride to be treated like a pet), but you'd think that she'd be eager to get to the work she loves doing. And she does love it. Several years ago when Josh was working on a ranch at Beaumont I rode Molly to help one day. It was my first time on the ranch and the owner, as is common with new help owners don't know much about, had put me at the tail end of the herd of cows and calves. Up ahead the lead cows (always the liveli-est) were doing their best to avoid being driven toward the pens (it doesn't take a cow long to learn that good things don't usually happen to them in pens). Molly and I were at the back with the slow cows, but her eyes and her mind were on the leaders an eighth of a mile ahead, where her tensed muscles wanted her to be. Later, after we had them in the pens, Sam Brady, whose keen eyes missed little around cattle, said something to me about how that "catty little mare" sure hated to miss out on the action. (Sadly, a few years after that Sam, one of the best pasture cowboys in the southern Flint Hills and a genuinely nice man, was killed in a freak accident when a young horse he was loping across a smooth pasture stumbled and fell.)

In her prime Molly was a good pasture-roping horse, quick al-though not as fast as a longer-legged steed. And she'd do whatever you asked of her. She could pull a steer that came within a couple of hundred pounds of her own weight into a trailer so hard and fast that his head would bang like a pinball on the front panel. And she was sure footed. She seemed able to pick her way through the thickly strewn rocks that cover the Hills; seldom did you hear the clank of steel horseshoe against flint rock. I was particularly thank-ful for her agility one time when I was trying to rope a wild steer the first year that Josh and his cousin, Warren Kruse, had started their ranching venture, the Flying W Ranch, with headquarters just south of Clements in Chase County. Half a dozen steers had eluded the first gather in a pasture that had everything bad in it—rocks, brush, timber, streams, steep canyons, old stone fences. I jumped a steer out of some trees along the road and headed him north along a flat area where I would have a chance of roping him. I was barreling after him, rope whirling and Molly at full speed, through the weedy bottom when I saw a draw just ahead. I later determined that it was about five feet wide and four feet deep, but when you're running flat out, going way too fast to stop or turn, a little draw like that looks like the Palo Duro Canyon. I grabbed the saddle horn with my rope hand (rope still in it) and kicked loose from the stirrups. As high as the weeds were, I figured that even if the mare did see the ditch, it would be too late to avoid a wreck. I threw Molly her head and ducked my own, hoping to be thrown free and roll and not be smashed between the saddle and the side of the ditch. But

Molly sailed through the air, landing on the other side as smooth as a steeplechaser. I wish I could say that I shook the loop out and latched it onto the steer, but by the time I got my heart out of my throat, he was disappearing into the timber.

When Molly was seventeen and I had younger horses that needed riding, I turned her over to my wife. Cathy likes to ride, but came to it somewhat later than I. She likes Molly because she's willing to go but also controllable. In 2003 Molly's arthritic right front shoulder got a little worse, so Cathy switched to Rosita, another lively sorrel mare that likes to work cattle, and now Molly is the kid horse. I never thought that she would be gentle enough for that, but like a lot of horses she can tell if the person on her back needs to be coddled or challenged.

Molly might be my all-time favorite horse, but in absolute terms the best horse I ever rode was a big red-dun gelding that we raised. My sister, who first owned him, named him Travis. When I got him, I changed his name to Claude but never called him that. He was always One-Eye or, like most horses his color, Old Buck. Here's his background story:

Along about the time I hit high school, maybe a year or two before, our jack, Old Black Joe, escaped his pen and got into the Little Pasture where we kept milk cows overnight and—more to the point in this instance—where the saddle horses ran. It was quite a lucky break for Joe, for of the four horses in the pasture, three were willing mares. Eleven months later we had three mule colts, one of them belonging to Rusty, Dad's best cow horse. She was out of commission for the summer and, as it turned out, her working days were over. Dad started riding other horses and Rusty, along with her sister mule-mothers, became a brood mare.

About two years after the mule episode, in the mid-1950s, Dad hauled Rusty and Star (a little bay mare I had ridden when I was younger) up to Matfield Green to breed to a good stallion that Wayne Rogler was standing, Sutherland's Fire Hair. Star had a roanish little sorrel filly colt with a bald face and wide-set front legs. I called her Jan (after Jan Howard, the country singer) and made a bulldogging horse out of her. Well, actually I didn't have much to do with it; she was a natural. On her maiden run, I took her past a former roping calf, a two-year-old Ayrshire that had grown a decent set of horns as he aged, then jumped him on the second run. That was all it took. She'd lay her ears back as she ran past that Ayrshire and pull you right up under his horns every time. Unfortunately, although she was quick, she wasn't fast. She was a good practice horse on slow steers or at a lap-and-tap dogging. I only took her to a couple of rodeos, winning a second place at Council Grove and overshooting a set-up steer at Countryman's.

Rusty had a horse colt, Buck, which Dad gave to Rita. He was a solidly built dun, a lot bigger and heavier muscled than his half sister, and a little edgier, too. I bought him when he was a three-year-old and Rita was getting married and moving to western Kansas. By that time he had had the first of two operations to remove a large, eyeball-sized, wartlike growth just above his right eye. When I got the horse, the wart had grown back just as big. I didn't want to spend the money to take him back to K-State, so we hauled him to the vet in El Dorado. The growth didn't return, but as a result of the operation his eyelid drooped, the eye was a little cloudy, and the tear duct continually dripped. But that horse could see more cow with his bad eye than most horses can see with two good ones.

He was a little bronky by the time I started riding him. It was the winter of 1961, the year I had graduated from K-State. Mother was teaching school in El Dorado, Dad was looking after the cows, and I wasn't doing much of anything. Just hanging around home, waiting to be drafted. Some of my friends had taken their physicals in May and were called up the next month, so when I took the physical in June, I figured I'd soon be in the army, but the call never came. Earlier that fall after shipping was over, I had ridden for Wayne Rogler, looking after Mississippi yearlings that Wayne had taken in to winter on the Frew pastures near the county line. It was a cold, drizzly fall, the cattle were sickly, and I got in plenty of roping practice doctoring them. I'd get up each morning and drive the dozen miles from our place to Wayne's, then catch either Pockets (a leggy three-year-old bay thoroughbred) or Mary Ann (a nice little sorrel mare, also three years old) and head to the pasture. The yearlings were pretty much straightened out by mid-November, so I quit to go to the Chicago rodeo. There I won enough of the calf roping that I didn't have to work for a while (not that the win was so big, but that my living expenses in those days of 25-cent-a-gallon gasoline, 50-cent beer, and seven-plays-for-a-quarter juke-boxes were so low), so I was hanging around home helping feed the cows in the daytime and following my coon dogs through the timber at night. (At one point that winter I realized that in the evenings Dad had for some days been reading aloud the want ads from the *El Dorado Times*. I also realized, much more quickly, almost instantaneously in fact, that this was not something he was doing for his own benefit or entertainment. So after feeding the next morning I went off visiting rodeo buddies in Halstead and Brookville for a couple of weeks and by the time I got home, he was glad to see me again.) At any rate, I saddled Buck up one day after a big snow and headed out to check on the cows. About halfway to the pasture he stuck his head down and started bucking, but instead of trying to pull him up, I did what I had heard bronc riders in North Dakota and Montana did and headed him toward a snow bank. After a few lunges through the drifts he bogged down and only bucked a couple of times after that.

Buck was not only an excellent pasture horse, surprisingly quick on his feet for as big as he was, but also good in the arena. When I was in graduate school at Columbia, Missouri, Cathy and I rented a pasture on Perche Creek just west of town so that we could have some horses to ride and thus keep a connection to the prairie while in the midst of all those trees. For three of the four years we were there, we ran steers in the summer. Among other horses, I took Buck over there so I could do a little roping. We didn't have time to go to many rodeos, but I did win a team roping at Queen City. The rodeo at Pilot Grove was particularly memorable, not for the arena action (I missed my calf) but because the rodeo clown had a camel for one of his acts. I didn't know about the camel, naturally enough, but as I was riding from the horse trailer to the arena before the rodeo started we happened upon the beast just as he was standing up. I doubt if a steeplechaser could jump any higher, faster, or farther than Buck did when he saw that strange creature. My next-to-fondest memory of our time in Missouri, after the birth of our daughter, was being awarded my Ph.D. one night and winning the calf roping off Old Buck at the Williamsburg rodeo the next.

There were a bunch of horses between Buck and Molly, some of them—Hector, Cinnamon—pretty good, but none to compare to those two. As I said earlier, Molly is now semi-retired and doing duty as a kid horse for grandchildren Henry and Lucy (a third grandchild, Josie, living on a ranch, has horses of her own). When

Buck got up around twenty, Dad traded him off. Right now I'm riding two little gray mares, both out of Jay Young's gray stud. Pudge (she started out with the name Lucy, but when Farrell and Larry picked that name for their daughter, the horse got a name change) is out of Molly, and Tica is out of Cinnamon, which makes her relationship to Pudge a bit complicated because Molly's mother was also Cinnamon. I guess Pudge and Tica would be half sisters from the sire's angle, and some sort of aunt-niece from the dam's. I like them both, and if I could combine their qualities I'd have another great horse. Tica has more natural cow in her than any other horse I've owned. The first time I used her with cattle, as a two-year-old, we were helping Josh and his wife, Gwen, move a bunch of cows about eight miles. I was at the drag end, which is the best place for a colt, and by the time we were halfway home, Tica was reaching out to nip the stragglers, her ears laid back. She doesn't need reining to turn cattle and she has a nice slow lope for traveling. But she's not very fast and not (yet, at least) a good rope horse. Pudge, on the other hand, needs a little reining when working cattle, but she's better looking, quicker, faster, and much better for roping. I guess what I have is a pen horse and a pasture horse. I reckon I can get by with that, and at this stage of my life they should last me as long as I'll need a horse.

Six

The Whirlaway Mare

Just north of the county line, about three and a half miles from Cassoday, the highway angles slightly northeast on its way to Matfield Green, bisecting a trace that, unless you are looking hard, is visible only when the East and South Frew pastures are burned each spring. I used to ride those pastures when I worked for the Rogler Ranch, but I hadn't noticed this dim, straight rut until years later when Wayne pointed it out to me. I had been visiting with him at the ranch house, asking, as I often was, about some obscure point of Flint Hills history.

Wayne Rogler was the son of Henry and the grandson of Charles Rogler, who had walked into Chase County before the Civil War and established the farm that would, under Wayne, become one of the most prominent ranches in the Flint Hills. A former state senator, Wayne was always abreast of current affairs, political and

Horse race at the Cassoday Fair, 1909.

agricultural, and he knew more local history than anyone else in his part of the Hills.

On this particular day he pointed out a couple of large, flat, long, smooth chunks of limestone as he walked me to my car. Those, he said, were the drag stones for the racetrack up on the county line. What racetrack? I asked. And thus the story of the Scribner Gray and the Whirlaway Mare.

Cassoday lies on the flats, west and south of the more rugged breaks in Greenwood and Chase counties. About a mile north of the county line a ridge extends out into the draws and canyons that descend toward Jack Springs and Mercer Creek. Along that level ridge, running roughly northwest to southeast, is where early residents of Cassoday, Bazaar, Matfield Green, Wonsevu, and other communities in the area used to gather to settle disputes about the relative speed of horses. As is usual in such amateur affairs, the races were of the match variety—one horse against another. Thus two parallel tracks between a half and three-quarters of a mile long were laid out a few feet apart. The two big rocks I had seen in Wayne's yard were dragged back and forth to mark the tracks by knocking down the bluestem. Over time, and many races, the tracks cut into the ground like a cow trail, or Santa Fe Trail ruts, still visible (to a discerning eye) a century after their last use.

Rules for these races could vary slightly from match to match, but in general the two horses would be lined up in the open (no starting gates) on one end and, at a signal from the starter once he had determined that both riders were ready, head toward the other end, each in its own track. Two judges, mounted on their own horses, marked the finish line, with the winner being the first horse to cross between them. Spectators lined both sides of the track, with the biggest crowd, naturally enough, clustering around the finish line.

During the latter part of the nineteenth century, one of the fastest horses in Chase County was a gray stud owned by the Scribners, a pioneer family in the Matfield Green–Bazaar area. Very few challengers even came close to beating the Scribner Gray. Arthur Crocker, who became one of the big-time ranchers in the Flint Hills, got his start loose-herding cattle out in the Camp Creek area and beyond, where Chase and Greenwood counties join. As was usual up into the 1890s, steers would be shipped in from Texas in the spring, herded on open range for the summer grazing season, then shipped on to Kansas City or Chicago in the fall. Along with other youngsters at the time, Arthur was hired by a pastureman to stay with the cattle and keep them from straying onto land controlled by some other pastureman. Arthur would come in every week or so for supplies, then head back out to open country. The young herd boys, as they were called, cooked over campfires and slept under the stars or in tents in the rain. They would occasionally cross paths in the course of their work, always a welcome break in the loneliness and boredom.

For a number of years, as Wayne relayed the tale, the Mulhalls from Indian Territory ran cattle west of Madison. Helping out with these steers was young Lucille Mulhall, who would later gain acclaim as an accomplished performer in rodeos and Wild West shows. It was she whom Teddy Roosevelt, following a successful coyote chase led by Lucille and her father, called America's first cowgirl—not only could she ride and rope with the best, but she was attractive as well. Arthur Crocker and his fellow herders were never unhappy when their cattle grazed toward Big Springs, for there was always a good chance that Mulhall cattle might be in the vicinity.

The Mulhalls were, as you would expect, well mounted, but Lucille's mare was particularly nice—and she was fast, of Whirlaway breeding. Lucille had no trouble at all winning the impromptu races that arose among the herders. As the summer grazing season drew to an end, Arthur and a couple of his friends did a little horse trading. Autumn found the cattle all shipped out of Bazaar and the boys headed back to Matfield Green leading the Whirlaway Mare.

Their plan, and it was a good one, was to pool their summer wages—and double them. They knew the Mulhall mare was faster than the Scribner stud; they had seen both of them run. So they challenged the Scribners to a race and bet every dollar they had earned. People in the area, tired of the Scribner dominance, were solidly behind Arthur and his friends. The day of the race found the Frew pasture crowded with people, nearly all of them cheering for the youngsters and hoping that the Scribners would finally lose a race. Arthur Crocker, mounted in a light stock saddle, rode for the boys. When the race began, it was immediately obvious that the Scribner Gray had met his match. The crowd could see that the Whirlaway Mare was every bit as fast as the boys had claimed, for by the time the two horses had reached the halfway mark she was two or three lengths ahead and steadily increasing the daylight between them.

As the mare sped toward the finish line, the crowd went wild, cheering madly, waving their arms, throwing their hats into the air. Ironically, it was this very enthusiasm of their supporters that was the boys' undoing. The Whirlaway Mare was a pasture horse, not a seasoned racehorse. She might have been fast as the wind, but she was also skittish, and she'd never seen, or heard, that many people before. Instead of dashing across the line, she spooked at the noise and, with young Arthur pulling helplessly on the reins, trying to steer her back on course or at least stop her, she ran off across the prairie. Meanwhile, the Scribner horse, ignoring the commotion, galloped across the line and won the race.

So Arthur Crocker's venture into racehorses didn't pay off, but other ventures did. Later, he and his brother Ed were among the nation's most prominent cattlemen with ranches in Texas and Arizona, in addition to their Flint Hills holdings in Chase, Butler, and Greenwood counties.

Seven

Gift Horses

It was not an uncommon practice during the Railroad Era of Flint Hills history for a Texas cattleman to occasionally send up a horse or two along with his cattle each spring. Sometimes he did it so he or his foreman would have a cutting horse he was familiar with to ride when he came up later in the summer during shipping season. Other times, because often the same Texan would have pastured cattle with the same Kansan for years, he might send a horse as a gift, a kind of bonus to strengthen the good relationship that had built up over the years. Often this gift horse was a good-blooded mare from which the Kansas rancher could raise colts. Many cowboys, particularly on some Texas ranches, preferred to ride geldings, so shipping a few excess mares to Kansas helped trim the size of the herd in Texas, especially during times of drouth in the southwest.

Chuck Hodges, a friend from my hometown, told me about a time that one Texas foreman probably wished his boss had sent a horse up in the spring. Jake Jordan (pronounced "Jurdan" in true Texas style) was foreman for Leo Welder and Claude McCann, out of Victoria. Welder/McCann sent a lot of cattle to the Flint Hills back in the 1950s, many of them to Frank Klasser, who ranched east of Cassoday. I remember Jake from my youth, a short fellow with a south Texas drawl who always wore a narrow-brimmed silver belly Stetson and khaki pants, the cuffs of which he tucked into his short-topped handmade boots. Leddy's, I suppose, or maybe Olsen-Stelzers. He would entertain us with stories from Texas while we sat around Opal's Cafe, waiting for the train to come in so we could load cattle. One thing that stuck in my young mind was his offhand reference to "the little horse trap behind the barn, only ten sections." My gosh, at four acres per head we could have run 1,600 steers on a pasture that size up here. It obviously took a lot of land to handle one cow in south Texas.

I recall seeing Jake cut out fat steers to send to Kansas City, but I don't remember his horse, although it was undoubtedly one he had borrowed. As a kid, it was usually my job to help hold the cut (the steers to be driven in to the railroad), although occasionally I got to help with the more exciting action in the big herd. Some men were better at (and better mounted for) cutting out just the animal they wanted, but others (usually, it seemed, a commission man from Kansas City or a ranch representative from Texas on a borrowed horse) would often drive three or four at you at once, yelling "just the one on the left" or "hold the brockle face and the muley," then get irritated if you let the wrong one (or ones) get by. Dad and Uncle Marshall had a sure cure for someone who overdid that kind of cutting—they threw everything back at the cutter until, realizing that they'd never get to the yards in time for the train at this rate, he started bringing only the ones he wanted.

It's not always but often true that the cattleman (whether a rancher or a commission man) does not have the riding skills of the ordinary cowboy. Thus the borrowed cutting horse was often a sight better than his rider. Chuck recalled that on this particular day, Jake's borrowed cutting horse was working so well that on one occasion he ducked after a steer and dumped Jake unceremoniously onto the ground. Jake took the spill in good humor, getting back on and continuing his work. Sitting around Opal's Cafe later that day, he was recounting the episode to a group that included his wife.

Kenneth Hoy on Brutus, late 1930s.

"Yes," Jake said, "Old Brownie was really working today. Why, when that big old horned steer turned back, Brownie was so quick he just cut right out from under me."

Jake's account was interrupted by Mrs. Jordan, who dryly re-marked, "Jake, that horse could have wired you two weeks ago what he was going to do and you'd still have hit the ground."

Back to the gift horses. A one-time neighbor of ours, Tom Miller, who was reared down in Greenwood County, told me this story. Sometime back around 1935 or 1940, some cowboys were unloading cattle, I think at Virgil, or it could have been Hamilton. As was often the case, these big Texas steers had arrived during the middle of an April night. The stockyards had lights, so unloading them wasn't much more difficult than in the daytime. The cowboys had emptied the last car and were getting ready to go home when they heard a noise coming from inside it. When they checked, they found a horse haltered and tied to the front of the stockcar. He seemed gentle, though a little stiff after his long train ride, and he led out willingly. Once they had him under the lights, they discovered that he was a well-made mouse-colored stud horse, recently shod all around, with white spots on his withers where saddle sores had long since healed. Assuming naturally enough that the Texas rancher had sent him up for use in the Flint Hills, they led him home in the dark and put him in the barn for the rest of the night.

Next morning the boss pointed to one of the hands to catch the new horse and ride him that day. The stud took the saddle calmly, didn't squeal at the mares, and stood quietly while the cowboy climbed aboard. But no sooner had his foot caught the off stirrup than the horse blew up, bucking and twisting and throwing the cowboy sky high. Shaken but not injured, at least not seriously enough to require an ambulance, the cowboy, following the un-written code that governs horsemen everywhere, climbed back up and, ready (although decidedly not eager) for the explosion this time, managed to hang on through the roughest storm he had ever endured on the back of a horse. After a couple of minutes the horse settled down and the crew headed for the pasture. Coming back to the ranch after a morning of riding pastures and checking cattle, the new-horse rider took his turn at opening a gate, but as soon as he had it shut and had mounted up, the stud bucked every bit as hard and as long as he had that morning. After dinner, it was the same story. The cowboy, swearing to ride the buck out of this bronc (and swearing also at the horse), rode him hard that long afternoon. The stud's coat was foamy with sweat and his head was hanging low, but when the cowboy remounted after getting off to open and shut the gate leading into the corral, the rodeo began again, the stud just as hard to ride at twilight as he had been the first time that morning.

He was a hell of a cow horse, Tom said: "You couldn't put a cow past him." He was a roping and cutting fool, smooth riding, tough, surefooted, quick and fast, able to jerk down and hold a bull, but it never once failed that if you got off that horse, no matter how many hours or how many miles he had been ridden, he would buck like a son-of-a-bitch every time you got back on. After that first day the other cowboys never expected the stud rider to open any gates, and more than once they would carry his food to him at noon so he wouldn't have to get off to eat. It even got so that whoever's turn it was to ride the grulla stud that day could be found at the barn a few minutes early, unlacing his stirrup leathers and shortening them a couple of holes so he could stand up high in the stirrups and twist to the leeward side when nature called.

A few years later the Texas rancher was at the Kansas ranch checking on his cattle. As he and his Flint Hills host stepped out of the house, he looked toward the barn and exclaimed: "Why, there's my stallion! I thought he was dead! The boys told me three years ago last spring that he'd been struck by lightning out in the pasture." The Texas cowboys, tired of fighting equine lightning every morning, had stuck him on the last cattle car they had loaded three seasons earlier and shipped their troubles to Kansas.

I wish I could have seen their faces when they saw that horse in their barn again.

Eight

Pasture Pranks

everal years ago I was in Reno, attending a meeting of the Western Social Sciences Association. I had gone through the twenty I had set aside for blackjack at the two-dollar table, and slot machines have never held any attraction for me, so I decided to go visit a Flint Hills cowboy. Jay B. Parsons was reared near Chelsea, about midway between Cassoday and El Dorado. I had never met him before, but I had heard Dad and Uncle Marshall talk about him, a calf roper and bulldogger who had done well in the RCA (Rodeo Cowboys Association). So I placed a phone call, got a welcoming response, rented a car, and drove across Donner Pass to Grass Valley, California.

When I got to his place near Rough and Ready (a good name for a Western town), they were working calves, J.B., then in his mid-seventies, catching heels and dragging to the crew. Later we talked in the office in his horse barn, and I found out a little more about his rodeo and ranching career. He had left the family farm after high school, taken jobs on ranches and dude ranches from New Mexico to Montana, rodeoed all over the country, and finally gotten into the racehorse business. Hanging on the wall was a photograph of a little mare named Lanty, who, along with some of her fast-running offspring, J.B. said, had paid for his ranch.

What about your rodeo career? I asked. Like most Flint Hills cowboys he wasn't too inclined to brag about his past successes, but when I asked how he got started rodeoing he had a good tale to tell.

It seems that J.B. got the rodeo bug as a high school kid watching some of the older fellows around Cassoday—Deke, Frank, Buss, and Jim Young; Dad and Uncle Marshall; Turk Harsh; and Wilbur Countryman. His mother, however, didn't want him rodeoing, not even the less dangerous timed events that he found especially appealing. So one day when his parents were gone, he got a friend, Chester Scribner, to come over and they set out for the pasture so J.B. could learn to bulldog. His father was pasturing some Texas steers that had pretty good horns on them, so J.B. figured that with Chester hazing, it would be easy to jump one out in the pasture.

Now the thing about bulldogging (or steer wrestling as the event is officially known) is that it happens fast in a rodeo arena (three or four seconds, if you want to win any money), and the uninitiated never see the subtleties, so unless you have someone to tell you just what to do, you're liable to have some trouble. It *looks* like the dogger jumps off on the steer's head, pulls him to a stop, then twists the horns to lay him flat, but in actuality you need to start down at the steer's shoulders and let your horse pull you up under the horns. If you jump directly onto the head, you'll drive it down into the ground (this maneuver is called a "houlihan") and run the risk of sticking a horn into the dirt. A horn driven into the dirt stops immediately, although the steer doesn't; his body flips literally head over heels, and if the horn doesn't come unstuck it might snap off, or the steer's neck might break. And so might the cowboy's.

Well, J.B. houlihaned the steer, but luckily he walked away from the wreck unhurt. Not so the steer. It was dead. J.B. said when he looked up, Chester was in a fast lope, headed for home. J.B., too, headed for the barn, worried sick about what would happen to him once his father got home. "I couldn't bring myself to tell him what I'd done," he said, "and I sure didn't have much appetite for sup-

Youngster thrown from a calf at Countryman's Rodeo, late 1950s.

per. I finally got a little sleep that night, and when Mother called me for breakfast, I still wasn't hungry. Well, about then my dad came in from choring and told my mother, 'You know, that little shower we had last night? It looks like lightning struck one of the steers.' I never said a word," he said, "and my dad never did know what really happened to his steer."

J.B.'s initiation into bulldogging reminds me of an episode in Dad and Uncle Marshall's young lives. It was a Saturday night, and they, like many young men in the Flint Hills in the 'teens and twenties, liked to ride into town for the evening. (I have a photograph from about the same time period showing a group of young horsemen calling themselves the "Burdick Roughnecks," the Saturday night crowd from that Morris County town on the western edge of the Flint Hills.) At Cassoday the young guys would hang around Al Gennet's (accent on the last syllable) barbershop, which was also a de facto pool hall, pitch and domino parlor, beer joint, and outlet for bootleg whiskey. I suppose some of the fellows had cars, but most of the crowd, at least the ones my father and uncle hung around with, were there horseback. Dad often rode Cap into town on Saturday nights, the only horse he ever owned, he told me, that would ground tie and never budge: "He'd starve to death with a bale of hay only ten feet away," was the way he put it.

On this particular night they were riding back home across pastures under the light of a bright full moon. The Sturgeon twins, or maybe it was the Plummer boys, were riding with them. Whether it was simply high spirits or perhaps a bottle or two of Prohibition beer, they got it into their heads to practice their rodeoing skills. One of them—I think it was Dad, but he was always a little vague on the subject—roped a cow and the others worked at rigging up a loose rope with which to ride her. Dad dismounted, probably to help hold the cow because both the Sturgeons or the Plummers, whichever it was, were younger and smaller than the Hoy brothers. Somehow in the moonlight and the confusion of an uncooperative cow, Dad's horse (unfortunately, not Cap that night) spooked and jumped. Like nearly everyone else in the Central Plains during that time period (in fact from the 1860s to the 1960s), Dad was tied on hard and fast. The cow got jerked down, which further spooked the horse, and he took off, dragging the cow across the prairie. The others gathered up their horses as quickly as they could and finally stopped the runaway. They figured the cow was dead, but after a little while she managed to catch her breath, find her feet, and stagger off.

The boys split up and headed for their respective homes, their high spirits well dampened. About a week later Dad Hoy (my grandfather) and his sons were in town when they ran into the neighbor whose cow had been roped. After some general conversation the neighbor remarked, "Frank, the damnedest thing happened. Lightning hit one of my cows the other night and burned the hair clear off one side. Made her a little stiff, but it didn't kill her." Dad said that, like J.B., he and Uncle Marshall never breathed a word.

Nine

To and from the Stockyards

owboys and railroaders are arguably the two most colorful folk figures in America, and the Railroad Era brought them together in what I like to think of as the Golden Age of the Flint Hills. During shipping season there was always a lot going on at the stockyards. A woman from Alta Vista once told me that for entertainment after church and Sunday dinner, her father would drive the family in to Volland to watch the cowboys load cattle. I doubt that would fly with today's preteens. But the stockyards were exciting places—dusty cowboys whooping at snorty Brahma steers, an occasional bronc ride, hopping onto a caboose for a look around.

Young fellows would often hang around the stockyards on spring weekends when cattle were coming into the Flint Hills, hoping to get hired to help drive them to pastures. That's what happened to Andy Olson, who was reared in northern Morris County. Andy told me that he and a friend were on their horses in White City (or

Leaving the Matfield Green Stockyards, 1944. From left: Arthur Crocker; unknown; Andy Tarrant; Wayne Rogler; unknown; Jess Bailey; Henry Rogler; William Blackmore; Mary Ann Rogler. (Chase County Historical Society)

maybe it was Dwight) late one mid-April afternoon when a couple carloads of cattle (just under a hundred head, as I recall him saying) came in. The rancher who received them asked the two young cowboys if they would drive these steers to the pasture, about ten miles out of town, and they naturally took the job.

Now in those days (the 1930s), most of the Texas steers that came to the Flint Hills for summer pasture were three or four years old, tall and lanky. They had plenty of frame (skeletal structure), but in the spring of the year after a hard winter on a drouth-stricken Texas ranch, there wasn't much flesh on that frame. Some were so weak that they had to be tailed up out of the cars (i.e., a couple of men would go into the stock car and push on the steer while twisting his tail in order to make him stand up) so that they could wobble down the unloading chute. Some were dead on the cars, and their bodies would be shoved out, farmers hauling them off for hog or dog feed.

Some of these sick and weak steers died in the first week or two, especially if it was a cold, rainy spring. But if the weather was warm and the grass coming on, the cattle could recover quickly. Paul Patterson, an old-time cowboy storyteller and poet from Crane, Texas, once told me about accompanying a trainload of his brother's steers to the Flint Hills, at roughly the same time period that Andy Olson was telling me about. (I'll get back to Andy's story in a little while.) "They were so poor and weak they could hardly stand," Paul said. "We had to lift about half of them out of the cars. But after they had grazed out about fifty yards on that new grass, they were feeling so good they were wringing their tails, shaking their horns, and looking for something to hook." Like many humorists, especially those from Texas, Paul occasionally exaggerates, but the point he made is a valid one: Those big, weak Texas steers made remarkable recoveries and weight gains on Flint Hills bluestem.

One more digression, and then back to Andy. Edgar Templeton, who farmed in the Cole Creek neighborhood southwest of Cassoday, told me that as a boy he often saw cattle that had been unloaded at DeGraff in the spring being driven to the pastures at Cassoday. Thousands of steers over several weeks would make this fifteen-plus-mile trek, but those that were too weak or sickly would be left by the wayside. Afterwards a man, hired for the purpose, would start at DeGraff and drive those steers that had recovered some of their strength on toward the pastures east of Cassoday. He knew which brands went to which pastures. Some of these steers would make it the whole way, others he could drive only a few miles before they gave out, so he'd pick them up again on a later day. It took about a month, Edgar said, for all the cattle to finally reach their summer homes. Edgar also said that if it were a rainy April, the unpaved DeGraff Road would become rutted from the hooves of steers, each one having stepped into the track of the steer in front of him. When these waves of deep ruts dried, they were so rough that his father had to drive their car in the pastures beside the road when he went to town.

But to return to Andy's story of taking similar steers to spring pasture: It was nearly dark when he and his friend finally got to the pasture, and it had not been a pleasurable trip. The weather was cold and the steers were weak. Every so often some would give out and the two young cowboys would leave them behind as they pushed the others slowly down the road. "We might not have made it," Andy said, "except my friend had a bottle of hot water with him and every little while we'd take a drink of it." Now by hot water, Andy was referring not to temperature but to proof—about 90 for that particular batch of bootleg.

When they arrived at the gate, only about a dozen head of the steers were still in front of them. After pushing the cattle into the pasture, the two cowboys sat down at the side of the lane to finish off the whiskey. The bottle was a little bigger than they realized. "We woke up next morning there by the gate cold, stiff, and hungover," Andy said. "I told my friend, 'Well, I suppose we better ride back and get the rest of the cattle.' And he said, 'Yes, but first maybe we ought to see what's in the pasture in case some of the others came in during the night.' So we counted them, and you know, every single one of those steers was in the pasture. They'd trailed after the others on their own. Those old Texas steers would stick together, not like these yearlings today."

Andy is sure right about today's yearlings. Working with yearlings compared to those old Texas steers is like dealing with rebellious or sullen teenagers compared with cooperative working adults in their late twenties. Maturity has something to do with it, particularly the experience that comes with age. Those older cattle had been gathered several times by the time they got to Kansas, where they would again be gathered several times before all of them had been shipped to market. They were used to being rounded up, and they knew how to act like a herd. Martin Gnadt from Alma remembers back when only two men could cut a hundred head out of a herd of five hundred big steers, one man cutting and the other holding the cut. Genetics also played a role. Sometimes a few Mexican cattle, corriente types, would show up back in the Railroad Era, but primarily we worked with four beef breeds and mixtures thereof: Hereford, Shorthorn, some Aberdeen Angus, and Brahma (Brahman, to be punctilious; braymies, to be colloquial). Brahmas and Brahma crosses, with their long, floppy ears and humps and their tolerance of heat, were particularly popular in south Texas, where a lot of our summer cattle came from. We thought they were wild, and they could be, but if you didn't rile them up they handled well. Again as Martin Gnadt observes, Brahmas might break back once, but then they'd settle down and not give any trouble. Today there must be nearly a hundred different breeds from every corner of the world on American ranches. Ever since the Charolais was introduced and started the exotic fad, we've been inundated with Chianinas and Fleckviehs and Gelbiehs and Salers and Belgian Blues and Simmentals and Limousines and on and on. Limmies are the worst, the most high-strung, the least manageable of them all. Most of these exotic breeds are European and have been bred and raised in European style—small numbers, kept in barns, cared for by hand. Here in the West they are raised in large numbers, kept in large pastures, and they run at the sight of a horse.

Several years ago my son filled a pasture with around four hundred Limousine-cross heifers from Texas. He had pulled a portable unloading chute down the pasture, but I doubt if more than a hundred hooves touched it—those heifers were so wild they leaped out of the truck as soon as the endgate was pulled up and most of them landed a dozen feet beyond the chute. ("They wouldn't be in such a hurry to get out if they knew they weren't in Texas," drawled one jingoistic trucker. It must have been his first trip to the Flint Hills or he would have known that a hundred days later each of those heifers would be 250 pounds heavier.) A week or so later, Josh and Gwen and I, returning from dragging calves down at Howard, stopped into the pasture to check the heifers. A bunch of them took off at a run as soon as they saw us a quarter of a mile away, and they were still running when we left the pasture an hour later. Not all of them were that goofy, but every bunch we rode up to would scatter like quail. Josh was worried sick about how he'd ever get them gathered at shipping time. These young cattle, compounded by their exotic breeding, knew nothing about bunching up and acting like a herd. So Josh decided to train them. A week or so later, he, Gwen, Cathy, and I unloaded in the pasture early in the morning. As soon as the heifers saw us and started running, we got behind the others and pushed them after the leaders. We circled the pasture a time or two, then tried putting them in a corner, but they scattered, so again we pushed the stragglers hard to keep up with the wild ones in front. At about the third or fourth attempt to hold them in a corner, they were tired enough to not try to break out, so we backed our horses up, turned toward the trailer, and left the heifers there to move out as they pleased. After that they no longer ran when we rode into the pasture, and on shipping day they were rambunctious, but we got them to the pens without a spill. They still weren't as tractable as the old Texas steers, but they had learned to herd up.

Back to the stockyards stories. This one took place in eastern Greenwood County over around Virgil where a rancher and a cattle buyer began to play pitch while waiting for the cowboys to gather the steers and drive them to the pens. They started out playing cut-throat pitch: eleven points a game, six cards and four points to a hand (high, low, jack, and the game), no draw, no widow—just like we used to play on the school bus as we were traveling to basketball games. Except we played five-point, counting the off-jack (the jack of the same color but not the same suit as trumps) as the extra point. The minimum bid for each hand was two, and if no one else bid, the dealer was stuck with it and often went set.

The beginning stakes between the rancher and the cattle buyer were a nickel a game and a nickel a set, but by the time the cattle reached the pens they were playing for a dime a game and a dime a set. After weighing and loading the cattle, the two adjourned to the pool hall in Yates Center where the stakes began at quarter-quarter, then progressed to dollar-dollar, and by the end of the evening they were playing for twenty dollars a game and twenty dollars a set. Now pitch, especially cut-throat, is a fast-paced game, and I don't know how many hands they must have gone through by the time the beer joint closed. The rancher, who is the one who told me the story, said that his wife wasn't too happy when he walked into the house a little after midnight, but that her mood brightened when she learned he had won over a thousand dollars in the marathon card game. Which, he told me, was more money than he cleared on the two truckloads of steers he had sold that day.

As I said earlier, back in the days when cattle were shipped into and out of the Flint Hills by train, the local stockyards was a bustling place. Whether at Hymer, Cassoday, Volland, or Matfield Green, whether on the Katy, the Santa Fe, the Frisco, or the Missouri Pacific, whenever there were cattle in the pens, there was often some excitement on the ground—a Brahma steer on the prod, a cowboy's horse suddenly breaking in two, a scuffle between humans.

The late Glen Clopton of Madison told me once about how as a teenager he stood up to one of the big cattlemen. Clopton had been with a crew that got to the Hamilton stockyards first that day, and after weighing their cattle they had put them in the pens closest to the loading chutes so that they could load out first. As a kid, he had been left to watch the cattle while the older cowboys on the crew went to eat. While they were gone, the boss of an outfit that had arrived later started to move the steers so he could put his own cattle in the priority loading pens. "I stood in the gate and told him he'd have to move me first," Clopton told me. "He was madder than a wet hen, but he backed down."

Not too long ago I ran across an account of a big fight in 1899 at the Bazaar stockyards. The scuffle was not about loading steers, but about ownership of a steer. Here is the *Chase County Leader-News* account, verbatim:

> The greatest fist fight that ever occurred in Chase or adjoining counties took place in one of the pens of the stock yards here last evening. Several parties were shipping cattle when Sam Stotler, living near the county line on the Verdigris, and Evander Bocook, living at Matfield, got into a dispute over the ownership of a steer. Bocook said if Stotler would make affidavit that the steer was his or under his control, he (Bocook) would let him have it. Stotler furnished the necessary evidence and Bocook, who was on the fence, said "the steer is yours, but you are a——!——!——!" Stotler returned the epithet and Bocook leaped to the ground but before recovering himself Stotler planted two blows in Bocook's eyes. Nothing daunted, Bocook recovered his equilibrium and tackled Stotler. John Leonard and Lewis McCrary were the only persons in the pen with the fighters and they attempted to part them, but they refused to be parted, and the battle was renewed. For 28 minutes they pounded each other, Stotler getting in mostly on Bocook's face, while Bocook showered blows on Stotler's breast and stomach, until both fell exhausted. Stotler broke his right hand and his breast and stomach was badly bruised. Bocook's eyes were nearly closed and his face cut and lacerated. Geo. Leonard dressed Bocook's wounds and he rode home in the Matfield carry-all. Stotler left for home on a horse.

> We hope the fight is over but some think they will renew the battle the first time they meet.

The combatants are pretty well matched, each weighing in the neighborhood of 200 pounds, but Stotler is the oldest and heaviest. Bazaar has been the scene of many a set-to in which the manly art of self defense has been introduced to show how battles are lost and won, but the last was the best, the men giving and taking punishment like veteran pugilists.

Ironically, at the time of the fight the newly created Kansas Livestock Association had a detective investigating both men for cattle theft. Neither man was ever caught in the act, but it's obvious that neither had a very high opinion of the other's character, either.

One story I've heard about a near-fight at the Cassoday stockyards involved Frank Klasser, whose ranch was in Greenwood County about a dozen miles southeast of Cassoday, and Slockie Brazel, who came from Eureka and cowboyed in the Cassoday-Rosalia area. Klasser, like a lot of cowmen (and unlike the typical cowboy), hated a rope. That didn't stop him from hiring Dad and Uncle Marshall to help with wild cattle that might need roping, although they were good enough cowboys to get the steers to the pens without having to rope them. And it didn't stop us from carrying a rope on our saddles (a cowboy might as well be naked as not carry a rope), but Dad made sure that my sister and I knew never to take it down to throw at weeds or heels while we were driving Klasser's cattle.

This particular day in the yards, Slockie was carrying a coiled lariat as he counted carloads of steers into the loading chutes as they were being driven up the alley. As the right number would go through the gate, he would toss the coils at the ones coming up behind them to scare them back. When Klasser looked out from the scale house and noticed him doing this, he yelled, cussed, picked up a two-by-four, and headed for him. Brazel scooped up a couple of rocks, then whizzed one right past Klasser's ear when he got fairly close. Frank stopped and said, "If I had my gun I'd fix you right here and now." Slock's reply: "I wish you did have it. I need a new gun." When Klasser went down to the telephone office to call the law (no cell phones in those days), Brazel got on his horse and rode away.

Martin Gnadt told me a good story about Herman Sommers and a railroad engineer. Martin himself was just a young cowboy at the time, the early 1940s, helping to drive a herd of three- and four-year-old steers to the stockyards at Hessdale from pastures to the north. Herman, who worked for the Wagstaff Ranch near Alma, had lost a hand to a buzz saw but, with an iron ring on the end of his arm to guide the ax handle, he could sharpen a thousand hedge posts a year, Martin said. Herman had another iron prosthesis, not exactly a hook but a kind of pincer, that allowed him not only to saddle and ride horses, but shoe them as well. On this particular day he was, as usual, riding ahead of the cattle on his big buckskin horse when the train pulled in with a string of cattle cars in tow. As he passed the herd, the young engineer, who hadn't had much if any experience with a cattle train, gave the steam whistle a couple of blasts. Those old tip-horn steers, perhaps recalling their long confinement in crowded stock cars when they had last heard that sound in Texas, broke back and scattered like quail. While Martin and the other hands were getting the herd back together, Herman ran his horse up to the engine and leaped aboard. Shoving his iron claw into the engineer's Adam's apple, Herman said, "Sonny, when you see cattle coming into the yards, don't you *ever* blow that horn!"

The cattle that got off the stock cars in the spring weren't always thin and weak. Wayne Rogler remembered unloading some South Texas Brahmas at Matfield Green one spring. "They were so wild that as soon as we opened the door, they didn't wait for us to put in the bullboard and take out the bar [i.e., the two-by-six-inch board that fit across the doorway so that cattle would be held in while the bullboard was taken out or put in and the door slid shut or open] but started leaping over the bar and running down the chute. We finally got the bullboard in for the last few head, but by that time the first ones out had bounced off the back side of the corral and run back up the chute and into the car."

I've already told (in *Cowboys and Kansas*) about the outlaw steer that Dad and Uncle Marshall brought into the Cassoday stockyards for Jim Teter, but it's a story I think is worth retelling. It was in 1938 and a big Brahma steer had jumped the fence north of the yards when the Teter crew brought their herd across the tracks. I don't know if the Hoy boys had been helping somebody else ship or if they were just hanging around the stockyards on a Sunday afternoon, but Jim Teter asked them if they could get his steer, which by that time had jumped a couple more fences and was well on his way to Chase County, three miles away. They sent my mother (she and Dad had been married a couple of months earlier) to tell Dad Hoy to bring the truck, then took out after the steer. By the time they saw him, he was across the county line in one of the Frew pastures, headed down into a ravine. Uncle Marshall, the better roper, told Dad to wait while he loped to the head of the draw, then bring the steer to him. He latched his horns, Dad caught his heels, and they had him tied up by the time Dad Hoy got there. The nearest ditch where the truck could be backed into so that the bed was low enough to load the steer was a little way off. Dragging the steer to the truck burnt off a big patch of hair on his shoulder, but they got him loaded. Back in the stockyards someone asked how they were going to get the steer turned loose. "Easy," said Uncle Marshall, as he tied the lariat rope on the horns to a heavy post. Dad Hoy gunned the engine and drove out from under the steer, the sudden drop knocking the breath out of him long enough for Dad and Uncle Marshall to get the ropes off. Jim Teter came running up, protesting the treatment of his steer, whose aggressive attitude was proof aplenty that the only damage from the rough treatment was to his pride, not his body. "What are you complaining about?" Uncle Marshall told him, "Your cowboys couldn't even get him into the pens."

One of the most unusual stockyards stories I've heard came from Chet Unruh, whose family moved from Kiowa County to a farm south of Cassoday at the end of the 1930s. This was toward the tail end of the Dust Bowl, and Chet, who was in high school at the time, said that moving into the Flint Hills region from western Kansas was like moving from a desert to the Garden of Eden. Chet was accused of being as windy as his native High Plains when he told about having seen cattle in the Greensburg stockyards that had weeds growing on their backs, but he was vindicated later that spring when some green-backed Texas steers were unloaded at Cassoday. The cattle had apparently gone through a sandstorm on their way to the railroad pens in Texas, the wind driving both dust and weed and grass seeds deep into the hair of their backs. Either in the Texas pens, or perhaps when they were temporarily offloaded en route for feed and water, a rain shower had soaked their hides. Body heat, combined with the warmth of close quarters in the stock cars, acted like a greenhouse and caused the grass and weed seeds to sprout. I don't remember Dad ever saying anything about green-backed steers, but he did remember cattle coming in with Texas sand so thick in their hides that it was nearly impossible to brand them.

A random memory of my own: Often today as we move cattle in summertime, their hooves stir up an odor from the crushed leaves and stems of the fetid marigold. Every bit as much as madeleines acted on the mind of Proust, the pungent aroma of this prairie wild-flower invariably floods me with memories of the days of railroad shipping. That pungency of the trail is succeeded in my mind by the warm smell of creosote oozing from posts and boards as we approached the railroad pens, which itself gives way in memory to the sharp acridity of the gourd vines that sprangled along the siding on which the cattle cars were lined up, awaiting the arrival of the engine that would pull them into position for loading. As the train pulled in, coal smoke, or, later into the 1950s, diesel fumes, would briefly dominate. Over it all hung the not unpleasant (to a young cowboy) odor of dried manure.

A random memory from a woman who had attended Coyote School: Coyote School was a one-room wooden building not quite halfway between Burns and Cassoday. Officially named Prairie Dell (although no one ever used that name), it was literally out in the middle of nowhere, set in the midst of bluestem pastures. Both students and teacher rode horseback to get there. In the early 1920s Burns had a railroad, but Cassoday didn't, so, as at DeGraff (and Bazaar and Sallyards and Rosalia), cattle would be unloaded there in the spring to be driven to the pastures near Cassoday and Matfield Green. As a little girl, Catherine Olberding Brown remembered that for what seemed like nearly a month beginning in mid-April, she would hear cattle bawling all day long. From the time she arrived at school until she left, she could look out the window and see herds of cattle stringing by Coyote School. At noon and at recess, cowboys would sometimes ride up to say hi to the kids and get a drink of water from the pump in the schoolyard.

Here's a story I heard about a cowboy and a brakeman and how they resolved a little problem with loading cattle. The man who told me the story said that the cowboy was Cliff Cannon. If there was a tougher, more capable cowboy than the late Cliff Cannon, I don't know who it was. He and his wife and young daughters lived on the Henley Ranch southeast of Cassoday when I first knew

Coyote School.

him—I suppose he was around thirty or thirty-five at the time and I was just a kid not even ten years old. He was a good pasture hand, and pretty tough in the arena as well. I suppose he had ridden rough stock in his younger days; his brother Harry rode bulls at Madison Square Garden. I remember Cliff roping calves at Countryman's Rodeo, riding a nice little buckskin gelding that someone at the rodeo offered him a thousand dollars for. This at a time when a hundred dollars would buy as good a using horse as you could want. Cliff turned the would-be buyer down, and Wilbur Countryman's laconically incisive comment, delivered in his inimitable style, was: "That's where two fools met."

Sadly, Cliff contracted polio in 1952 and had to spend the rest of his life in a wheelchair, not on a horse, but he was still no one to mess with. He ran beer joints and pool halls, supplemented with bootlegging, at Toronto and Latham. Just after he had opened for business, the Toronto city marshal stopped by his place and drank a couple of beers, then started to walk out. "Wait a minute! That's seventy-five cents," Cliff said. The marshal replied that he didn't have to pay at the other tavern in town. "Then," said Cliff, "that's damn well where you'd better drink your beer because it costs you here." The lawman fussed around before finally coughing up the money, and as he left he threatened to give Cliff a lot of trouble. Cliff's rejoinder: "You'd better give me trouble, you son-of-a-bitch! That's what I'm paying taxes for!" Another time in his first year of operation a man threatened to go get a gun and come back and kill Cliff. After he left, Cliff called the law and reported the incident. The marshal, thinking Cliff wanted protection, told him that when the man came back, stall him and not give him any trouble. "Trouble, hell," said Cliff, "if he comes back you can pick him up at the undertaker's. I'm calling for his protection, not mine." The man never came back.

As to the scuffle in the stockyards, Cliff himself told me it never happened to him, and as is obvious from the foregoing paragraphs, Cliff was the kind of fellow who would have told the story on himself if it had happened. Anyhow, whoever the cowboy was, on this particular day at the Cassoday stockyards the train was late. Real late. Usually at Cassoday you'd get to the yards around noon, weigh the cattle, go down to Opal's Cafe to eat, and be back at the yards when the train came in around 2:00 or 3:00. But on this day the train wasn't there at 2:00, or 3:00, or 6:00. Back in that pre-daylight-savings-time era it got dark about 8:00, but the stockyards had lights, although they tended to be used more in the spring when cattle came in at all times of the night rather than in the summer and fall when shipping time was more carefully controlled. But the train wasn't there at 8:00, trouble with a hotbox or something like that the depot agent said, and it finally rolled in around 10:00. The lateness of the hour wouldn't have mattered so much if the cowboys hadn't been facing another day of shipping on the morrow. As it was, this particular cowboy had about a twelve-mile horseback ride home, where he would get to sleep about two hours, if he was lucky, before getting up the next day to ride half a dozen miles to the pasture they were shipping that day. A few people at that time, the mid-1940s, had one-ton trucks with stockracks they used for hauling horses, but they were the exception; everyone else rode to the pasture and rode home.

So when the train finally pulled in, the cowboy was not in a particularly happy frame of mind, nor was his mood improved when they started loading cattle. Now, you need to picture in your mind the setup on a railroad loading chute. The platform was maybe four feet off the ground, and a couple of feet from the stock cars when they pulled up to the chute. The chutes (there were always two, spaced so you could load two cars at the same time) slanted up from ground level to platform level, and would be connected to the stockcars by way of two heavy wooden gates hanging on either side. The gates themselves were extendable so that if the stock car happened to come to rest a couple of feet beyond the center of the chute, you could pull the extension out (not very easily, but it could be pulled out—or at least the men could; us kids didn't have much luck with them) in order to direct the cattle through the door of the stock car. To keep cattle from falling into the foot-and-a-half gap between the platform and the car, there was what we called a bullboard (I've heard some call it an apron) made of heavy lumber. This bullboard was five feet wide on the chute side, cut down to four feet on the railroad side so that it would fit into the four-foot doors of the stock cars, and three feet across with cleats on the bottom to fit snugly between platform and stock car. And heavy? It must have weighed nearly a couple of hundred pounds.

Now if the engineer could handle the train, and if the brakeman or the conductor could spot cars, then the stock cars would line up directly opposite the loading chute every time. Which meant that the extensions on the chute gates never had to be touched and the bullboard had only to be lifted out and back a foot or two. But if, as on this particular night, the brakeman and the engineer weren't communicating too well, then the cars would first be three feet past the chute on one load, then two feet off center the other way the next time, then back the other way by a couple of feet for the next load. The cowboys working the chute gates and the bullboards not only had a lot of extra physical exertion to go through, but they were also losing several minutes with each load. And if you've been up since three in the morning, rounded up a pasture full of lively Texas steers, cut out ten loads of the fattest ones, driven them fifteen miles to the pens, then waited eight or nine hours for the train to come in, and if you have a dozen miles to lope before you get home, where you then have to put up your horse, find something to eat (if you're not too tired to eat), crawl into bed for an hour or so, and then get up at 3 a.m. the next day to do it all over again—well, you're not going to be very tolerant of stock cars that aren't being spotted correctly.

Which pretty much explains why the cowboy didn't have too much patience with how the railroad was doing things: "What the hell's wrong with that engineer? Doesn't he know how to drive this train?" The brakeman responded with an inaudible mutter, which brought this from the cowboy: "Or maybe you don't know how to signal with that lantern."

The brakeman wasn't in a very good mood himself. It wasn't his fault they'd had trouble down the line, and he'd just as soon have been home in bed several hours ago, too: "If you think you could handle this lantern better, why don't you just do it yourself?"

"Why you smart aleck son-of-a-bitch," the cowboy came back. "Somebody ought to teach you some manners."

To which, the brakeman: "Come right ahead."

When the cowboy lunged for him, the brakeman came around about 300 degrees with his lantern and caught the cowboy alongside his hat, knocked him down, jumped in the middle of him, and started pounding. The cowboy never landed a blow, but when the other cowboys came running up, he hollered out: "Get me away from this guy before I hurt him!"

Well, the brakeman started laughing and the fight was over. The cowboy got back up, the brakeman signaled the engineer, and they started loading cattle again. Thereafter, every time the cars pulled up and stopped, the brakeman would ask, "How's that?"

"Close enough," the cowboy would say, and they'd load the cattle.

Not every day at the stockyards was as exciting as that, but I think you can see why I miss the days of the trains.

Ten

The Little Houses

Just north of Matfield Green on the west side of Kansas Highway 177 and along the east side of the railroad tracks stands a long, low building with its roof caving in. William Least Heat-Moon, in *PrairyErth*, describes this structure as "a low stone building, gray and grim like a barracks. It has eight rooms, ten doors, five chimneys, and is built like a double-footed L on its side, and between the two longer end rooms is a roofed porch, and in front of it, a covered well. The stone blocks are, in fact, concrete cast to look like hewn rock.... Built without plumbing or insulation ... the building is the last of its kind in the area."

In fact, this section house, for that is what it is—or was, is to the best of my knowledge the last one to be found anywhere in the state of Kansas. I know for sure that it is the only one remaining of at least ten that once stood on the stretch of the Santa Fe line (technically back then the Atchison, Topeka, and Santa Fe, now the

Burlington Northern Santa Fe, although we still call it just the Santa Fe) that ran through the Flint Hills from Emporia to El Dorado. In addition to the one at Matfield, some of the housing units along this stretch were located at Chelsea, Cassoday, Bazaar, Gladstone, and Elinor.

Section houses were built by the railroad to provide shelter for section hands and, for those who had them, their families. As I recall (but dimly), during my school days at Cassoday the Solis family and some single men lived in the section house there, while the section boss and his assistant lived in the two much larger frame houses that were also built on the right-of-way. Leo Westerhaus was the first section boss I remember, and he was my great-uncle, married to Ivah Breidenstein, my father's mother's sister. I know that we must have visited them many times, but I cannot recall what the inside of the house looked like.

Uncle Leo was a good section boss, one of the more humane ones, according to Chet Unruh, also of Cassoday, one of whose first jobs was working the section from Aikman, where the Chelsea gang took over, to north of Cassoday about halfway to Matfield. One section foreman he worked for, Chet told me, carried a sidearm, both to enforce discipline and for self-protection because he was so hated by the workers he bullied. His favorite ploy when there were a number of new men in a gang was to take the handcars to the farthest reach of his section of track, then immediately fire the biggest, toughest-looking of the new men and force him to walk back to town. It's a little hard to use fists against a man armed with a pistol, so the victim, no matter how angry, would be forced to trudge back to town, and the rest of the crew would be intimidated into full and immediate obedience to the boss's will.

Most of the section hands on the Santa Fe, at least in my part of the Flint Hills, were Hispanic. I don't know whether or not the late Manuel Leal was born in Mexico, but for most of his life, including retirement, Cassoday was his home. (I'm not sure how Manuel himself pronounced his name, but the Anglos at Cassoday said "manual," like an instructional booklet.) I think that he may even have worked on Uncle Leo's gang. From 1949 until 1952, however, he worked on the Matfield Green section, and he lived in the section house there. At that time, he told me, the ten-room house was divided into five apartments. No families lived there then, just eight

Section house at Matfield Green, 1990s.

bachelors who made up the gang. They were assigned to work an eight-mile section of track, four miles each way from Matfield, where their segment of the line met that of Cassoday to the south and Bazaar to the north. The crew traveled on open handcars powered by small engines that burned a mixture of diesel fuel and gasoline.

The Matfield Green section house, Manuel said, like all the others along the Santa Fe, was not weather-tight; it was cold in the winter, hot in the summer. Heat in winter came from small coal stoves, the coal from the Santa Fe. Drinking water came from a well with a hand pump in front of the house, while wash water was piped in from a tank on the hill to the west, across the tracks. He recalled that the only items of furniture provided by the railroad were bunk beds and big sacks, which the men would stuff with hay or straw to form mattresses.

Section work involved long hours and was physically demanding—exhausting might be a better term. The major duty was to maintain the tracks and right-of-way, keeping the tracks level, the roadbed firm and secure, and the right-of-way clear of weeds. Ties had to be solidly embedded in the road grade with the rails firmly and securely attached to the ties. Even on Sunday and in any kind of weather someone had to walk both rails of the track, making sure that all the spikes were tight. The tracks also had to be level. If one track was off as little as an eighth of an inch, the gravel ballast had to be worked and adjusted and the track raised to bring it up to true. Rail, I've been told, could weigh as much as 140 pounds for a three-foot section. Tools used included a maul for driving spikes, a claw bar for removing them, and a lining bar to raise and line up the track.

Deteriorating ties had to be replaced, and each new tie was marked with a short, thick, broad-headed nail, the head containing two numbers, signifying the year the tie was put in place. Out in my shop and in a tool drawer in the house are several of those numbered spikes, including a couple from 1923, the year the Santa Fe line finally extended from Bazaar south though Matfield Green, Cassoday, Chelsea, El Dorado, and on down into Oklahoma. I have a memory (I was probably in early grade school at the time) of riding with Dad in a hayrack to pick up ties on the Maguire place a mile or so northeast of Cassoday. Quite a passel had been replaced and Uncle Leo had told Dad to go get however many of the old ties he wanted or could use. At that time used ties were given free of charge to anyone who wanted to expend the energy to load them. Those that weren't hauled off were piled and burned. Today used ties are bundled up like so many sticks, fastened with flat metal straps, and loaded onto trucks to be hauled away and sold; anyone caught picking them up from the right-of-way would probably be arrested. At any rate, Dad, never one to pass up a usable item if it was offered, picked up a bunch. He had a pair of ice tongs with which he would lift one end up onto the hayrack, then go to the back end of the tie with the tongs and lift and shove it on. In later years when I was old enough to help in this salvaging operation, I learned just what a difficult and hard job loading ties could be. Our mules, and later our truck, got a good workout carrying ties, and we ended up building several sets of corrals with them, stacking them up horizontally and holding them in place with hedge posts.

These pens were solid, stopping both livestock and wind. The only animal that ever escaped in the decades that those walls stood was a Brahma roping calf. I was in my late teens at the time, and I think I had bought this bull calf at the El Dorado livestock auction. I had practiced on him and my more usual assortment of dairy calves (they were much cheaper to buy) all summer, then gone off to college. When I came home for a weekend and decided to run a few calves, this now-not-so-little gray Brahma calf not only outran my horse, but when he got to the far end of the roping pen he left the ground and sailed over the tie wall without even touching it. I think we had a name for this calf, but I don't remember it. He grew up to be the prototype of what a Brahma bull should look like—short backward-curving horns, broad forehead, gray hair with black points, and a classic hump between his shoulders. When he was a two-year-old we sold him to E.C. and Ken Roberts for their rodeo string. As I recall, Gene Peacock came to pick him up. We figured he'd make a dandy bucking bull, but I guess being something of a pet around our place—although we darn sure kept a wary eye out when we walked into his pen—took the buck out of him. He ended up meatloaf and hamburger.

The other major duty of a section gang was to maintain the right-of-way. In addition to keeping down weeds in the warm months, the crew also had to burn fireguards from the tracks to within fifty feet of adjoining farm or pasture land in order to minimize the chance of an accidental prairie fire caused by sparks from an engine or from a hotbox. These accidental fires, especially during the winter, were a significant hazard and could burn thousands of acres. Part of right-of-way maintenance also included fence building and repair and cattle guard installation at crossings in order to keep stray livestock off the tracks. In recent years railroad companies seem to have lost interest in keeping rights-of-way cleared and neat. After Uncle Leo had retired and he and Aunt Ivah had moved to Marion (this was in the early 1960s), Aunt Ivah used to complain about how the railroad was just letting the right-of-way go to pieces. I can't imagine what she'd say if she were around to see the sagging fences and unmown ditches along the tracks today.

Here in Emporia there were once at least four section houses, each built according to the plan of the Matfield Green structure, which I recently walked through. Its roof is sagging and missing in places, while only a remnant or two of the inside walls that once divided it into ten (not eight) rooms survive. The five chimneys served two rooms each, and there are two air vents on the roof. I stepped off the two end rooms, on the north and south, at six by three paces—about 18 feet by 10 feet. The other eight rooms were about 12 feet long and 10 feet wide. Not much space for even a single man, much less a couple or a family. The doors of the eight smaller rooms open to the east, that of the south end-room to the north, and the north end-room to the south, all of them opening onto a porch with a concrete floor that is about 84 feet long and 5 feet wide. The outside dimensions for the structure are approximately 105 by 18 feet. There were once windows on the west side of the building, facing the tracks, but all the glass has long since been broken out.

The section houses at Emporia were erected in 1926 and razed in 1960. In 1979, a site near where the houses once stood on the north side of west South Avenue was turned into a city park with the name Las Casitas—the Little Houses—which is what their Hispanic occupants called them. Each building housed three families, with each family occupying from two to five rooms, depending on the size of the family. Each room had only one doorway, which led to the outside, so if you wanted to go from one room to another, you had to first step outside. A wooden porch ran along the entire front length of the building, and two buildings faced each other, forming a kind of courtyard in between, reminiscent, perhaps, of architectural design in Mexico.

A hand pump in the center of the courtyard provided well water for washing, bathing, cooking, and drinking. There was no indoor plumbing, only two outdoor toilets at the north end of the courtyard to serve all the occupants in both buildings. Neither was there any gas or electricity until the 1940s, so until that time families used wood or coal stoves for cooking, heating water, and household heat. Refrigeration was provided by iceboxes. Each family did have a garden plot for its own use. These plots ranged in size from very small to some with hundreds of plants, depending on the energy and ability of the gardener.

Today Las Casitas Park includes a playground for children, tennis and basketball courts, a shelter house, and a bandstand. Ironically, considering the primitive nature of the original section houses, it also has running water, flush toilets, and a sewer line. But no gardens. Each year a fiesta is held at Las Casitas Park to celebrate

Mexico's independence from Spain. I hope that during this celebration the older residents of Emporia's long-time Hispanic community tell the children and the more recent arrivals from Mexico how the park got its name.

And I hope that the remnants of that last surviving section house in Matfield Green escape the bulldozer.

Postscript

My hope has been realized. I was told a while back that "a couple of attorneys from Chicago" had bought the section house and were turning it into apartments to rent. As usual, the gossip was only partly right, but the good news is that the section house is indeed being preserved and renovated. About the time of the Flint Hills rodeo this spring (2005), Cathy and I were driving to Matfield Green to hear Wes Jackson, whose Land Institute has a branch there, speak to members of the Kansas Rural Center. As we rounded the curve toward town, I saw a pickup parked at the section house and a man carrying a board, so I stopped. The man was Pat Moss, a carpenter from Chicago (originally from Hays) and one of four partners involved in the project. We were short on time for talking, but Pat gave me the name and number of the prime mover, Bill McBride, who is an architect in Chicago.

When I called McBride, he told me that, although originally from Ohio, he loved the plains and a few years ago started looking for a retirement spot in the wide open spaces. After trips to North Dakota and the Nebraska Sandhills, he read Heat-Moon's *PrairyErth* and came to Chase County to look around. In 2001 he and his wife, Julia (a management consultant), joined with Moss and Karl Rohlich (a public defender from Milwaukee) to buy the section house and forty acres of former railroad property from Wes Jackson. Renovation started sometime after that.

The plan is to keep the exterior of the section house looking historically accurate, but to turn the interior into three modern apartments. At the time I spoke with Moss, two of the units were shaping up well, but the space for the third was still something of a shambles. The McBrides plan to move to Matfield Green in the spring of 2006. Their new dwelling will undoubtedly be smaller than what they are used to in Chicago, but they will have the pleasure of being able to watch the sun rise every morning over the valley of the Southfork. And they will have the satisfaction of living in a structure of historic significance and of knowing that they have helped preserve the last section house in Kansas, if not the country.

Part three

Ranching in the Flint Hills

William Kansas Waugh, Bud Kraus, and Wendall Tranter unloading Texas cattle at Eskridge.

Eleven

Winter in the Hills

Not anything much prettier than the day after an ice storm in the Flint Hills, a day so pretty it hurts your eyes. Cold, maybe even bitter cold, but no wind. It's calm after a big storm, the wind gone into retreat to gather its strength for another day. Of course it's really the sun, not the beauty, that hurts your eyes, makes you squint them almost shut. But even with your eyelashes fuzzing the outlines of everything you see, the beauty filters through. In the distance the trees along the creeks droop with sparkling loads of diamond ice; in front of you the transparent crystal leaves of the tallgrass reflect the brilliant sun like a thousand prisms. It's like you're looking into the face of God. And out there on top of a hill, miles from the nearest house, a lone hawk circling the winter sky, a few head of cows wending down for a drink at a spring in the valley—maybe you are.

That's the more pleasant side of a Flint Hills winter. On the less pleasant side it can be just plain cold and windy, day after day with maybe some patches of snow scattered among big splotches of bare ground that will turn into mud hubcap-deep once the sun climbs high enough to take the frost out of the ground. You need to get out early to feed on these days.

All in all winters in the Flint Hills are relatively mild, at least they have been in recent decades. We sometimes go a whole winter with only a few skiffs of snow, and often we'll have no more than a couple of bad storms. Rarely nowadays does the ground stay completely snow covered for more than a few days, which is sure not how I remember winters as a kid. Dad always liked to feed our cows on snow, and most of the time we did that all winter long.

Or so it seems. Exaggeration of childhood memories, especially of tough times, is a near-universal human trait, as those of us who grew up hearing our parents and grandparents talk about the hardships of the Great Depression well know. So it is with memories of winter weather. Several years ago I interviewed Floyd Fisher of rural Cottonwood Falls, who told me how when he was growing up he used to have to walk two miles to country school, "uphill both ways," of course. In the winter, he said, holding his hand in front of his waist, "the snow was clear up to here. Now," he continued, dropping his hand below his knees, "it never gets any higher than this." I thought at the time, but withheld comment, that snow waist-deep on a small boy isn't much more than shin-deep on a grown man.

Still, I do think that Flint Hills winters are not as snowy now as they were when I was growing up in the 1950s. Since we moved to the country south of Emporia back on the second of January, 1976, we've had only two or three winters where we really needed to use our four-wheel drive to get the eighth of a mile from the mailbox to the house. But one of those years was a doozy. It started snowing on New Year's Eve, 1978, and it snowed hard for the next several days. Our kids were in second and fifth grade, and I'd pull them down to meet the school bus on a sled. For three weeks we had to park at the road and walk back and forth to the house. Our neighbor would, Sisyphus-like, plow our road out, but it would blow full again almost before he had gotten out of the driveway. For almost a week, at the end of January, we were able to get to the house, then another storm hit and for three more weeks we walked, sledding our groceries from the mailbox to the house. Funny thing—not a one of us caught a cold that winter.

How deep was the snow? Well, one morning we got a call from a neighbor three-quarters of a mile west telling us that we had a horse on the road. It was, as I figured it would be, Rebel, the kids' kid horse, half Welsh pony and the other half ornery. After I caught him and led him back in, I went to check the gates, but they were all closed, so I set out to walk the fence, assuming there was a break in the wire somewhere. Instead, at the southwest corner of the pasture I found hoof prints on a snow drift, a drift so high that it was only a couple of inches below the top wire of the fence. The big horses would have broken through the drift, but the lighter pony had walked over the top of the packed snow and right out onto the road. Nothing like the Dakotas, of course, but occasionally we do get some serious snow in the Flint Hills.

Snow-covered ground is good for wintering horses the way we used to do it back home. Usually we kept only one or two saddle horses around the house during the winter, along with a team of mules to pull the feed wagon. In early November we'd kick the rest of the herd into the Funk Pasture, a section of grass half a mile north of the home place. There was a pond on the northwest side and a springy draw along the south fence. We didn't feed them a forkful of hay all winter, and Dad never worried about breaking ice for them as long as there was snow on the ground. Unlike a cow, horses will paw through the snow to get to the old grass, and they'll get enough water from the snow to keep them healthy. They would stay in good flesh all through the winter and only start losing weight along about the first of March when the cool-season grasses would begin to push up and the horses would quit eating the old grass. Once the bluestem came on in late April, however, and the wild oats burgeoned in May, the weight would go back on in a hurry.

Several years ago I ran a little unintentional experiment. We had four horses on the place. A couple of them I let run in the barn, kept hay in front of them, and fed them oats several times a week. The other two ran in a pasture with a little timber for a windbreak, and all I did for them was break ice when I had to. The interesting thing was that the horses with access to the barn never went inside, even when it snowed. After a storm both sets of horses would be snow covered for hours, their heavy winter hair acting as insulation to keep their body heat in. Both the welfare and the rugged-individualist horses were in about the same body condition when March

My grandfather's barn, with Uncle Marshall on the hayrack, Aunt Cleda and Aunt Jeruah by the wagon, and Grandmother and Aunt Virginia in the doorway.

came, which is when I brought the pasture horses in for hay so they wouldn't lose weight while looking for the early dabs of green.

Nowadays I keep our horses around the house during the winter. They run to a big-round-bale hay feeder and a tub of Crystalix. Guess I'm getting a little soft hearted. I even bought an electric tank heater and keep open water in front of them instead of making them drink at the creek, if it's running, or from a hole in the ice at the pond. But some people still winter horses the old way; in the winter I will usually see three or four different small herds of saddle horses in the big pastures along the turnpike between Emporia and Cassoday. And they look just as well fed and content as mine. There's something to be said for the precarious benefits of a free-running life.

I doubt if any Flint Hills farmers and ranchers would want to feed cows the old way, even if they could. Protein pellets and big round bales hauled to the pasture on a flatbed four-wheel-drive pickup truck have replaced bundles of kaffir corn and loose alfalfa hay delivered on a hayrack by a team of mules. Like most everyone else in the Hills we called our pastures by name, and the forty acres across the road west of the house was the Cowlot, one of the winter homes for our hundred head of cows. The other was on the east side of the road, the south half of the eighty that my great grandparents had settled when they first came to Kansas back in the 1870s. We sometimes called this the Cemetery Pasture because the Cassoday cemetery, which my great grandmother had donated to the community, is located on the southwest corner of the property. Alternatively, we called it the Cave Pasture, referring to the small, roofed, semi-dugout where the Santa Fe workers who constructed Fox Lake, a mile east of town, had stored dynamite. The dynamite had been used to blast out a limestone quarry on the south bank of the Walnut where it crosses the road into the Cowlot, the stone being used for the spillway of the lake, which itself had been built to supply water for steam engines.

About a fourth of the Cowlot was timber, a third was grass, and the rest was bottomland used for crops—sometimes oats, sometimes corn, sometimes alfalfa. The timber provided a windbreak and there was a spring on the west end for water. The north side of the Cave Pasture was also timber-lined, and although there was no spring, water often stood in some of the deeper holes of the riverbed. The only time the Walnut River, which ran from east to west across both pastures, carried water was after lots of rain; the river went underground about half a mile east of our property and resurfaced about half a mile west on the old Parsons place. North of the river was cropland with the house, barn, sheds, and corrals in the northwest corner.

Dad had built a couple of big feedracks on the Cowlot and one between the cave and the quarry in the Cave Pasture. In the summer we would stack alfalfa and prairie hay in the Cowlot racks, prairie hay in the Cave Pasture. In winter we could ride a horse over to pitch loose hay from the stack to the feedrack, but when that supply ran out (or if Dad was saving it for bad weather) then we fed with mules and a hayrack. Sometimes that feed was alfalfa and sometimes kaffir bundles, either of them usually supplemented with prairie hay.

A typical winter morning went something like this at our place: Dad would be first up and get the fire going in our wood-burning stove. Meanwhile Mother was stirring around in the kitchen, all this before the sun had risen. Dad would holler at Rita and me, his wake-up calls later seconded by Mother if we hadn't appeared soon after he had left the house. I'd go out to help milk our four or five cows and then run the separator. The cream was poured into five-gallon cans and stored in the storm cellar east of the house, the skim milk reserved for the calves. While Rita and I bucket-fed them, Dad would be feeding and harnessing the mules.

Then we'd have breakfast: pancakes and steak. Every day. Some-times eggs instead of steak, but no ham or sausage or bacon—Dad was allergic to pork; got that way from having to eat too much of it as a kid; gave him back trouble, so he said. I don't know how much of this was scientifically verifiable, but it resulted in good breakfasts as far as I was concerned. Mother made her own syrup from sugar, water, and maple flavoring, and we got butter from the cream truck when it came by to pick up our full cans and leave empties. For sev-eral weeks during the winter we'd have sourdough pancakes, made from starter Mother kept in the refrigerator. I never cared much for their flavor, but Dad liked them. As for the steak, it came from about anywhere on the cow and was always fixed the same way.

The first onset of really cold weather, usually a little before but sometimes after Christmas, signaled butchering time. I remember seeing Dad Hoy and Dad butcher long before I was old enough to start helping. I even remember Dad Hoy butchering hogs and Grandmother rendering lard and making cracklings. But as I said, Dad didn't eat pork, so all our butchering was of cattle. The steer that had been fattening in the south pen would be driven into a small corral next to the barn, Dad would trace an imaginary X between his horns and his eyes, then put a .22 bullet at the crossing of the X. Using a block and tackle (and, later, the Farmhand stacker mounted on our tractor), he would immediately hoist the steer up and slit his throat. Once bled, the skinning began, which I first got to do the Christmas I found a hunting knife in my stocking. After the steer was skinned and gutted, Dad would split him in half by sawing down the middle of the backbone, then he'd quarter the carcass. Three of those quarters were hauled a dozen miles to Burns, where the locker plant would cut, wrap, freeze, and store the meat for us (federal and state health regulations were different in those days), and the fourth quarter, sometimes hind but more often front, Dad would carry to what we called the bunkhouse (actually just a storage shed, drafty and bare-walled) and hang it from a rafter cross-bar.

Each morning, before he went out to chore, Dad would go to the bunkhouse, lower the haunch of beef onto a heavy table, and cut off a steak, sawing through bone and frozen flesh if the weather had been hovering around zero for a while. Technically, the cut might be from the sirloin, the T-bone, a shoulder, the chuck, or even the brisket area, but he always cut it like a round steak, and Mother always took a hammer and pounded the hell out of both sides (which sure tenderized the tough cuts) before flouring it and frying it. (I can still hear the sound of that hammering, which was better than an alarm clock for making me jump out of bed onto a cold floor and into my chore clothes, because that meant that Dad was on his way to the barn and I'd better be there by the time the cows were in their stanchions. It was hard to leave a warm bed when there was ice on the windowpane and little skiffs of snow had sifted onto the sill, but if he ever had to come back to the house to get me, it was, in his words, "Katy bar the door.") I don't know how old I was before I found out that a steak could be grilled, or even fried without flouring.

Breakfast out of the way, it was back outside to hitch up the mules and start feeding. In the summer we used two teams for haying, but in the winter we turned Flossie and Tessie (both bay molly mules) out and just kept one team up—Andy, a lazy brown horse mule, and Mickey, a white mare. Mickey was a worker, but touchy about her ears, so when Dad bridled her he'd lift the bit far up against the corners of her mouth, then quickly and firmly pull the top of the headstall back over her ears before she had a chance to jerk away. (I never did get onto this maneuver, although I might have mastered it if a mule's ears were as short as a Quarter horse's.) Mickey's position was on the right, Andy's on the left as they straddled the tongue to have the neck yoke fastened and the tugs hooked to the doubletree.

An empty wagon affords a cold ride on a stormy day, but once you filled it with alfalfa or prairie hay from the stacks that had drenched us with sweat during the summer you could burrow down into the hay and get out of the wind. We usually fed prairie hay every day and alfalfa or kaffir corn bundles every other day. The cows needed to be in decent shape to throw a healthy calf along about February or March, but you didn't want them fat.

A major change in winter feeding in the Flint Hills occurred with the availability of affordable alternative sources of protein—first cottonseed cake and soybean meal, and then protein pellets. We kept bags of cake and soybean meal in the salt house; I liked the smell of both and I particularly liked the taste of the soybean meal. No additives to worry about in those days. Raymond Prewitt had become a dealer for the Gooch Feed Company in the 1950s, and Dad got his cake through Raymond. Rita and I made Dad fasten the metal tag he gave us, "Don't feed 'em, Gooch 'em," onto the stockracks of our one-ton GMC truck, and it stayed there through a couple of trades, another Jimmy and finally a Ford.

Dad was pretty conservative in his approach to cattle care. He did feed cake and meal to any steers we were planning on butchering, but he stayed with the prairie hay and alfalfa regimen for several years after Uncle Marshall had started wintering his cows on prairie grass and pellets. (Uncle Marshall also went to Angus cows while Dad stuck with Herefords. It was probably in the 1960s before he put Angus bulls on our cows to get black baldy calves. His last herd was colorful, all former Brahma roping calves.) Sometime in the later 1960s Dad began feeding pellets on grass on a regular basis, although he still gave the cows plenty of prairie and brome hay.

Another major change in feeding practices in the Flint Hills resulted from the invention of the big round bale. Roll 'em up in the summer from the comfort of an air-conditioned tractor cab, then roll 'em out from the comfort of the heated cab of a four-wheel-drive pickup in the winter. You can go through the entire haying cycle, from mowing to feeding, without ever touching a blade of hay with your hands. Sure not like stacking loose hay.

We hardly used any baled hay at all until we bought an Allis-Chalmers Roto-Baler in 1952. One advantage of the small round bales was that they could be left in the hay meadow until you needed to feed them, which was fine for prairie hay (which is cut once in a season) but didn't work well with alfalfa (which produced three or four cuttings and thus had to be hauled off after each cutting). So we continued to loose-stack alfalfa and bale prairie hay (about half of which we did store in haysheds and half we left in the field) until about the time I was out of college. In the 1960s Dad cut down the size of his cow herd, so all the hay he needed could be baled and shedded instead of loose stacked.

Dad never did go to the big round bales. He continued to bale hay with the Allis until he was eighty-one years old. That was the summer (1985) he lost his right arm to the Roto-baler. After all those years of being careful. After all those years of warning me to keep my hands away from the rollers. His first words to me when I got to his side at the hospital in Wichita were apologetic, not angry or self-pitying. To this day I am ultra sensitive to the oft-heard offhand remark, "I'd give my right arm for...." Trust me, you wouldn't. For several years after the accident Dad got along pretty well one-handed. In fact, he could saddle and mount a horse as well as anyone. He bought a small, light saddle with a lightning fastener that he could easily toss on Fibber's back and cinch up. And he could pull bales from the shed onto the back of the pickup, then throw them off as Mother drove.

As you drive through the Flint Hills countryside today, you'll often see large metal bins standing on stilts, usually by a barn or machine shed but sometimes out in a pasture. These bins are for storing protein pellets. A typical bin holds twelve tons of feed and is square with a pyramidal top and bottom, the latter sloping down funnel-like to a small door in the center. Call the feed company and they'll send a driver out to auger pellets from the delivery truck into the bin. Then drive your four-wheel-drive flatbed pickup under the bin, line up the motorized cake feeder fastened to the bed just behind the cab, open the top of the feeder, pull open the door at the bottom of the bin's funnel, fill up the feeder, shut off the flow from the bin, drive out to the pasture, turn on the electronically operated motor that activates the auger on the feeder (which can be calibrated to deliver the pellets at varying rates and amounts), drive along as the pellets spill out onto the grass, shut off the feeder motor when you've fed the right amount, and head for the gate and the next pasture to repeat the process.

These mechanized pellet dispensers, like many items of equipment on a farm or ranch, had their origins, I would bet, on the tinkering of people like my father. In earlier years Flint Hills cowmen winter-fed protein supplements from sacks—hundred-pound gunnysacks of cottonseed cake, then fifty-pound paper sacks of protein pellets. Bulk feed is cheaper, however, so Dad had pellets delivered to a small round grain bin, from which he would shovel pellets into the bed of his pickup to be shoveled off in the pasture. It didn't take him long to salvage the hopper from an old Allis-Chalmers Gleaner combine and rig it up into a gravity-fed feeder that he mounted onto the back of his pickup.

Pellets are scattered on old grass or where hay has been fed if the weather is snowy. As I said earlier, well into the 1950s we'd hitch up the mules after breakfast, fill a hayrack with alfalfa or prairie hay, then drive to the Cowlot or the Cemetery Pasture and pitch it off. In the mid to late 1940s (where my first memories begin) we also fed kaffir corn.

Kaffir was a good crop for the Flint Hills, a drouth-resistant grain sorghum that grew well in the climatic and soil conditions here and one that had a variety of uses. In the early part of the twentieth century, El Dorado celebrated the grain with a Kaffir Corn Carnival, an annual event that lasted over two decades. It included a Queen of Kaffir, band concerts, parades, booths and floats decorated with kaffir stalks and grain heads, a rodeo, and a turtle race, among other events. The first Kaffir Corn Carnival was held October 18–20 in 1911 and drew some twenty thousand spectators on the first day alone. Geneva Houser of Cassoday was chosen the first queen. She and eight attendants rode in an elaborately decorated float in the parades, and she wore a white satin pearl-trimmed gown, which a year later served as her wedding dress when she married Dwight Harsh.

I don't know this for a fact, but I wouldn't be surprised if milo, the most common grain sorghum raised nationwide today (and for the past half century), was developed from kaffir. But whereas kaffir grew tall with a medium-sized head of grain, milo is short so that more energy goes into producing a bigger grain head and less stalk. Kaffir was a row crop, whereas cane was often sown, the purpose of both sorghums being to produce fodder and grain for livestock feed, although some Flint Hills people would press the juice out of cane stalks to make molasses. Once kaffir had matured, it was cut with a grain binder and the bundles placed into conical shocks. The grain from kaffir could be threshed and fed whole to hogs and chickens or it could be ground to feed to milk cows or fattening steers. Or the heads could be thrown whole to chickens and hogs. The chickens pecked out the grain, while the hogs would eat the entire head.

If we wanted grain for the chickens or to grind in the hammer-mill, Dad would drive to the field north of the creek at Dad Hoy's on a hayrack fitted out with a hand-operated header that was something like a guillotine. He would pull up beside a shock, Dad Hoy would lift the handle of the header, Dad would stick the grain end of the bundle over the header bar, and Dad Hoy would behead the stalks. Dad would then restack the headless bundles horizontally into a flat stack rather than a conical one. The grainless bundles, although not as nutritious as before their decapitation, were nevertheless good cow feed. I don't recall ever cutting heads off kaffir after Dad Hoy died in 1952, probably because there were no longer any pigs to feed. We did, however, continue to grow kaffir for cow feed for a number of years.

As a kid I found feeding kaffir corn much more entertaining than feeding hay, although a load of hay was better for burrowing into to get out of the wind. Mainly I preferred kaffir because of the wildlife. It took a long time to get to the bottom of a haystack where the mice nests and tunnels were, but if you pitched a dozen shocks of kaffir onto the hayrack there were a dozen colonies of mice for me and the dogs to wage war against. And wage war we did; I never shared the sympathy of Robert Burns for the "wee timorous beasties." If a mouse was foolish enough to attempt to run to another shock once his cover was blown, he was a goner. If the dogs didn't get him, I'd hit him with the tines of my pitchfork. Some shocks were mouseless, but most showed signs of habitation if not actual mice. If the dogs were still digging at an earlier shock, I'd whack the mice that ran from the one we were working on and then dig up the dirt where the shock had stood with my pitchfork, hoping to unearth those rodents thinking they had found refuge there. Very few escaped.

Dad didn't mind my taking time for mouse hunting, so long as I got to the next shock in time to pitch my share of bundles onto the wagon, because he did not like mice. In fact, he was squeamish about them. Not phobic; he didn't scream or quake or run when he saw a mouse, nor did he start the way I usually do when I see a snake. But he hated mice. I can't remember any other thing he was goosey about except mice. He'd had some bad experiences with them, like the time he had ridden over to Madison to help Dow Gilbreath ship cattle and was spending the night in some oil field shack out in the middle of a pasture near Kenbro. He was awakened in the middle of the night by mice running around his head, and when he found on the pillow pieces of his hair the mice had bitten off, he got no more sleep that night. Then there was the episode I witnessed, one that occurred one late fall day in the kaffir field just north of the creek on Dad Hoy's place. We were loading bundles when I heard Dad yell. And I mean yell. I looked and he was bent forward, clutching himself with his right hand just below where his belt encircled his Lee Riders. Unbuckling his belt with his left hand, he jerked open his pants, revealing a bloody spot on the surface of his long underwear just below his waist. He turned his pants inside out as he opened his right hand, and a dead mouse fell out. It was hamburgered, the blood, guts, and life literally squeezed out of it. It had crawled past his work shoe and up his pants leg between the long johns and the Lees, but Dad was unaware of it until it had been stymied by the tight waistband. So as I said, he was happy for the dogs and me to eliminate as many mice as we could.

That reminds me a story I heard Dad and Uncle Marshall tell one night out on Glen Kirk's ranch near Sallyards. The Flint Hills Overland, which sponsors covered wagon excursions into the Flint Hills, had started up a few years earlier, and the operators had retained these two old cowboy brothers to be outriders, ostensibly to open gates and scout the path for the wagons, but more likely for the local color they provided. And they were colorful. On this particular evening Uncle Marshall, his grandson Rick Remsberg, Dad, my son Josh, and I had settled into our bedrolls beside the horse trailer, but no one was particularly sleepy, so the reminiscing that had started around the campfire continued under the stars.

Sometime after one o'clock (an insomnia that did nothing to keep them in bed after 5:00 the next morning) their talk moved from the corncob fights in the barn on the neighboring Schuler farm (Kenneth and Herman versus Marshall and Frank) to a big rat killing on Dad Hoy's place. The rats had made a network of burrows under one of the sheds, so Dad and Uncle Marshall got Herman and Frank to come over and they took some pitchforks and clubs and started digging up burrows and killing rats. About three hundred of them, or so they recalled more than six decades after the fracas. The hero of the day was a terrier dog that would grab a rat, shake it dead, then grab another and shake it, all so fast that the dog literally collapsed from heat exhaustion. So the boys threw water on him and the dog jumped up and went right back to killing rats as fast as he could.

There was a pause in the storytelling on this cool July night, then Dad asked, "Was that our dog or Schulers'?"

"I don't remember," Uncle Marshall replied, "but it was our rats."

Back to winter feeding. On many mornings prairie chickens would fly from the tops of the tepee-like kaffir corn shocks. About once a winter Dad would get hungry for prairie chicken and stick the .22 rifle Mother had brought to the marriage (why she ever owned a gun I never knew) into its canvas case and hang it from one of the upright two-by-fours on the front of the hayrack. If there were chickens in the field that morning, he would stop the wagon a couple of hundred yards away, half-hitch the reins around one of the wagon uprights, unsling the rifle, leave me with the wagon to hold the dogs, and begin stalking. Prairie chickens, like the bison before them, weren't generally frightened away by noise, but they were by motion, so he always kept a shock between himself and the birds. When he was within range, a shock or two away, he would carefully ease the rifle out from around the shock, take aim, and pick off a chicken. I particularly remember one time when there were three chickens on the same shock. He shot the one sitting on the very peak of the shock, which tumbled over the other two on its way to the ground, but they didn't fly so Dad picked off another one.

Even after we had quit raising kaffir and stacking hay, we still used the mules for winter feeding. Ubiquitous as they are now, four-wheel-drive trucks weren't generally available for farms and ranches until the 1970s. We had a one-ton truck and a half-ton pickup, but it was pretty easy to get them stuck in snow or mud and besides Dad actually enjoyed working with mules. After the teams I remember from boyhood had long since made their way into dog food cans, Dad raised a pair of buckskin mules from the granddaughter of my old kid horse Dusty, which he had named Miss Dusty but which my little nieces mispronounced Mr. Dusty. Like their mother they were long-legged, and could those long legs walk! In the 1960s and 1970s we had a hay meadow three miles southwest of home. We could leave the barnyard, pick up a load of bales, and be back to the Cowlot in under two hours; Buck and Blue were traveling an average of six miles an hour, half the trip with a full load and never getting out of a walk.

Some Flint Hills ranchers and farmers, particularly those pasturemen who handle summer cattle exclusively, don't have to worry about winter feeding. I have heard of some Flint Hills houses in earlier years that weren't even winterized because the rancher lived in town during the six-month off-season. Today, it seems that I see more cow herds throughout the Hills, and some ranchers are contracting to keep cattle for other owners in winter as well as summer. Generally speaking, however, winter is a more relaxing time for cattlemen here. Although not dormant, as are the Hills themselves, they too are getting a chance to rest.

My father always said that every warm day in winter was one less cold day until spring. I hate to complain about warm winters, but December and January highs in the upper 60s just don't seem natural. But Dad would also say, after we'd had a few of those warm days in a row, that winter was a long way from being over.

Twelve

Down at the Crick

The Walnut River rises a mile east of Cassoday in what is known as the Lake Pasture, a section and a half of bluestem on which the Santa Fe Railroad built Fox Lake back in '23 to supply water for their steam engines. It empties into the Arkansas River at Arkansas City after flowing through El Dorado, Augusta, and Winfield. The Walnut runs through our home eighty, a mile west of town. Well, sort of. The river*bed* runs through the home eighty; the river itself goes underground half a mile east of our line, surfacing again on the Parsons place a quarter of a mile or so west of the Cowlot forty that lies just across the road west of the home place. There's a small spring on the west side of the Cowlot, a little patch of open water lying in a cut-off horseshoe just to the south of the riverbed proper. This water hole, as I remember it growing up, was always a little murky. Not stagnant, but the spring wasn't forceful enough to supply sufficient fresh water to keep the silt and decaying leaves from permeating the lagoon. I guess it was more of a seep. There was enough water to keep our cows in the winter, but unlike flowing springs, this one would form ice. It wasn't usually as thick as on the ponds, but still it had to be broken in zero-cold weather to provide access to the thirsty cows. The Spring, as we called it, was the only thing resembling open water on our place, except in times of heavy rain. Then the Walnut would flow through our property like a real river.

The only times I remember the river (or "crick," as we termed it—how can you call something a river when water is only running down it a couple of times a year?) flooding really bad were in 1950 and 1951, when it spilled over its banks, filling the bottomland south of the house with water and making the road impassable for several days. Impassable by car, that is; we could still ride out horseback if we needed to, but there was rarely a need. It was about that time that Grandpa Rice and Dad made a "trash burner." They made this contraption by covering a heavy woven-wire cylindrical frame with chicken wire, closing off one end, and constructing an inverted funnel of chicken wire in the other. On the inside, just behind the funnel, Dad would wire a dead rabbit, a chunk of beef spleen (what Grandpa called the "melt"), or a chicken carcass, then, when the flood had subsided but the river was still flowing, throw the thing into a hole west of the house, the funnel end on the downstream side (fish always swam upriver, according to Grandpa—I never thought to ask him how they got downstream to begin with), and anchor it to a tree with a long piece of number 9 wire. Next morning we'd usually have a nice mess of catfish: channels and bullheads (the junk fish, suckers and carp, we threw out on the bank, a kind of dry drowning, I suppose)—something to tide over our appetite for fish between visits from Grandpa. We tried the contraption in the pond in the Big Pasture once, too, but all we caught were a few salamanders. Water dogs and mud puppies, Dad called the ugly, weird-looking things.

Grandpa Rice was an avid fisherman. He and Grandma drove up from Conway Springs several times a year, but always during the warm months. I don't ever recall them visiting in winter. In Sumner County Grandpa was a stream fisherman—Slate Creek, the Ninescah River. But in our country he fished ponds for bullheads, with an occasional foray onto the Walnut on the Parsons place west of the Cowlot where the river rose and there were a couple of deep holes. He had his favorites—the pond in the northwest quarter of the section-large Funk Pasture, the Orient pond northeast of town on the east side of the old railroad grade, the big pond on the Butler side of the county line where Highway 13 ran east and west for a mile.

Grandpa was a line-and-bait fisherman—put a worm on a hook, or a chunk of melt or, his favorite bait, fresh chicken guts if fryers were in season, toss it out into the pond with a sinker to hold it on the bottom where the bullheads lolled (no bobbers on his fishing poles), then sit and wait for a bite. He usually fished two poles, sitting on a folding stool (he was a large man) and watching for the twitching at the end of a pole that signaled an interested fish. He would then deliberately pick up the pole, tighten the line, and wait for the erratic but sustained jerking that told him the nibble had turned into a real bite. When he felt that bite, he'd give a sudden jerk and, keeping the line taut, unhurriedly reel in another bullhead. Grandpa had patience, and rarely was he skunked. I, on the other hand, had little patience and spent most of my time looking for frogs or crawdads along the shore, or exploring the ditch below the dam and spillway. Or, if the sun was warm and the wind still, I would lie on the bank and daydream or doze. I loved going fishing with Grandpa, but I was skunked often.

Dad Hoy used to fish, too, but not like Grandpa Rice. Only once did I get to go along on one of Dad Hoy's fishing ventures, which employed a seine instead of a pole, but the tradition was passed down through my father to me and my son. Not that we have ever been a threat to the fish population with our less-than-once-a-year fishing excursions, which usually took place on the property of one of the fishermen involved. But not always. When Dad Hoy was young, I'm told, he and some of his friends would venture up into Chase County near Clements when the Cottonwood was in flood and string a span of chicken wire across Coyne Creek upstream from where it fed into that river. When the water receded, some of the big river cats would be left behind in the deeper holes of the creek, where they could be easily seined out. The one time I remember getting to tag along (I was probably about six or eight), Dad

Hoy, Dad, and half a dozen other men hit a couple of draws that drained into Fox Lake. As I recall, they caught a few fish, but what mostly stays in my mind is that this was the first time I ever heard much profanity. It was good natured, what today would probably be termed locker-room talk, but new to my young ears.

For a number of years about the time I was high school age, our family would go fishing with the Countrymans, who lived on Durachen Creek half a dozen miles south of Cassoday. Every Fourth of July Wilbur and Virginia (and Gene, Ginger, and Terry) put on an annual rodeo that our family helped with, and the fishing trip was everybody's way of letting down after the stress of the rodeo. Durachen Creek had some nice holes, and we would usually catch a pretty good mess of bullheads and a few channels, but the real treat was snapping turtle. It seems like every year we'd get at least one big snapper (Grandpa Rice also occasionally pulled one in from a pond). Dad had figured out how to dress them—get them to bite a stick and stretch out their necks for the ax, then plunge the carcass into a tub of boiling water (like you would a chicken for plucking), and cut the bottom shell away from the top one. For years we had turtle shells baling-wired up on the side of the salt house, clattering in the breeze like a wind chime. The legs and the neck were meaty, and Dad always cut them out carefully in order to avoid contamination with any musk sacs. Mother would use a pressure cooker to get the meat tender, then finish it up in a frying pan. As I remember, some of the meat was light colored, some dark. It was good.

Wilbur had an unusual way of catching snappers, far different from Grandpa's. When a turtle got on the line in a pond, Grandpa would slowly reel him into the bank, then, using the fish line if it had swallowed the hook or getting it to bite down on a stick if it hadn't, maneuver the turtle into a bucket or a gunnysack to bring home. Wilbur's method was more daring. He seemed to have a knack for kicking against a turtle with his gumboots in the waist-deep, thoroughly opaque waters of Durachen Creek. He would then hold the turtle down with his foot, reach down into the water, feel around the shell for the turtle's tail, grab it, and lift him out. How he knew which end to grab is a mystery to me, but he never once got bitten.

Exploring the creek was one of my favorite pastimes. I'm sure that one reason I got to go there when I was little was because

Mother didn't have to worry about my falling into the water. It's pretty hard to drown in a dry riverbed. Actually, even though it wasn't running, there were a few holes that held water for quite a while after a rain, and those holes were a great place to get minnows and tadpoles with a homemade seine made of lath and gunny sack. Usually I put them right back into the hole, but sometimes I'd take a few up to turn loose with the goldfish in the horse tank.

I don't remember just how old I was when I got a Red Ryder BB gun for Christmas (or maybe my birthday, ten days earlier), but I must have been pretty young because I got a shotgun (single-shot 20 gauge) for Christmas when I was 12. I loved going down to the creek with the BB gun and the dogs, Hank and Shep (and later, after Hank died, Shep and Speck). We'd go to the Cowlot crossing west of the house and walk the creek west to the water gap where we bordered Hacklers (who owned the Parsons), then we'd go along the south side of the creek all the way under the bridge and over to Whithams on the east line of the home place. Sometimes I'd go up to Dad Hoy's and walk that creek to the Robinson Pasture. The dogs would jump rabbits and squirrels, well out of range of a BB gun, so most of my shooting was at tree trunks or rocks sticking out of the creek bank. Later, with the little pump Remington .22 or my 20 gauge, I'd bag rabbits and bring them home for Mother to fry, but the only animal I ever killed with the BB gun (other than sparrows and starlings at the barn and the hay shed) was a skunk. The dogs had treed him in a hollow stump between the rock quarry and the cave (a man-made semi-dugout where dynamite had been stored when they had blasted for rock to make Fox Lake long before my birth). Shep got pretty thoroughly sprayed, but I escaped contamination. I would run up to the stump, poke the gun barrel down, fire, then run away, cock, and run back and shoot again. I don't know how many times I repeated this action, but we did kill that skunk.

I liked wandering the creek bed, looking for unusual rocks. I always hoped to find an arrowhead but never did. I did, however, once find a geode with a crystal center. Most geodes I've found in the Flint Hills have a center of chert.

One of my early memories of the creek occurred just after Christmas, probably my sixth or seventh one. I'd gotten a little hatchet that year, and I took it along when Dad and Dad Hoy went over on the Forty (the alternate name for the Cowlot) to cut firewood. Dad had just gotten a chain saw, one of the first in our part of the country. It was a huge thing, yellow in color and heavy as the devil. Hefting it years later, I thought that cutting timber with an ax or a crosscut surely must have been easier. I guess not, though, for Dad preferred the saw. I suppose it was faster. At any rate, Dad Hoy was using an ax to trim up branches of trees Dad had cut down. We would then haul or drag them up to the house and cut them into stove-lengths with a buzz saw powered by a tractor and belt. I spent the whole afternoon hacking on what seemed to me a big tree, although in later years when I looked at the waist-high stump I saw that it was only about three or four inches in diameter. I circled that tree, cutting all around it until it finally toppled over. I was proud as a jay until Dad Hoy said it looked like beavers had chewed it down. My crest drooped a bit at the time, but my ego suffered no permanent damage.

A little room is an everywhere, says John Donne. That half mile of dry riverbed was not my whole universe, but it was darn sure my Africa, my New-found-land.

Thirteen

Good Fences

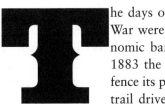he days of open range that followed the Civil War were numbered once a practical and economic barbed wire was patented in 1878. In 1883 the giant XIT Ranch in Texas began to fence its pastures, and by the end of the decade trail drives from Texas north were essentially over. Whereas the original cowboy scorned the fences made from the "devil's hatband," by the turn of the twentieth century building and riding fence had become an accepted part of the cowboy's job description, despised though those tasks were, especially the former.

The earliest fences in the Flint Hills, particularly in the uplands, were stone walls, or, in the flat bottomlands of the streams, living fences of Osage orange (also called bois d'arc or, more commonly, hedge). In the northern Flint Hills of Wabaunsee County, a Kansas State Historical Society road sign along K-99 draws attention to the many miles of limestone fence that line that highway and commemorates the hundreds of miles that were built in the Hills during pioneer times. The ten-thousand-acre Tallgrass Prairie National Preserve (Spring Hill/Z-Bar Ranch) in Chase County once had some thirty miles of stone fence, while just north of Matfield Green the Rogler Ranch maintains the mile or more of stone wall that separates the highway from the corn and alfalfa fields along the east side of K-177.

We still have a couple of short stretches of stone wall around the corrals of the home place near Cassoday, but nearly all of what once stood there is now gone, the victim of our pilfering rocks for other purposes, or collapsed from a century and a quarter of weather and use. A large percentage of the stone fence in the Flint Hills met a different fate, however, being ground into dust after World War I. I have seen a 1920s photograph from Cowley County showing a machine crawling the length of a limestone wall, its combine-like maw literally eating its way through the flat rocks and reducing them to powdered lime, which was then spread onto fields being prepared for the sowing of alfalfa.

I've often noticed when driving from the eastern half of Kansas into Oklahoma that the hedgerows that dot the Kansas landscape suddenly disappear when entering the Sooner State. Why? Because Kansas opened for settlement in 1854, long before economical and effective wire fencing was available, while Oklahoma remained Indian Territory, unoccupied by white farmers until the last decade of the nineteenth century. Thus Kansas farmers fenced their quarter-section homesteads, and Flint Hills ranchers often fenced the small pastures around their headquarters, with hedge. A good hedgerow will easily turn cattle and horses, and if the thorny branches are thick enough and close enough to the ground they can even discourage the passage of pigs and goats. An unexpected advantage of having a good hedgerow was that once barbed wire did come onto the scene, hedge proved better for posts than any other wood, lasting decades longer than its nearest competitors, catalpa or treated cedar or pine. And hedge grows back quickly, so you can cut posts out of the same hedgerow every fifteen or twenty years. Its hard wood withstands not only rot but also a fast-burning prairie fire, and hedge will hold a staple well—if you can manage to drive one in without flattening it. I've heard it joked that the main difference between a hedge and a stone post is that it's easier to pound staples into the stone one.

Even after the introduction of barbed wire, open range in the Flint Hills did not immediately disappear. Tom Watkins near Cassoday and Arthur Crocker east of Matfield Green herded summer steers in the years just before the turn of the twentieth century, while Harold Harvey's first job when he moved from Indiana to Kansas in 1902 was loose-herding cattle near Beaumont, as was Shorty Nurnberg's when he first started working on the Nation Ranch in southeast Chase County in 1910. Sometimes referred to as "herd boys," these youngsters earned something like fifty cents a day for a grazing season that ran from six to eight months. Under open-range conditions the farmer has the responsibility of fencing his crops in order to protect them from foraging livestock, but under the provisions of the fence law, the livestock owner is required to confine his livestock. When the Kansas Legislature passed a fence law (sometimes referred to as a herd law) in the later nineteenth century, it was on a county-option basis. Thus in some Flint Hills counties cows could roam freely, while in others they had to graze behind fences.

Even though no full-scale fence war broke out, as happened in the Gypsum Hills along the Oklahoma border, the Flint Hills were not without trouble. Folk custom holds that the landowner, standing on his own land and facing his neighbor's, is responsible for building and maintaining the right-hand portion of the fence. Fence law, however, doesn't specify which half, just so each owner does his share. Ill will often resulted when a landowner with a creek flowing through the property would build (or rebuild) on the left-hand side because water gaps are much harder to construct and maintain than fence on level ground. Or sometimes one landowner would simply not keep his fences up. If repeated and prolonged difficulties between the two could not be resolved, the fence-keeping landowner could pull back from the property line a few feet, build a fence all the way through, and the other landowner was prohibited by law from turning out any livestock until he had built a complete fence an equal number of feet back from the property line. The resulting space between the two parallel fences is sometimes called a spite fence, but in the Flint Hills it is commonly referred to as a

Devil's lane in Chase County.

"devil's lane," I suppose because the two feuding landowners are inspired by hellish rather than heavenly forces. Or were so inspired: devil's lanes often outlive their builders by decades. The two Flint Hills devil's lanes I recall from my youth—one southeast of Casso-day a couple of miles and the other about ten miles west of Elmdale on the south side of K-150—are both gone now, whether because of a change in landowners, reconciliation of past differences, or the death of one or both of the cantankerous parties I don't know.

Fence troubles sometimes led to more than just extra work. Be-fore Chase County passed the herd law, at least one Marion County man was killed in a grazing dispute near Cedar Point, according to a story I have heard. Not wanting to build a fence to restrain his cattle, as Marion County law required, he drove his herd across the line to let them run free—and free of charge—on the unfenced uplands of Chase County. Not surprisingly, the Chase Countians didn't much care for trespassing nonresidents and their cows, and when the dust eventually settled there was one less Marion County cattle herder. Good fences might have made good neighbors in New England, but no fences made dead neighbors in the Flint Hills.

When I was growing up, nearly every cowboy in our neck of the Flint Hills carried a saddle hammer and a staple pocket. My grandfather may have loose-herded cattle, but by the time my father and uncle were cowboying, riding fence was part of the job. Not a very exciting one, but necessary if you wanted to keep your cattle in and the neighbor's out.

Steel posts had not yet become common in my youth. Each spring, after pasture burning and before turning out, we would drive around our fences (sometimes by truck, sometimes with mules and wagon), replacing any posts that had burned off, splicing barbed wires that had broken under the tautening of zero weather, and putting in new staples where the old ones had fallen out. In the summer we would ride pastures to check on the health and numbers of our cattle. If we were short on the count, we would look for a broken wire or missing staples on the border fence with neighboring pastures when we went to look for our stray. Even if we had our count, we still often rode a stretch of fence just to check for loose wires.

A good barbed wire fence can last a long time. We have one on our place that I remember being built in the later 1940s. It could stand replacing, but it's still plenty serviceable. Out east of Cassoday along the south side of the Teterville Road about half a mile east of Fox Lake, Johnny Green's six-wire, double-barb fence, hung on sturdy hedge posts, performed its duty well for eighty-plus years, supplanted by a new five-wire, steel-post fence only half a dozen years ago. Since 2000 we've replaced over half of the fences on the home place, fences that had to have been thirty or forty years old when I was born. And they needed it, much more than did John Green's. Over half the thickness of the wires had rusted away, and some of them were so brittle with age that they wouldn't bend without breaking. I don't know what the percentage is of fences in the central Flint Hills that have been rebuilt in the past couple of decades, but it has to be pretty high.

At least partly because of this recent replacement fencing, most of the fence maintenance nowadays takes place in the spring without much fence riding in the summer. In fact, very few people ride pasture horseback today. It seems that not many people carry a staple bag or a saddle hammer anymore, either. If anything, they carry a pair of fence pliers (mine are a smaller version of the bulldog type, manufactured by Moore Maker, Matador, Texas). In general, fence pliers are handier than a hammer, particularly for taking off and putting on the clips that hold barbed wire to a steel post, but they are not so good for pounding staples into, or pulling them out of, a hedge post. Moreover, steel posts don't seem to lose clip wires as much as hedge posts lose staples. Thus as steel posts have replaced hedge, fence pliers have replaced saddle hammers, just as pickups and four-wheelers have replaced horses for riding pasture.

Saddle hammers differed from a standard carpenter claw hammer in that they usually had a smaller head and a shorter handle. Dad carried an even smaller than normal saddle hammer (I've not seen another like it), which he also used for shoeing horses. The head was only about half as big as a regular saddle hammer, and the slim, short handle ended in a smooth taper rather than being flat across the bottom. On that taper he had carved our brand, a Flying H. Sometime around the late 1960s or early 1970s it bounced out of the leather keeper and was lost for over ten years. And then he found it one day while riding across our pasture in section eight, a couple of miles northwest of the home place. Rather than take a chance of losing it again (he was pretty much through with fence riding by his late seventies, anyway), he hung it on the wall. Today it holds down papers on the top of my desk.

Riding fence is often a tedious chore, but building fence is damned hard work, even with all the conveniences of contemporary mechanical equipment. Ideally, a corner hedge post should be set four feet in the ground, hedge line posts (if you're not using steel posts) at least two-and-a-half, both kinds tamped solidly with dry dirt. Digging such holes with jobbers or a hand auger and tamping posts with a length of oil field sucker rod is good aerobic, muscle-building, callous-inducing exercise, but it gets old awfully fast. When I was little, we had a neighbor, a colorful old fellow with a big handlebar mustache named Will Fluke. My sister and I would occasionally stay all night with Pa and Ma Fluke, as we called them, and

I vividly remember Pa eating almost everything (yes, including peas) with his table knife. He also, like my paternal grandfather, saucered his coffee rather than drinking it from the cup. Anyway, Pa Fluke had a solidly built bull corral on the east side of his barn. The Goerings lived half a mile south of the Flukes, and he hired a couple of the sons to dig the post holes, deep ones, for that pen. He told them that when the handlebars of the augur reached the ground, there would be a quarter at the bottom of the hole. In other words, he paid the Goering boys twenty-five cents per hole. Hard work, but not bad pay for a kid back in the 1940s. I don't know if that quarter included tamping or not, but a well-tamped post took almost as much work as digging the hole. Dad always insisted that good tamping required more dirt than had come out of the post hole.

Nowadays fence builders use motor-driven hydraulic augers to dig post holes and special rock bits to drill through the limestone layers that often lie just beneath the surface of the Flint Hills. A four-foot hole without much rock to go through can be dug in a minute or so. Add another two or three to clean out the loose dirt with a pair of jobbers, and you can dig a hole and set a post in it in under five minutes. Even tamping has gotten easier. Empty a couple of sacks of fly ash into the hole, mix in some dirt and gravel, add water, and stir it all up, and when the mixture dries the post is solidly set without the sore muscles and strained back of tamping. As for steel posts, in many places the hydraulic scoop on the tractor or skid-loader can press a steel post in the ground much more quickly and easily than driving it in by hand.

Although many Flint Hills farmers and ranchers build their own fences, many others hire professional fencing crews to do the work. According to Kansas Department of Agriculture figures, the statewide average for having a mile of five-wire fence installed early in the twenty-first century would run $4,480. In the Flint Hills, however, undoubtedly because of the rocky ground, the uneven terrain, and more water gaps to build, the cost was significantly more: $5,760 per mile. I assume those figures include corner posts and braces, but if not then the price would be even higher.

Water gaps. The most aggravating part of fencing. They're hard to build and hard to maintain. A water gap too often is just that—a gap in the fence line where it crosses a stream because a rain storm has caused the waterway, anywhere in size from a small draw to a

Water gap in northwest Chase County, near Burdick.

small river, to wash out the fence. And cattle can walk right through gaps whereas they have to squeeze through a hole in the fence.

A draw or ravine might well be dry 364 days a year, but a gully washer can roar down a draw and take out the gap, and by the time you get to the pasture the next day half your herd might be on the road or mixed with those in the neighboring pasture. If the fence line crosses a running stream, then a good rain is liable to carry enough run-off trash (dead grass, brush, tree branches) to knock out the water gap and even mash down the fence on either side of the gap. Fixing water gaps often requires wading out into water waist deep or higher in order to clear debris or restring the wire.

Usually a water gap will have a heavy post set on either side of the watercourse with a guy wire of some sort (sometimes a cable, sometimes several strands of barbed wire) strung from the tops of those posts over the stream to hold them straight and also to help hold up the detachable arrangement of barbed wire that runs across the stream and is attached to the posts like a big gate. Often one end of that panel of wire will be loosely attached so that it breaks loose when the onrush of water and trash hits it, carrying the wire out and along the side of the stream, thus making it much easier to clean off and reattach than if it had been solidly fastened.

Over the years I have seen many innovative water gaps, all of them designed to be more likely to withstand an onslaught of flood water. Some are free-hanging barbed wire panels, some are wooden panels, some are pipe, nearly all of them fastened at the top and designed to be pushed upward with the rising water, then drop back down into the gap when the water lowers. For instance, where the Walnut River runs under Satchell Creek Road on our place, Dad hung a wrought-iron fence panel that had been discarded from the Cassoday Cemetery. It's been in place thirty years or more and still works fine. I've also heard that back in the early years of the twentieth century, a series of poles were laid lengthwise with the Walnut where it crosses the DeGraff Road, rather like the grid of a cattle guard. It's a little hard to visualize, but I'm told that it worked like a cattle guard in keeping cattle from going downstream. Like cattle guards, water gap devices tend to be the product of folk ingenuity and thus exhibit great variety in design and material.

I like a high-pole gate, especially if the poles are big, heavy hedge posts. High-pole gates are usually found where two pastures come together or else in a fence line some distance from a corner, and they are useful as landmarks for giving directions in a strange pasture: "You'll see a high-pole gate once you cross that ridge over to the east." The chief advantage of a high-pole gate, however, is that it saves a lot of work when building a fence. A regular gate requires brace posts and braces on either side of the gate posts, which means that at least four deep holes have to be dug, four extra-heavy posts set, and a stout brace securely fastened between the gate post and the brace post on each side of the gate. All this because each of those sets of posts has to withstand the pressure of five tightly stretched wires a half mile or more in extent. I remember how scornful my father could be of some unknown fence builder if, while driving along some road, he would see the wire between a brace post and a corner post or a gate post angling sharply upward, a sure sign that the posts were not properly set and braced. But high-pole gates don't have to be braced. The five wires attached to each pole might extend half a mile on either side, but the strands of heavy wire at the top of the poles, twisted taut, maintain a continuous pressure along the whole length of the fence. Only if that top wire breaks is there a danger of the poles being pulled loose.

It seems to me that a high-pole gate reflects the ethos of the Flint Hills: It stands out from the rest of the fence, colorful but not ostentatious, just as the landscape of the Hills is distinctive but not spectacular. Whereas the beauty of mountains, for example, is a barren beauty, the Flint Hills, like high-pole gates, are attractive but utilitarian and productive.

Fourteen

Chapman Posts

Many aspects of folklife in the Flint Hills area are distinctive (e.g., grazing transient cattle, ranch sizes and configurations, and pasture burning), yet there are probably more similarities than there are differences between ranching and cowboying in the Flint Hills and ranching and cowboying in other parts of the American West. So, too, farmers, oil field workers, railroaders, and citizens of small towns in the Flint Hills all share similarities to their counterparts in other parts of the state and country. Ranching gear, equipment, and work methods vary among regions of the country, but an outsider observing a man on horseback tending cattle would likely miss the details that distinguish a Great Basin buckaroo from a Texas ranch hand from a Flint Hills cowboy; all such mounted herders in the West would blur into a composite cowboy in the mind of the average American. To put it bluntly, there is no style of chaps or boots or saddle, for instance, that is immediately recognizable as "Flint Hills."

Still, from all that I have been able to learn, there is at least one item of Flint Hills ranching folklife, a particular type of fence post, that is unique to our area. I have sometimes heard this post referred to as a "pipe-in-rock post," a "rock-and-iron pipe post," or a "patent post," and I myself often call it a "Chapman post" from the name of the man who obtained the patent, but it has no generally accepted name, just as its uniqueness goes generally unremarked by residents of the central Flint Hills where it originated and where most extant Chapman posts are to be found, some still in use and others lying discarded beside a new five-wire, steel-post fence.

There are three different types of Chapman posts—a barbed wire post, a woven wire post, and a corner (or gate) post. Most common is the one designed for use in fencing cattle pastures with barbed wire, another one is intended for corrals or for pastures where woven wire is needed, while the third is a corner or gate post to which strands of fence-line wire are attached and stretched. What makes all three types different from other posts is that (1) they are constructed from a combination of steel pipe and limestone and (2) they are intended not to be set into the ground, but rather to sit on top of it. In fact, the two fence-line posts are essentially, although not easily, portable. The barbed wire post is constructed by either finding or quarrying a large squarish chunk of limestone roughly a couple of feet on each side and about a foot thick, drilling a hole in the middle of the rock (which weighs in the neighborhood of 300 pounds), and inserting a three-and-a-half foot length of one-and-a-half or two-inch pipe into the hole. Sometimes the pipe is driven into the hole to wedge it tightly, the top of the pipe often banged up from the blows of a sledgehammer, while other times, if the hole is larger than the circumference of the pipe, concrete is poured between the pipe and the hole to make it secure. In a typical post four groups of double holes are drilled into the pipe, the top hole of which goes all the way through the pipe. The first of these groups is just below the top of the post, the second about a foot lower, the third a little less than a foot lower, and the fourth about nine inches below that, which puts the lowest wire about six inches above the rock. Large (six-penny) nails are inserted through the pipe, then bent upward over a strand of barbed wire, the tip of the nail being forced into the upper hole just above the wire, thus holding it in place once it has been stretched. Often the top of the post is capped with concrete in order to keep rainwater from entering and rusting out the bottom of the post.

The woven wire post is the only one of the three for which I have been able to locate a patent, #733,150, issued to Philip Chapman of Council Grove on 7 July 1903, about eight months after he had filed his application on 3 November 1902. The major difference between this post and the one for use with barbed wire is in the stone base. Instead of a two-foot-square base a foot thick, this post has a base about a foot square and a foot-and-a-half long. A slot about six inches long and two inches wide is cut into the top of one side, and halfway down the slot a hole is drilled horizontally into the stone. In the middle of the top of the stone a vertical hole is drilled straight down to intersect with the horizontal hole. An anchor bolt with a hole in its end is inserted through the base of the pipe and into the horizontal hole, and a metal pin is dropped into the top hole so that it enters the hole in the end of the anchor bolt, thus fastening the pipe to the stone. In some of these posts the horizontal hole is drilled completely through the rock and the post is fastened by placing a bolt through the hole and securing it on the other side with a washer and nut. The stone can be set on top of the ground, or it can be set a few inches into the ground to make it even more secure. With the pipe thus fitted flush against the flat side of the anchoring stone, woven wire can be attached that will reach from the top of the post all the way to the ground to form a hog-tight or sheep-tight barrier. On the barbed wire post, however, the lowest wire is around a foot above the ground, good enough to keep cattle in but leaving plenty of room for smaller barnyard animals to wriggle under.

A typical corner or gate post in the Flint Hills is of hedge wood and is set firmly and deeply into a hole in the ground. The Chapman corner post is unusual in that it sits on top of the ground. It is constructed by first putting into place a very large flat chunk of limestone, then drilling a vertical hole into it and inserting a heavy steel rod. Next, a stone post a foot or more square and close to four feet in length is quarried and a hole drilled into the center of its bottom side. This large post is then lifted up and fitted onto the steel rod in the center of the ground stone. Or perhaps the rod is first placed

Woven-wire Chapman post, Lyon County.

into the stone post and then placed into the hole of the ground stone. Once in place, it is practically immoveable. Sometimes stone or pipe braces are fastened into place between the upright post and the ground stone, sometimes not, but the corner and gate posts that I have seen, after nearly a century of service, are still withstanding the pull of four tightly stretched barbed wires.

Almost all of these patent posts are in the central Flint Hills area around Dunlap and Council Grove, although some are also to be found in Geary, Riley, and Wabaunsee counties. These latter posts, however, can be traced back to a common origin at Dunlap, an Exoduster community on the Lyon-Morris County border. The Dunlap Exodusters, freedmen who moved to Kansas in the 1870s (some

Barbed-wire Chapman posts, Morris County.

of whom are listed in the 1880 census as stonemasons), are closely associated with Chapman posts. A couple of the necessities that mothered this invention included the enacting of herd laws, which signaled the end of open range in the Flint Hills, the rocky topography of the Flint Hills that made drilling or digging holes for typical fence posts difficult, and the financial straits of the Exodusters.

Topsoil in much Flint Hills pastureland is thin, very thin. Digging post holes when you hit rock only an inch or two below the surface is extremely onerous. Driving steel posts is somewhat easier, unless you strike a solid layer of limestone several inches thick. But neither steel posts nor motorized hydraulic post-hole diggers were available when herd laws were passed in some Flint Hills counties in the 1880s, laws that required cattlemen to fence in their livestock. Thus the Chapman post, because it did not require a post hole, was an ingenious adaptation to geological conditions necessitated by legal requirements.

No written records survive, but oral tradition credits the former slaves who settled at Dunlap with the invention of the pipe-in-rock post. No one knows for sure the name of the inventor, but the name that surfaced often in my queries to area residents was that of Harrison Fulghum. Fulghum, remembered as likeable and cheery, did build miles of patent post fences on the Chase and Aye ranches in Geary and Riley counties, respectively, but he may or may not have had the original idea for their design. When I first became aware of the possible uniqueness of this post, I drove out to see London Harness, an old cowboy who was the last black man to live in the Dunlap community. He knew of no special term for the posts, other than "patent fence," but he did say that Harrison Fulghum, along with Levi McCoy and the Tipple brothers, were some of the first to make them.

Harness witnessed some of the posts being made and fences being built. Other people, such as the late Russell Klotz, knew about the process only by what he called "hearsay" (which, of course, is what we folklorists would call the oral tradition), but all the accounts I have heard differ in only the most minor of details. If the posts were made on site, then a crew of black workers would go out with mules and wagons for a week at a time, sleeping on the ground and eating at a campfire. Using only hand tools, they would locate a good vein of limestone in or near the pasture to be fenced, peel off the thin layer of topsoil with a horse-drawn slip, quarry blocks of stone, feather them out with hammers and punches, then use winches to load them onto a stone boat (a sort of low wooden sled) or use a sling to hoist them up under the running gears of a wagon. When Harrison Fulghum built the fences on the Chase and Aye ranches, he would haul four blocks at a time to the site of the fence, line them up straight, then drill holes in the blocks and pound pipes into them. I have been told that a crew could make several barbed wire or woven wire posts a day but that the corner posts took longer to build, up to four days from initial quarrying to final placement.

Russell Klotz said that the crew received a quarter for each completed post placed in a fence line, while Tom Moxley, whose ranch today encompasses many of the old forty-acre plots originally allotted to Exodusters, recalls that his grandfather said that he paid a dollar for each post he contracted. Other estimates I have heard have ranged from a nickel to eighty cents per post and a dollar fifty for a corner post.

Perhaps not so much from the expense as from the weight, Chapman posts were spaced much farther apart than steel posts are today. A good contemporary five-wire fence will have posts twelve, at most fifteen feet apart, but Chapman posts ranged in distance from twenty feet to three rods. If the latter distance, then a hedge post was usually placed halfway between, which meant a post about every twenty-five feet, which seems to be the typical distance between the patent posts I have seen that are still in service today, although some are up to forty feet apart.

Harrison Fulghum was living in Dunlap when he was contracted by the Chase and the Aye ranches to build what became known in the northern Flint Hills as "Fulghum fences." After completing them, he settled in Geary County. He is also said to have built some fence on the Dewey Ranch, now the Konza Prairie Research Natural Area, but I have not seen any of his posts there, nor have personnel there recollected seeing any.

Whether Harrison Fulghum or some other black Dunlap resident invented the rock-and-iron post, it was Philip Chapman who took out the patent. Chapman is listed in the 1880 census (which is probably about the time that the first posts were being made) as a twenty-eight-year-old farmer from Missouri, married to twenty-year-old Clara and father of two sons, the elder of whom had been born in Missouri two years earlier and the younger, ten months old, born in Kansas. Several years ago I visited with A.H. Hermstein of Council Grove, Chapman's grandson, who as a six-year-old boy accompanied his grandfather when he built his last fence in 1920. Hermstein's job was to stuff each pipe with corn shucks so that a concrete cap could be poured in the top. In the winter, Hermstein said, his grandfather had a kind of factory set up at Dunlap where black workers would make posts. Then in the spring and summer he would take a crew out to set them up and build fence. Harrison Fulghum is also said to have made posts during the winter for later use in warm weather. I have been told, but doubt the story, that during the Great Depression, out-of-work cowboys near Manhattan made posts for twenty-five cents each. It is most unlikely that any Chapman posts were made after the early 1920s.

If he had run out of premade posts and was quarrying and building on site, Philip Chapman would sometimes line up a whole mile of fence before boring holes in the blocks and inserting a pipe in each one. The pipe, by the way, came from boiler flues used in steamships, which Chapman first went to St. Louis to buy, then later had shipped by rail from Kansas City.

Hermstein believed that his grandfather had invented the posts, although everyone else I spoke with thought that the original posts had been developed by the Exodusters. Hermstein also believed that his grandfather held patents on all three kinds of posts, although I have been able to track down a patent for the woven wire–type post only. It could well be that the barbed wire and the corner posts were already in use in the area before Chapman arrived in 1879, which would explain why he didn't patent them but did patent the woven wire post because he had in fact developed it himself.

Other advantages of a Chapman post, besides being portable and not needing post holes, include imperviousness to rot and to fire, which is no small thing in an area where pasture burning is an annual practice. A curved fence line that tends to pull a hedge post fence over is, I have been told, easily handled by Chapman posts. Moreover, a gully washer that tears out water gaps or snaps off hedge posts merely lays a Chapman fence down; go along and knock the debris off, set the posts upright, and the fence is as good as new. One rancher near Junction City told me that he has, when far from a gate, tipped two or three Chapman posts over, driven his pickup across, set the posts back up, and gone on. And it didn't take much longer, he said, than opening and shutting a gate. The only major mishap I've heard of concerning a Chapman fence occurred on the Aye Ranch where two bulls started fighting across the fence, tipped over several posts, and caused the two herds to get mixed. It took a little time to sort the cows, but not very long to set up the posts. The continuing problem was that the bulls kept fighting all summer, which meant a lot of sorting.

In addition to the concentration of patent posts in the Dunlap–Council Grove area and those in Geary and Riley counties, I have also heard of a few in Wabaunsee County near Bradford, Harveyville, and Dover. The fence of the Chalk Cemetery is held up by both Chapman corner and woven wire posts. A couple of Chapman posts, along with a big ball of old barbed wire, decorate the parking area in front of the Emporia Veterinary Hospital. There is also a patent post near the reconstructed Kaw cabin on the grounds of the Kaw Mission museum in Council Grove. In the mid 1980s I was driving I-70 from Manhattan to Topeka and saw a large number of Chapman posts at a roadside business, a cafe I believe. I pulled off and talked to the proprietor, who told me that the 250 posts lining his parking lot had originally been on the Aye Ranch. He had bought them for ten dollars each (not a bad rate of return on an original purchase price of twenty-five cents) and moved them with a backhoe and front-end loader (much easier than with a block-and-tackle and wagon).

The most unusual use of a Chapman post can be seen on the road that leads to Lake Kahola, built by the WPA during the Depression to provide water for Emporia during times of drouth. Along that road you can still see a few of these posts with a pipe some ten feet tall, rather than the usual three or four feet. Look closely and you'll see an insulator near the top of the pipe: These were early-day telephone poles set up by a rancher who wanted phone service and had to install his own line. (This was not an uncommon practice on some remote Flint Hills ranches. As late as the early 1950s Frank Klasser ran a line from Cassoday to his ranch a dozen miles east of town. He did not, however, always hang the wire high but instead ran a large part of it along the tops of hedge posts of fences that separated the big pastures in that area.)

After eighty to one hundred years a few Chapman posts are still holding up wire on Flint Hills fences, but many of Harrison Fulghum's and Philip Chapman's creations either lie in ditches or adorn parking lots. I wouldn't mind having a couple of discarded ones here at home, but it would take a much stronger set of muscles than I have to hoist one up onto a pickup bed. I don't need one in my yard, however, to appreciate what I believe is a unique aspect of the material culture of the Flint Hills. Although I would not claim to have been exhaustive in my search, still I have not found evidence of a similar fence post anywhere else in the world. The closest thing I have seen to a Chapman post was on the Isle of Harris in the Outer Hebrides. There, someone had drilled a hole into a piece of granite that had broken through the surface of the ground and had set a pipe into the hole. The pipe with barbed wire attached at first glance resembled a Chapman post, but the chunk of rock in which it was placed was not a small block of moveable limestone resting on the surface, but rather a huge underground granite boulder with, like an iceberg, only the tip showing.

Fifteen

The Flint Hills Firestick

I t's kind of interesting—a little brush fire in California or a few thousand acres of forest ablaze in Colorado will lead the evening news on the national networks, but here in the Flint Hills we burn a million or more acres each spring and nobody outside the area—or inside, for that matter—even notices. Fire, in one of its mythic manifestations, symbolizes destruction and ruin on a biblical scale; the next time around the earth will perish by flame, not flood. But in another sense fire not only sustains all earthly life (no sun, no life), but it is also an agent of renewal and regeneration. Consider bluestem grass: like the fabled phoenix, it rises from its ashes, but even more miraculously it does so annually, not once every five hundred years. The farmers and ranchers who set these vernal fires don't think of their actions as mythic or ritualistic; they're just doing what's been done here since territorial days.

The first prairie fires I remember were not intentional pasture burns but wildfires that broke out along the railroad right-of-way

Beating out a backfire near Bazaar Cemetery.

during the summer. Dad would throw a fifty-gallon drum on the back of our truck, fill it with water, grab a couple of buckets and some gunnysacks, and away we would go to help beat out the fire with wet sacks. I've been fascinated by prairie fires ever since.

I'm not the only one. Years ago I read a *Harper's Magazine* essay, "Field Guide to the Synthetic Landscape," by philosopher Frederick Turner, about the attempt to reconstruct a native prairie on forty acres of used-up Wisconsin farmland. That article contained this passage on fire that pretty well summarizes, in more high-toned language than they would, the reasons that farmers and ranchers in the Flint Hills burn their pastures:

The old prairies were dependent on periodic fires to clear the thatch, fertilize the soil, and above all to kill the tree saplings that would otherwise quickly cover the ground. The richest mix of species occurs only on burnt prairies. Before the settlers came, a prairie fire could burn all the way from Illinois to the banks of the Wabash. As William R. Jordan, the editor of *Restoration & Management Notes*, once told me, "Remove the fires caused by lightning or set by Indians, and you have to replace them, or the prairie will quietly vanish, not in a roar of machinery, but into the shadows of a forest." Accordingly, the Wisconsin arboretum burns its prairies—every two years at first, but now more irregularly, as nature might. It is said to be an unforgettable sight with flames leaping up thirty feet, and it is gradually taking on the status of a ritual for the professionals and volunteers who set and manage the fire. I myself can remember from my childhood in central Africa the spring burning practiced by the Ndembu tribe, and the air of festival it conveyed; it is associated for me with the smell of grass smoke, harsh native honey beer, the hunters' rites and dances, and the delicious little ground-fruits that we village boys would find among the burnt grass roots. Perhaps one day prairie burning will be one of the great ritual occasions of the Midwest, a sort of festival of Dionysus, the god of inexhaustible life—an occasion for drama, music, poetry, and storytelling.

It is remarkable how passionate the true prairie restorationists are on the subject of burning. The discovery of the need to burn, I believe, emancipated the naturalist; burning can even be seen as a sacrificial rite of redemption for our ecological guilt. The patient, careful labor of copying the natural prairie called for the medieval virtues—humility and obedience to nature, poverty and chastity of the imagination, sensitivity, self-abnegation, self-effacement. Burning showed that nature needed us, needed even those most Promethean and destructive elements of ourselves symbolized by fire.

These two paragraphs contain ideas that are as true for the Flint Hills as they are for a restored prairie in Wisconsin: The most teeming prairies are those that are burned; an unburned prairie inexorably becomes a forest; before the advent of modern agriculture prairie fires could, and did, burn vast areas (substitute Oklahoma and the Kaw for Illinois and the Wabash); prairie ecologists are passionate about burning (as are Flint Hills graziers, only without the intellectualization); burning of the prairie can take on attributes of cultural if not religious ritual (e.g., Chase County's annual Prairie Fire Festival). Imbedded within these concepts is the century-long conflict over intentional burning that was waged between ranchers and agricultural scientists, between custom and folk wisdom on one hand and scientific opinion and experimentation on the other, a conflict that in the past few decades has been resolved in favor of folk practice.

Pasture burning may well be a traditional practice in the Flint Hills, but the methods of setting fires have varied widely over the years. Some ranchers, in a manner similar to the Kaw method of dragging a burning ball of dead grass across the prairie, have wrapped a log chain around a bale of hay or an old tire, poured some kerosene or diesel fuel on it, stuck a match to it, and dragged it behind a pickup. Others have wrapped a piece of burlap into a tightly twisted ball or taken a corn cob, soaked it with kerosene, attached it to a length of heavy wire, then tied the wire to a lariat rope and dragged it behind a horse. My father would set a clump of old grass on fire, then use a pitchfork (others use a rake, preferably one with a piece of pipe for a handle) to drag old burning grass along to set a line of fire. Slim Pinkston told me that in years too wet for driving through a pasture, he and his brothers would start fires from horseback, riding along, striking matches on their saddle horns, and throwing them onto the ground. The matchstick, however, had to be broken in half because a whole match, Slim said, would just lie on top of the grass and flicker out whereas half a match would drop down into the grass and catch fire. Slim said that on February and March evenings he would often sit in the kitchen and break matches by the boxful, getting ready for burning season. Wayne Rogler often "patched" (i.e., set fire to spots in a pasture that hadn't burned the first time) by throwing half-matches out the window of his pickup, the floorboards of which were littered with the bottom halves of matchsticks. Wayne, always an innovative thinker, ordered maritime matches from a company in Maine, matches with wax-coated sulphur heads twice as large as ordinary kitchen matches. Other pasture burners have used propane branding-iron torches, kerosene weed burners, and even army surplus flame throwers to start pasture fires.

Without question, the most distinctive method for setting grass fires here is a device of folk technology variously called a fire pipe,

Close-up of the drip end of one of Jane Koger's firesticks.

a drip pipe, a pipe burner, a fire starter, a fire setter, or, most commonly, a firestick. Unique (as far as I know) to the Flint Hills, the firestick is simplicity itself: a length of ordinary steel pipe sealed at one end, plugged at the other, and filled with gasoline. A small drip hole is sometimes drilled into the removable plug, but usually the drip hole is created by using a file or hacksaw to cut a notch across the threads of the plug and another across the threads of the pipe. When the plug is screwed in almost all the way, the two notches are aligned so that gasoline can drip out; tightening the plug a final quarter turn shuts off the gasoline. To use the firestick, a pasture burner will first use a match to set fire to a clump of grass (the firestick is never lighted directly), then the drip end of the firestick is dropped into the burning grass and dragged along the strip of prairie to be fired. As gasoline bounces out of the drip hole, it simultaneously catches fire and falls on some leaves of dead grass, immediately setting them ablaze. To extinguish the flame, the firestick is simply turned straight up into the air; when the gasoline on the surface of the plugged end has burned up, the flame goes out. A gloved hand clapped over the flame will expedite the extinguishment. To restart the firestick, simply drop the plugged end back into burning grass and start dragging.

Sounds like a bomb, doesn't it? Government personnel (county agents, Konza Prairie Research Natural Area workers, and rangers at the Tallgrass Prairie National Preserve) eschew the firestick for commercially manufactured drip torches, widely used by the U.S. Forest Service, while farmers and ranchers scorn the idea of buying a slower-burning drip torch (which uses a wick fed by a cooler mixture of three-quarters gasoline and one-quarter diesel fuel) when they can make their own faster-burning firesticks. Despite the qualms and warnings that have been expressed by government burners, I have yet to learn of a single firestick that has exploded. The reason they don't, I am told by those who use them (as I now do myself), is that oxygen cannot get into the pipe.

I saw my first firestick on 2 April 1987, when I went out to observe and document Slim and Phill Pinkston and Slim's son Larry burn a couple of Chase County pastures, one near Bloody Creek and the other just north of the Bazaar cemetery. As is often the case, some neighbors were helping, both to exchange work and to protect their own pastures—Charley Trayer on Bloody Creek, Tom Burton and some hired hands from the Rogler Ranch at Bazaar. Needless to say, I was fascinated by the firestick. Despite my nearly lifelong residence in the Flint Hills region and despite the pasture I had helped burn as a youth, I had never before seen or even heard of such a thing. I saw some three firesticks that day, each one varying slightly from the others, mainly in length and circumference of the pipe.

No one that day, or since, could tell me where and when the firestick originated or who invented it. Tom Burton said that Roglers had been using one for about ten years and that before that they had used a cumbersome kerosene-fired weed burner. Slim Pinkston said he thought they had been using theirs for about fifteen or twenty years, he wasn't sure, and that they got the idea from Bud McLinden.

So a few days later I went over to see Bud, one of the best-known pasturemen and ablest cowboys in the Flint Hills. His home was in eastern Marion County and most of the pastures he looked after were there and in Chase County, but I have heard ranchers and cowboys from Latham and Beaumont in the southern Flint Hills to Skiddy and Junction City in the north praise his skills. I have heard my dad and Cotton Rogers, neither of them slouches with tough horses or wild cows, speak approvingly (as close as either of them ever came to effusively) of Bud's ability to ride and rope. Anyway, Bud had some good stories to tell about firesticks, which he'd been using for a dozen or more years, he thought. When I asked about potential explosions, he told me about the time he had finished setting a head fire in a large pasture about dark and had then driven to the gate. When he got there, he discovered that he had bounced his firestick off the back of his flatbed pickup, so he drove back to look for it. As he drove over the blackened earth, he saw flames intermittently shooting skyward in the distance, "like Old Faithful geyser erupting," was how he put it. As he got closer, he saw it was his firestick. The headfire had burned over it and the intense heat had compressed the gasoline, which was shooting out in spurts and sending flames into the air. "If ever a firestick should have exploded, that was it," he said, "but it didn't. I don't think you could explode one." When I asked where he had gotten his firestick, he said he had made it, so I amended the question: Where did you get the idea? "Well, I think I saw one on Vestrings, down at Cassoday."

Continuing the quest, a few days later I went to see Bob Vestring, who lives near Burns but runs pastures at Cassoday as well as some in Chase and Marion counties. Bob, the last of three brothers (Jim and Jack), is, with the help of his three sons (Rob, Steve, and Louis), continuing the cattle business begun by his father, Louis, in the early years of the twentieth century. When I asked about firesticks, Bob said they had been using them since the 1960s or 1970s, he didn't remember for sure, but he did recall that the first one he ever saw was being used by the Pinkstons.

With my search for the originator of the firestick coming full circle back to the Pinkstons, and unable to find any published scholarship about the device, I decided to try another approach. I checked with county agents, got the names of seventy-five men who regularly burned pasture, and sent questionnaires to them. The forty-two (56 percent) who answered represented fifteen counties, mostly from the Flint Hills (ten from Chase; five from Morris; five from Lyon; four from Greenwood; three from Marshall; two each from Riley,

Marion, and Butler; one each from Ellsworth, Chautauqua, Clay, Coffey, Elk, Geary, and Wabaunsee; and two who didn't give a location). Of these, fourteen used firesticks—six from Chase County; two each from Morris and Greenwood; and one each from Butler, Marion, Lyon, and Ellsworth. The earliest any of the respondents recalled seeing a firestick was in the 1960s, but all agreed that they did not fully come into common use throughout the Flint Hills until the 1980s. In fact, three old-timers I talked to in 1987 made me feel a little better about not having known of firesticks. Glenn Pickett of Emporia, long-time executive secretary of the Kansas Livestock Association, born in 1900 and reared at Hymer in the heart of the Flint Hills, had never seen one. Neither had R.L. Anderson of Burdick, who said that he had been burning pasture for over fifty years. Nor had Frank Frey, also born and reared in the Hymer neighborhood. He was ninety years old when I talked to him and said he was only seven when he first helped burn pasture.

Since 1987 I have probably seen three or four dozen firesticks and also had Wayne Bailey make one for me. Wayne and his brother Darwin look after cattle in the Matfield Green–Teterville area, following in the footsteps of their father, Durwood, and grandfather, Jess. Wayne's mother, Opal, once told me that her job during pasture-burning season was that of chip kicker—going along after a backfire had been set and kicking the smoldering cow chips away from the edge of the unburned into the burned area so that a gust of wind wouldn't start a new fire. (The Baileys are tough hands who can ride anything with hair; Darwin rode bulls in his younger days, and Wayne was a good bronc rider and bulldogger.) Wayne, instead of using regular steel pipe, makes his firesticks out of muffler exhaust pipe, which is thinner and lighter. He also welds a triangular handle on the sealed end to make dragging the firestick, whether by hand or from a four-wheeler, easier.

One of the most unusual firesticks I've seen was made by the late Al Wills, a Texas Panhandle native who came to the Flint Hills to cowboy for the Price family (who, like many Flint Hills or Texas cattlemen, had ranching interests in both states) and ended up staying here. The top six feet were of lightweight plastic pipe while the plug end, about a foot and a half in length, was regular steel pipe. Somehow or other Al had been able to seal the two materials together so that there was no leak at the join.

Most firesticks I have seen, although they vary in length and other details, are made from regular steel pipe, from an inch to an inch-and-a-half in diameter. Lengths have ranged from ten feet to half that, with the average around seven feet of inch-and-a-quarter pipe. The advantage of the longer, larger pipe is that it holds more fuel, but it is also much heavier that a smaller one. Some ranchers drag the longer pipes behind a pickup and use a smaller one for hand work. Some firesticks are straight; others are angled (from 45 to 90 degrees) at the plug end, which makes them easier to fill. An angled plug tends to point the drip hole up from the ground so that it is less likely to become clogged from the damp earth of a gopher hole or from a cow chip. I've seen a couple that have had ten- or twelve-inch curved prongs welded onto the plug end in order to hold the firestick up off the ground, and one with a small rod cage welded around the bottom to keep it from snagging on rocks and out of gopher mounds.

I've also seen a firestick with a petcock for a drip hole instead of filed grooves. If the drip hole is too large, the firestick has to be refilled more often (and, with high gasoline prices, costs more to operate), whereas if it is too small the fuel won't trickle out fast enough to sustain a flame. A six-foot, one-and-a-quarter inch firestick with a properly adjusted drip hole pulled behind a pickup or four-wheeler can fire over a mile of prairie. A common problem (at least in my experience) is that the vibration caused by dragging the firestick will cause the plug to loosen and fall out. Murle Teter of Eureka solved that problem by fastening a small chain with swivels to both plug and pipe.

In the decade and a half since my first encounter with a firestick, I have been able to push the date of the prototype back to the 1930s. This is well before the first forest service drip torches went on the market in the early 1950s. The drip torch looks something like a small, portable weed sprayer, only the tank holds fuel instead of herbicide. A tube coming out of the top of the tank is bent into a complete circle in order to form a safety loop so that fire cannot be sucked back into the tank. At the end of the tube is a nozzle containing a wick. When saturated, the wick is ignited and drops of burning fuel (a mix of gasoline and diesel) fall to the ground to start a fire.

The Wisconsin Natural Resources Department uses a fire-starting device called a drag torch in maintaining the Crex Meadows prairie. The drag torch, which seems to have been created in the 1960s, looks something like a firestick but operates like a drip torch. It is a long tube, three or four inches in diameter, with a handle along its mid-length, a wick at one end, and an air valve at the other. It burns a fifty-fifty mixture of gasoline and diesel fuel.

From what I can tell, firesticks began to be used with some regularity by people like the Pinkstons, Vestrings, and McLindens as early as the 1960s, although, as noted above, it took some three decades for that usage to become widespread. As early as the 1940s, I am told, an old-timer (Brown I think was his name) near Olpe would take a kerosene-soaked corncob and shove it into a pipe, then fill the pipe with kerosene, light the corncob, which acted as a wick, and drive through his pastures in a Model T Ford, dragging the pipe out the door and holding his hand over the top to keep the kerosene from splashing out.

The earliest firestick-like devices I have learned of, however, were being used in the 1930s and 1940s by section crews of the Missouri Pacific and Santa Fe railroads. Back then one of the regular duties of a section gang, besides keeping the track and roadbed in shape, was to maintain the right-of-way—keep up the fences and burn the dead grass between the fence and the tracks. The reason for keeping the right-of-way cleared of old grass was that sparks from steam engines often set prairie fires, which meant that the railroad had to pay landowners for the damage these fires caused. Chet Unruh, who as a young man started working on the Santa Fe at Cassoday in the later 1930s, said that they were supposed to use matches, rakes, and wet gunnysacks to set and control the fires. Instead, they would use a pipe filled with the gasoline-diesel fuel mixture used in handcars to start the fires. Fuel-saturated cloth at the bottom of the pipe acted as a wick when set alight.

These unauthorized devices, which Chet said were made surreptitiously for them by workers at the Santa Fe shop in Newton, were similar to the ones that Alva Fuller of El Dorado used when he began working on the Missouri Pacific section in 1933 (at thirty-two cents per hour, he told me). Here is how he described what he termed a "torch":

It was made of 3/4 inch pipe with a curve in the lower 12–14 inches. The lower end was plugged with cloth which had been pulled in from the bottom with a length of baling wire. As to the fuel ... we used the "company gasoline" furnished for use in the two-cycle motor cars. This came already mixed with 50-weight motor oil, which cuts down the "flash point" considerably. In use, the foreman (usually) would carry a one gallon can of "gas" which was carried in one hand for refilling in the open top of the torch. The foreman, mostly walking backward, would drag the curved torch through the grass, watching closely to see how well we "section snipes" were keeping the backfire out, the slight variables in the wind direction (burning toward the track), etc. It was officially a no-no to use a torch, although the roadmaster knew that we kept and used them. When we saw an official motor car coming down the track, we blew out the torch, laid it down, and set the fire by using hanks of grass (hay) until they were out of sight.

Chet also said that if he saw a handcar with a supervisor coming down the track, he would hide his pipe in the grass and go back to using a rake to set fire until the higher-up had gone on.

Just where and when the first firestick was created is, and will no doubt remain, a mystery. It does, however, seem to have originated in the Flint Hills, although on the railroad, not on a ranch. It is a pretty amazing invention, when you stop to think about it. Who in the world would ever have had the temerity to put straight gasoline into a pipe, drill a hole in the bottom end, and intentionally poke the dripping thing into a clump of burning grass? With what trepidation (if any) would such a brave, nay foolhardy, soul first have tested his invention? We'll never know.

Sixteen

Teter Rock

The bluestem grass running down off the slopes is so tall that it's hard to see the fence rows. In the distance ribbons of light green mark the benches, the natural terraces that stack one on the other to form the Flint Hills. A light blue haze blurs the horizon in all directions as I switch off the pickup and the tremolo of Emmylou Harris, its poignance perfectly matching the moment and my mood. The hilltop knoll toward which I walk is some sixty feet across and covered with buffalo grass, broom weed, and a scattering of ragweed. Nearly a mile away, the crest of Teterville Hill (I've heard it called Teter Hill, and today some people call it Texaco Hill, but to us it was always Teterville Hill) marks the horizon to the north; otherwise the eye can see ten to fifteen miles in all directions: south to Sugar Loaf Hill, northwest almost to Matfield Green, west halfway to Cassoday, east toward the old abandoned oil field camp of Burkett. In the sky between me and

Fall River to the east a string of geese, their formation spread out a quarter of a mile at its ends, circles over a large watershed pond. Their V undulates and twists, like a string twirled through the air by a child's arm, as it banks over a patch of dark rose and purple where sumac covers the crest of a ridge. A dozen geese break off, heading on south before the winter sure to come, hinted at in the faint edges of chill on this pleasant morning. It's early October, the fourth, but it feels like a cool morning in late May or early June. An occasional elm or Osage orange tree dots a draw, while a big cottonwood at the head of a canyon reaches down to water far beneath, forcing its roots between cracks in the rocks where even the grass can't grow. A few other trees are scattered along the banks of draws that wind south and eastward to the head of Fall River, its own banks thickly lined for miles with oaks, hickories, and sycamores.

On the ground are some small grasshoppers. Green flies dot a recent pile of cow manure, while an occasional monarch butterfly swoops along, heading south like the geese in the distance. Nothing sounds except the whir of grasshopper wings, some chirps of insects, and the slight rustle of wind through the grass. In the pasture to the southwest cows and calves graze, while a couple of hundred yards east in the pasture where I stand half a dozen steers come up the slope between the hills to the northeast, curious about the pickup. They pause idly to look at me, then move purposefully north—but to *what* purpose? There are three herefords, a black, a black baldy, and a limousine cross. One breaks into a lope for three steps, catching up with the lead steer. Again, for what purpose? But then what purpose does an exuberant yearling need?

At various places, some near and some farther away, you can see rim rock, limestone chunks so regular in their shape and positioning that it seems a giant has laid out the foundation of a stone wall. These huge blocks, trapezoids and rectangles, some of them ten or twelve feet long and over two feet thick, outline the ridges. The breeze gusts up to maybe ten miles an hour, then drops back to a faint gentleness. The smell—well, there is no smell, at least none detectable to someone for whom existence without grass is incomprehensible. The air is totally clean, as pure as Eden before the fall. Some swallows come dipping through this ether, flit by and around, their shadows playing tag along the grass. Then they are gone, as

Teter Rock, near Teterville in Greenwood County.

quickly and swiftly as they came. The geese, too, have disappeared beyond the south horizon.

Only a solitary hawk remains, sitting, as she has since I first stopped the truck a hundred yards away, atop the monolith.

A standing stone. Here, in the middle of the Flint Hills, thousands of miles distant from Cornwall or the Hebrides. Solitary, rising over fifteen feet into the air, leaning slightly to the northwest, but, unlike the Tower of Pisa, not much chance of an eventual fall for it is firmly planted in the stony earth and held in place on its flat sides by an eight-foot-tall boulder on the north and on the south by a five-foot-long stone some three feet high—a bench on which to sit, to wonder at the wide prairie before me. The standing stone is a foot and a half thick and eight feet wide at the base, angling upward and outward to ten feet at the top. Its western edge has been worn smooth as glass by cattle that, like the cowboys who tend them, have always scratched where it itched.

Other animals have left their marks on the stone, too. Recent visitors have with intention cut their initials, and an occasional brand, into the south face. Eons ago, when these Hills were an inland sea, this slab of limestone was silt and the creatures who swam above it died, their carcasses and shells sinking to the bottom and into that silt, ossifying into the three distinct and discernable layers of fossils before me, a kind of Permian graffiti, I suppose.

This limestone stele is visible from the road that crests on Teterville Hill, but only if you know where to look. What would seem a prominent landmark even at that distance is reduced by the scale and scope of the prairie, blending into the vastness of the Flint Hills, easily mistaken for one of the pumps that continue to pull oil up to the surface. But up close it is massive, awesome.

Why is it here? Who erected it, and when? Unlike the stanes of Scotland and the quoins of Cornwall, this is no artifact of the Iron Age. Here that era was skipped over, the flint knives and arrow points of the natives here replaced in little more than an eye blink by the steel tools and firearms of American pioneers. But this monument is even more recent, the byproduct of the petroleum industry that once permeated this part of the Flint Hills.

Teterville. A town, a thriving oil-boom town, stood fewer than two miles to the northwest. It was named after the Teters, a family lucky enough to have taken title to land that sat over a large pool of oil (not all those sea creatures became fossilized in limestone). The Teter Field and the Scott Field, a couple of miles to the south and west of Teterville, were as close as the oil ever got to Cassoday and Matfield Green. But to the east, there were fields at Burkett, at Kenbro, at Thrall—Golden Fingers, as the oilmen called these streaky pools of crude that reached here and there all the way to Madison and Hamilton and beyond. Wildcatters covered the area with holes, many dry but many more that flowed. Golden Fingers—not the massive underground lake of oil that constituted the El Dorado Pool in Butler County, where in 1915 Stapleton Number One ushered in the largest boom in the nation up until that time.

Nothing much is left of Teterville today. I'm not sure when the town was founded, sometime in the early 1920s, I suppose, shortly after oil was discovered, and over the next couple of decades the settlement flourished. I don't recall ever seeing Teterville when it was occupied, although I know that I must have because I remember riding with my sister and parents in our new car to visit Dow and Zula Gilbreath over west of Madison. I was eight years old in 1948 when Dad traded our old green Ford for a brand new Chevy. The approach from the west is gradual, but the road running down off the hill to the east curved in a wide S through pastures to the north and south. Just like a mountain road, the old trail up Teterville Hill had to work its way back and forth through a couple of hairpin curves (well, bobby pin, at least) so that both teams and automobiles could make the summit without undue stress. It was straightened out sometime around the mid-1950s, but before that I'm told that Model T Fords, with their gravity-fed fuel lines, had to back up the hill in order to keep their engines from stalling.

As late as the mid-1960s, maybe even later (it doesn't seem that long ago, but I guess it was), a filling station and small grocery store stood atop the hill on the north side of the road where an oil field worker, a cowboy riding pasture, or a pastureman taking small mercy on a crew droving cattle to the Santa Fe stockyards at Cassoday could pick up cheese, crackers, bologna, bread, and pop. The post office and the schoolhouse were located there by the road, too, but most of the population lived in the camp a mile or so down the slope to the northwest of the summit, just east of the Morris Pasture and half a mile north of the Teterville Road. (East

Teter Rock and cattle.

of here, so I've heard, folks call it the Cassoday Road; to us it was the Teterville Road. It actually comes out at Madison if you follow it on east and north.)

Every few years I'll drive up the lane that leads to the ruins, park, step through the barbed wire gate, and wander around what's left of the Teterville Oil Camp. The trees that were planted by hopeful mothers to provide shade from the hot prairie sun have finally grown tall and full enough to do their job. Too late now for people, but at least the birds can use them. Only the cottonwoods, some two or three of them in this grove, are native to the place, and they tower over the mulberries, catalpas, ashes, maples, cedars, elms, hackberries, coffee beans, and locusts. What had been streets are mostly overgrown with buffalo and cool season grasses. An occasional short strip of concrete marks a sidewalk, and some outlines of concrete and stone reveal where buildings—some substantial, most much less so—once housed roughnecks and roustabouts and pumpers and their families. Among such personal detritus as tin cans and scraps of shoe leather one especially poignant relic stands out, the skeleton of a baby carriage. What mother pushed that buggy? Was she young and hopeful as she took her firstborn out for a walk? Or was she worn out from many births and from rootless years in the oil patch?

As eloquently as did the stones of Gray's churchyard to him, so do the rocks and rubble of Teterville speak to me.

As does that limestone spire a mile south of the crest of Teterville Hill. I had heard that it had been placed in the ground by a pipeline crew, but why? I had also heard that it had been erected by Murle Teter in honor of one of his old cowhands. But which Murle? Father or son? Investigation produced some clarifying if conflicting information from Sally Osger, one of many volunteers who make Greenwood County's historical museum as useful as it is attractive, and from Eldon Teter, grandson of Old Murle and nephew of Young Murle.

There is indeed a memorial dedicated to the memory of a Teter cowhand, but not this rock. His edifice, much lower and more prosaic in appearance, stands on a lower slope in the Lanigan Pasture, a mile to the southeast of the standing stone. It is about seventy-five yards from the east fence of the pasture, looking like a rectangular tombstone, but of native limestone instead of marble. It is a little over two feet wide, a good foot thick, and nearly five feet tall. A three-rung metal-bar fence, apparently made from some cut-down portable cattle panels, encloses the monument, reinforcing the appearance of a burial plot, but there is no grave. Neither is there an inscription, not even graffiti, on this stone. The man in whose honor it was erected was named A.J. "Jake" Bugbee. Bugbee, an excellent horseman, had worked many years for the Teters, despite an early injury that had left one leg much shorter than the other. According to one story, a blizzard struck, a severe one, perhaps the very one that Turk Harsh remembered that froze cattle upright where they stood at Jack Springs, fifteen miles northwest of here. As Bugbee was attempting to move some cattle from the range to shelter, his horse slipped on an ice-covered rock and fell. Pinned down and unable to move either himself or the crippled horse, Bugbee froze to death.

Most likely, however, his death was more prosaic. Harold Wiggins doubts the blizzard story, if for no other reason than that Murle Teter would not have had any winter cattle; he, as was the prevailing custom in the Flint Hills at that time, would have pastured Texas steers in the summer, and his winter pastures would have been empty, save for the ranch horses and coyotes, both species fending for themselves in the snow. In fact, he died not in wintertime but in July 1925. "I didn't know Bugbee," Wiggins told me, "I'm just repeating what my father and neighbors said about him. All he ever did was look after cattle ahorseback. He never tied up a horse; all his horses was broke to ground tie. But when they found him, he had unsaddled and tied his horse to the fence by the gate." Bugbee himself was lying peacefully nearby, dead from the heart attack that he must have felt coming on. He is buried in El Dorado's Bella Vista cemetery, his plot near those of some of the Teter family. In respect for his cowhand's dedication and in honor of his years of faithful service, Murle, Sr., placed the monument on the southeastern slope of Teter Hill on the spot where the old man's body had been discovered.

The monolith on the top of the hill, however, reflects a different sort of human interest story. The hill that later bore the Teter surname stands on the ridge that separates the drainages of the Cottonwood River to the north and west, of the Verdigris River to the north and east, of Fall River to the south and east, and of the Walnut River to the south and west. During the 1870s when the massive westward migration that followed the Civil War was in full swing, many "movers," as the settlers in covered wagons were generally called at the time, stopped by the home of J.W. Teter to ask for directions to the Cottonwood valley. According to family lore, J.W. got tired of the constant interruptions and so erected a cairn of rocks on top of the hill to mark the divide among the rivers.

In the 1920s, in the early bustle of the strikes in the Scott and Teterville fields, some oil field workers, sent to gather rocks for concrete work, scorned to stoop to pick from the myriad of loose rocks that cover the entire Flint Hills and instead simply dismantled the cairn that Jim Teter had built, much to the chagrin of his son, Murle, Sr.

In 1954 an east–west pipeline was being laid south of Teterville Hill. Harold Wiggins told me that when the pipeliners got within a couple of miles of Young Murle's land, "he was out there every day." In the Dales Pasture, east of the Scott oil field, the route of the pipeline went straight through a bed of huge rocks. "I don't know how he did it," Wiggins told me, "but somehow he talked the company into moving that boulder two or three miles to the top of that hill." Wiggins, in fact, actually helped with the moving. "It took two big D-8 dozers to move it, one in front dragging with a cable and one behind pushing." Wiggins didn't know who erected the stone, how it was done, or how deep the stone is buried. Eldon Teter has heard that as much of the rock is underground as is above. Whatever the case, the marker that Murle Teter, Jr., arranged to replace his grandfather's cairn is much more impressive and spectacular than the original.

I knew none of this lore that morning as I walked around the stele, touching its hardness, communing with the primordial beginnings of the bed of limestone that forms the foundation of the Flint Hills, limestone and flint that have protected the Hills from the erosion that left other parts of Kansas level and that have protected them also from the plows that beyond the Hills ripped native grass forever from its natural moorings. I knew only the silent serenity, the calm beauty of the land—the grass, the sky, the animals wild and domestic, the rocks—all filled with life, yes, even the rocks.

Part four

Rodeo and
Other Amusements

Turk Harsh riding a bucking horse, 4 July 1920, at Cassoday.

Seventeen

Two Rodeos

In the later 1930s two rodeos debuted some thirty-five miles apart in the Flint Hills. One is still going strong, the longest continuously held rodeo in Kansas. The other ended after a thirty-year run, but still lives in folk memory. One was professionally sanctioned from the beginning. The other was open to the world. Both had precursors, and both were important in my life.

The officially recognized starting date of the Flint Hills Rodeo, held annually at Strong City, is 1937, but the originators, the Roberts family, had started holding rodeos on their place west of town several years earlier. Emmet (E.C.) and Clara Roberts had six children, four of whom rodeoed and three of whom were world champions. The children honed their natural abilities by riding every hirsute animal on the place—work horses, milk cows, hogs—to the point that E.C. started buying wild horses by the railroad car load out of Colorado, having the kids break them, then selling the gentled mustangs to neighboring farmers and ranchers. Once when he was selling a horse at an auction someone from the crowd called out, "Can a kid ride that horse, Emmet?" "My kids can," was his quick response.

The Roberts family, before moving to Chase County, had lived in the Chalk neighborhood east of Council Grove, near where Clyde Miller, a Wild West show operator from Iowa, pastured his bucking horses during the winter. When she was in her mid-teens, Marge, eldest of the six children, overcame her mother's reluctance to let her ride in the show during the summers by promising that she would return each fall in order to finish high school, a promise she kept. Marge went on to become a top competitor, winning in 1940 the last women's saddle bronc riding contest held at the Cheyenne Frontier Days rodeo. In the years before there were official world championships for either men or women, the cowboys themselves considered the winner at Cheyenne, the most prestigious of all rodeos, the de facto champion. Thus in the eyes of her peers, Marge would have been the equivalent of a world champion several years before either of her brothers attained that status.

Marge also was a trick rider, performing at rodeos all across the country. Her most famous stunt was one she developed called "the Dive." Standing upright on the back of a running horse, Marge would lean forward over the horse's neck at a forty-five-degree angle, arms outstretched with her hands cupped together, as if leaping from a diving board. Like many another successful invention, this one began by accident. Once while performing a simple running stand (simple for a trick rider, at least), she lost her balance and began falling forward. Instinctively throwing out her hands, the air pressure on her palms kept her aloft, although at a precarious angle. A picture from the 1950s shows her leaning so far forward that her fingertips are outside the frame of the photograph while the horse's nose is inside. Other trick riders later performed this stunt, but Marge originated it. She was inducted into the National Cowgirl Hall of Fame in 1987.

In later years people who were more aware of her brothers' successful rodeo careers than of hers would sometimes ask if she followed them into rodeo. Her quiet response was always, "No, they followed me." The first to do so was Ken, second oldest in the family, who was the world champion bull rider for three consecutive years beginning in 1943. He, too, honed his skills in Clyde Miller's

Ken, E.C., and Gerald Roberts. (Chase County Historical Society)

Wild West show before switching full time to rodeo competition. A top-notch saddle bronc rider in addition to bulls, his exploits in the latter event have become legendary. I have been told that one time in a Missouri rodeo Ken's bull rope broke midway through his money-winning ride, which he completed with sheer balance and the strength of his legs. Whether true or not, this story shows the respect his fellow bull riders had for his ability, guts, and determination.

Gerald, a two-time All Around champion (1942 and 1948), began his rodeo career at the tender age of thirteen. Several years ago

Marge Roberts performing "the Dive." (Chase County Historical Society)

I had a chance to meet and interview Gerald, who had fascinating tales to tell of the days when a rodeo cowboy led a gypsy life. This is the story he told me of how he started rodeoing.

When Gerald graduated from the eighth grade, he immediately set out for Nebraska to join up with Marge and Ken, who were riding steers and broncs in the Clyde Miller show. Everything went fine for a couple of weeks, and then, Gerald said, he got thrown pretty hard from a bronc and was knocked out for several minutes. At this point Miller, talking to Ken and Marge, found out that this kid, who looked several years older, was only thirteen. When Gerald finally came to, Clyde immediately sent him home.

But instead of staying home, he and a buddy went to a rodeo in Oklahoma, where they learned that a Wild West show in Nevada was hiring. So they hopped a freight and (illegally, of course) rode the rails to Winnemucca. They had to switch from the Santa Fe through several other lines to the Union Pacific, this during the Great Depression when out-of-work and desperate men were filling the hobo jungles of railroad towns.

His friend took off shortly after arriving in Nevada, but Gerald stayed and spent the summer riding broncs and steers. As the season came to an end, Gerald hopped another series of freight trains and headed home. As the train neared Strong City, Gerald could tell it was not going to stop, so he crawled on top of a boxcar and screwed down the brake. As the train came to a halt, he jumped off and hid in a corn field while the cursing brakeman looked for the problem (and the culprit) and finally got the train rolling again.

Gerald then walked back a couple of miles to his home where he found his mother fixing supper. As he walked in, Gerald said, she looked up and, in a tone as if he had just come in from doing the chores, said: "It's about time you got here. School starts tomorrow." Can you imagine the reaction of Gerald's English teacher if she gave the traditional topic for the first essay of the school year, "How I Spent My Summer Vacation"?

All of the Roberts started rodeoing at a time when the reputation of a rodeo cowboy was maybe just a shade higher than that of a carnival worker. Gerald said that when he and Ken were first starting out, frequently hitching rides to rodeos, they were often hassled by the cops and had more than one night's lodging paid for by whatever county the rodeo happened to be in. Later, after they had become successful, Gerald lived a fast life on the road. I've been told that he would pull into a rodeo town, pay his entry fees, take a room in the fanciest hotel, spend all his money throwing a party, then go out and win the bronc riding or the bull riding, getting enough money to hit the next rodeo and start the cycle all over again.

Gerald Roberts died at age eighty-five in 2004 on New Year's Eve, one of the biggest party nights of the year. It was an appropriate time for an old-time rodeo cowboy who enjoyed life and good times to check out.

The third son, Howard (nicknamed Jiggs), bulldogged, but did not rodeo as hard as his older siblings. The fifth and sixth children, Clifford and Gloria, were not drawn to the arena.

Toward the end of his riding career, which continued into his fifties, Ken went into partnership with E.C. in the stock-contracting business, producing rodeos chiefly in midwestern states. Many of their bucking horses came off Sioux reservations in South Dakota, and with those horses came a young kid who stayed with and worked for the Roberts family, crediting his apprenticeship in the Flint Hills with much of his later success. A few years ago Mark Potts took me to a barn on the old Roberts place on which he now lives and showed me where the kid had carved a pair of initials into the doorway: CT—Casey Tibbs.

Casey was a legendary character himself, and one of those legendary episodes comes from his youthful days in Chase County. As I have heard the tale, he had bought himself a brand new RCA-approved association saddle, and either Ken or Gerald had told him that the best way to break in a bronc saddle would be to soak it overnight in a horse tank. Casey, who was staying at the hotel in Strong City (which was destroyed by fire in later years), didn't have easy access to a stock tank, but he did to a bath tub, which was located in the communal toilet on the second floor of the hotel. So he put his saddle in the tub, filled it with water, locked the door from the inside so no one could interfere with his soaking saddle, then climbed out the window, shinnied to the ground, and went upstairs to bed. Later that night one of the other hotel guests found the bathroom door locked and assumed it was in use. A couple of hours and several door knockings later, the guest complained to the manager, who sent a maid upstairs with a key. When she opened the door, her eye went to the tub, filled with dark red water and a large object that in the dim light looked like a body. A scream and a faint brought more guests, including Casey and the manager, who was not amused. Casey rescued his saddle but spent the rest of the night in jail.

Among the bucking horses in the Roberts string was a big palomino gelding called Jesse James who typically left the chutes rearing so high he could knock a cowboy's hat off on the announcer's stand above the chutes. In 1961 Jesse James was named Bucking Horse of the Year by the Rodeo Cowboys Association, but sadly by that time he was owned by Hoss Inman, a Colorado rodeo producer. As a result of lawsuits following the collapse of bleachers at a Roberts rodeo in Mayetta, Kansas, Ken and E.C. were forced to auction off the company, including the bucking stock. Inman paid over $2,000 for Jesse James, at the time a record price for a bronc. Ken spent his last years running a dance hall east of Strong City where, I am told by one of my old college roommates who liked to play cards, high-stakes poker games went on into the wee hours. Ken died relatively young, a heart attack not caused but no doubt helped along by stress from doing what he could to pay off the court judgments. Because of his sense of honor Ken Roberts had refused to clear those debts by declaring bankruptcy.

I am told that E.C. Roberts, although he never entered a rodeo, could outride any of his three world champion children. If one of the wild Colorado horses he had bought kept throwing off Ken or Gerald, he would take the buck out of it for them. In later years when Gerald would drop by home in between winning championships at the continent's biggest rodeos, E.C. took great delight in bucking him off with one of the horses he (E.C.) used around the ranch. E.C. was named Rodeo Man of the Year for 1978. He continued his interest in horses even after leaving stock-contracting, running some racehorses and raising some colts. His house was just up the hill from the rodeo arena, which had been moved into Strong City in the mid-1950s from a mile west of town. When he died in 1992, his funeral was held in that arena with the mourners seated in the bleachers on both the east and west sides. There were hundreds of people there, nearly as many as on a typical Sunday afternoon performance of the Flint Hills Rodeo, and I counted at least half a dozen world champions in the crowd.

I don't remember seeing him do it, but Uncle Marshall roped and bulldogged at Strong City (broke a leg 'dogging there one year). In fact, I have only vague, dreamlike memories of the first rodeos held on a hill west of town, but I remember more clearly when the arena was moved to its present location on the north side of U.S. Highway 50 as it cuts through Strong City. I was in mid–grade school at the time, and on the first weekend of June for many years, probably until I was in college and would have been off rodeoing myself, we went to the Flint Hills Rodeo.

Those early memories are not all pleasant because they coincided with the annual visit to the dentist for my sister and me. Doctor Wilcox had an office in a small building on the west side of the street a block or so south of the river in Cottonwood Falls. If the concept of painless dentistry had come into vogue in the 1950s, Doc Wilcox sure hadn't heard of it, nor, apparently, of any kind of anesthetic, either. Although the inducement of going to the rodeo far overpowered the dread of the dentist's drill, I can still hear the sound and feel the heat of that drill. But we survived, and my teeth (knock wood) are still my own.

Often after the trip to the dentist and a stop at Jim Bell & Son to buy a new straw hat or a new pair of Lee Riders, we'd take in the parade, which started in Swope Park on the southeast side of Cottonwood Falls and went past the courthouse, up Main Street, across the Cottonwood River bridge, then up Kansas Highway 13 (now 177) the short mile to the south end of Strong City, continuing past houses and across the Santa Fe tracks and through downtown before coming out at the highway and onto the rodeo grounds. I don't think we ever rode in the parade, although Dad did in his later years. After the parade we might have a picnic, then go to the rodeo that night. After I was on my own, the night would end with the rodeo dance at the municipal building in Cottonwood, or maybe the one in Strong (the towns didn't get along all that well; they might cooperate in putting on the rodeo, but they drew the line on dances). And I remember seeing an occasional local twister (not one of the traveling rodeo cowboys) ride his horse into the Hole in the Wall tavern along about closing time.

For as long as I can remember, most likely from the beginning, the Flint Hills Rodeo has always been professional, sanctioned by the PRCA (Professional Rodeo Cowboys Association). It was also usually held on the same weekend as two other major regional rodeos, Fort Smith, Arkansas, and Sidney, Iowa, and it came in late spring, after the big indoor rodeos earlier in the year and before the even bigger outdoor rodeos later in the summer—Cheyenne, Calgary, and Pendleton. Thus Strong City often drew some of the top-rated cowboys of the day as they competed in three or four rodeos over a long weekend, attempting to overtake the leaders in the standings, or in some cases to add to their own leads. Over the years many world champions, past, present, or future, have competed at Strong City. In my childhood, besides the two Roberts brothers, I saw cowboys such as Shoat Webster, Jim Shoulders, Casey Tibbs, Buck Rutherford, and Willard and Benny Combs. Wayne Dunafon, a ranch-raised cowboy from Westmoreland in the northern Flint

Hills who came within a couple of hundred dollars of winning the bulldogging championship one year, often rode at Strong City.

In the early 1960s Dunafon signed on as one of the first Marlboro Men, so I know that at least one of those advertising symbols was a real cowboy. He told me once how he proved himself to some doubters at a television shoot on a Texas ranch one time. It was a large ranch, large enough to have its own railroad siding and stockyards. While the trains no longer hauled cattle, engines did come by every so often to pick up the tank cars filled with crude oil from the wells on the ranch. The first part of the filming took place at the main ranch headquarters, and the ranch foreman mounted Wayne on a pretty stocking-legged sorrel horse with a big blaze in his face. Then the shoot changed location to some pens at a line camp on a remote section of the ranch. The cameras were set to roll when the producer discovered that they hadn't brought the sorrel horse along for Wayne to ride. No problem, said the foreman. There was a nearly identical-looking horse at the line camp, and he sent one of the hands to bring him up. Wayne noticed that as the horse, which was easy enough to catch and seemed calm, was led from the pen, all the cowboys quit whatever they were doing and began quietly to congregate nearer to where the sorrel was being saddled. The look in the horse's eye and his tensed muscles, along with the gathered cowhands who were acting just a little too nonchalant, were a sure sign that this horse could explode. So instead of mounting immediately after saddling, Wayne took the bridle reins and ran the horse backwards a couple of hundred feet, knowing that this type of movement would wind the horse and take some of the buck out of him. Then he mounted and the sorrel walked right off, at which point the foreman came up and said to Wayne, "Well, I guess you have been around a horse or two in your life."

Later, in my teens, I remember seeing Larry Mahan getting his gear ready behind the bucking chutes, a couple of years before he started his long string of world championships. Two of those champions who rode at Strong City were friends, guys I had traveled with in amateur rodeos before they went pro—saddle bronc riders John McBeth and Bob Berger. Another was bulldogger Joel Edmondson, who had been a student of mine at Emporia State University back in the early 1970s. At that time we had a rodeo team, and all by himself Joel had us ranked among the top teams in our region.

I never joined the Association (as we referred to the RCA back then), lacking both the drive and the talent (particularly the latter quality), but have ridden a few broncs in the Flint Hills Rodeo arena—a couple of times practicing, once when they were paying mount money for trying out some potential bucking horses, and once as a contestant when they still had amateur bronc riding among the events. I came in second in both go-rounds, which most times will win you the average. Unfortunately for me, some fellow from South Dakota won first in both go-rounds.

The Flint Hills Rodeo is still going strong, although (unfortunately, in my opinion) far different in character than it used to be. As rodeo itself has become slicker, further removed from its ranching roots, so has the Flint Hills Rodeo gone to such changes as a cheerleading announcer who rides a horse around the arena with a cordless mike instead of sitting up in the crow's nest with the timekeepers where he belongs. I am particularly glad to have been at the Friday night performance several years ago when a couple of the cowboys surreptitiously loosened his cinch, with predictable results.

To offset this slickness in contemporary rodeo, cattle country took rodeo back to its roots a couple of decades ago by instituting ranch rodeo. Rather than the five standard events of professional rodeo (bareback and saddle bronc riding, bull riding, calf roping, steer wrestling), ranch rodeos have events, varying from region to region, based on actual work skills with contestants required to be actual working cowboys riding horses used on actual ranches. In 1987 the Flint Hills Rodeo Association initiated an annual ranch rodeo with events based on the work cowboys do out in Flint Hills pastures. The all-purpose skills it takes to doctor steers for foot rot, break a colt, heel calves and drag them to the branding fire, load a stray into a stock trailer, or rope and milk out a stock cow with an enlarged udder would be beyond the abilities of a hell of a lot of the top rodeo contestants going down the road nowadays. As Wilbur Countryman once observed, "A rodeo cowboy used to be just a cowboy and a horse; now he's an athlete on a racehorse."

That was not the case back in 1939 when Wilbur Countryman held the first rodeo on his ranch south of Cassoday. It was half a year before I was born, but I would bet that nearly every contestant in every event there would have been as comfortable pulling a calf,

Wilbur Countryman.

loading cattle on a stock car, or doctoring screw worms as he was in the arena. Especially the unplowed arena on the C Double Bar, which was located in the midst of a section pasture and twice the size of most rodeo arenas. The area immediately in front of the chutes where the grass had been worn away by the hooves of bucking horses and bulls was covered with gravelly flint rocks, which, combined with the native sod of the arena floor, provided added incentive for not getting bucked off.

Wilbur's rodeo grew out of the Cassoday rodeos, which trace back to roping and riding exhibitions and contests at the Fourth of July celebrations in 1906 and 1907. In 1920, when Turk Harsh realized that nothing was planned for Independence Day, he rounded up a dozen or so horses that would buck, built a couple of pens in the Cassoday Pasture, which bordered his place on the east side of town, then invited the community to bring a picnic and watch him and Andy Tarrant from Matfield Green ride broncs. Andy, at the last minute, went to a regular (i.e., paying) rodeo, leaving Turk to ride all the broncs himself, which he did over the space of a couple of hours. "I got throwed once," Turk told me, "saddle and all, but had a lot of fun."

Three years later Glen Watkins sponsored a two-day rodeo (along with a dance, barbecue, and polo match) to celebrate the coming of the railroad. An interesting feature of this rodeo was that calf ropers, instead of roping one calf as quickly as they could, had to rope, tie, and leave tied as many calves as they could in a set amount of time.

During the late 1920s and early 1930s the Young and the Hoy brothers put together some ropings and ridings just northwest of town in the Sunbarger Pasture for a little fun on the Fourth, but the real string of Cassoday rodeos began in 1932 at the instigation of Ruth Meyer. She and Ott had gone to a couple of the big professional rodeos that were part of El Dorado's Kaffir Corn Carnivals, and she told some of the local cowboys that they could do as well as the pros. So a bunch of them (Youngs, Hoys, Harshes, and Countryman) got together and built some pens, an arena, and a dance platform in Jick Reed's pasture bordering the town on the southwest. They gathered some cows, calves, and bucking horses and put out the word to cowboys. A gully washer fell the night before the rodeo, and it rained just enough on the Fourth for them to collect rain insurance but not enough to dampen the enthusiastic crowd (some six hundred, not counting kids). For the next several years Cassoday had a Fourth of July rodeo in the Reed Pasture, including a two-day show in 1936. The 1933 show was produced by Buss Young and Turk Harsh, the one in 1934 by Turk and Frank Cannon, and the rest by Cannon. (Cliff Cannon shared with me seven years' worth of records that were in his father's effects.)

Events included calf roping, steer riding, saddle bronc riding, bulldogging, wild cow milking, relay races, roping-horse races, and barrel racing. There were also pony races for both boys and girls (one of the latter won by my Aunt Jeruah). Unlike contemporary rodeo, the barrel race was not a woman's event, nor was it run in a cloverleaf pattern. Rather all contestants started simultaneously at one end of the arena, circled a single barrel at the far end, and raced back to the starting line. Roping and bucking stock was brought in by local people. In 1936, for instance, Frank Cannon was paid $157 for providing thirty-eight cows and twenty-nine calves. Bucking horse owners were paid $2.50 per horse, although my grandfather got $5 for a buckskin mare that was a spectacular bucker. She would go high in the air and sometimes come over backwards, which made her dreaded by the cowboys but loved by the crowd.

Contestants came from all over Butler and surrounding counties, as well as from Oklahoma and New Mexico. Over the years the calf roping drew more entrants than any other event, and ironically, considering his later reputation as one of the best calf ropers in the area, Uncle Marshall's name never appears in the roping standings. He did, however, win the steer riding one year and the wild cow milking another. He also won the bronc riding four times in seven years and the bulldogging five times. Dad was never the rodeo competitor that Uncle Marshall was, but he did win the bronc riding in 1935. That was the year that he drew Dad Hoy's high-rearing buckskin mare. I remember Dad telling me about how scared he was because she was so hard—and dangerous—to ride. But Uncle Marshall talked him onto her: "You can ride her, kid; you can ride her." And he did, to win.

In 1939 Wilbur Countryman took over the Cassoday Fourth of July Rodeo and moved it to his ranch half a dozen miles southwest of town, where it had a highly successful run of some three decades. That first year's competition was a little unorganized. As it came time for the rodeo to start, Wilbur gathered the cowboys together and said something on the order of "Okay, now, what are we going to do here? Who's going to rope calves and who's going to ride broncs?" The following year he filled out the program with other events and got my mother and father to act as secretaries, a job they held until the mid-1960s when Wilbur, following his divorce, had sold his bucking stock and was contracting the rodeo to another producer.

Wilbur Countryman, who was born in Osage County, Oklahoma, had always been crazy about rodeos, a passion that lasted his entire life. As a schoolboy he was hit by a car and nearly lost a leg. Because of that his bronc riding and horse breaking were severely hampered, but he made up for it by becoming an excellent roper. When he was in high school, the family moved to the ranch near Cassoday, later the site of his rodeo. As young men he and my father and uncle used to ride for Wilbur Stone, Wilbur's uncle, who had a ranch with headquarters east of El Dorado. Uncle Marshall told me about a time when he and Countryman were moving a bunch of steers from the ranch to some pasture near Rosalia. They were at the tail end of the herd, and Wilbur kept wanting to rope one of the steers. Uncle Marshall, who liked the idea but had some qualms, asked, "But what if the boss comes along?"

"Why, we'll just tell him that that steer looked like he needed roping, but after we got him caught we saw that he didn't, so now we're turning him loose."

Wilbur had a kind of nervous way of talking, often punctuating his speech with the expression "Well, ain't that a sight." He would also talk about how many people would "leak in" to his rodeo, so he felt no compunction to pay to get into anybody else's rodeo. He even walked past gatekeepers at the National Finals Rodeo when it was being held in Oklahoma City. He'd just pick up a halter or a lariat rope and walk purposefully through the contestants' gate. I doubt if he ever paid to get into a rodeo.

His house and barns were on the northern side of the southeast quarter of the section pasture in which he lived with his wife, Virginia, and their three children, Gene, Ginger, and Terry. The large arena was about a quarter of a mile southwest of the house. Ticket takers were stationed at the cattle guards on the south and the north entrances, but not at the high pole gate on the west side of the section. Wilbur kept part of his Hereford cow herd in this pasture, along with fifteen or twenty Brahma bucking bulls, some bulldogging steers, and thirty or forty broncs.

During the 1950s and early 1960s, he used those broncs and bulls to produce rodeos not only at his ranch, but also in places such as El Dorado, Halstead, Eskridge, Winfield, and Haysville. He also occasionally leased out bucking horses to RCA contractors. Many of these broncs were stocky blue and strawberry roans, hard buckers that traced back to the herd started by Tom Watkins in the late nineteenth century. Two of Wilbur's broncs, neither of them of Watkins breeding, are particularly memorable to me. One was Sambo, which Ernie Love would saddle and rope a calf off of after the horse had (usually) thrown his rider in the bareback bronc riding. The other was Flying Saucer, a grey saddle bronc ridden only a couple of times in his long career. I came close to riding him in 1962, bucking off just at the whistle. One judge marked the ride, but the other (a roper, as it happened) didn't. Good as Saucer was, he didn't have the fame of Saturday Evening Post, a dun-colored Brahma that was a run-of-the-mill bull until his photo appeared in a 1957 article about the Flint Hills, "They Don't Need Progress," by Myra Lockwood Brown. For the next ten years, he was ridden only a couple of times.

Rough-stock riders had tough animals waiting for them at Countryman's Rodeo, but so did the calf ropers. As at the earlier Cassoday rodeos, roping was the most popular event with contestants (although not with spectators, who preferred the action of bucking broncs and bulls). Usually from fifty to seventy ropers would be entered, many of them driving up from Oklahoma for Wilbur's show in the afternoon, then stopping at Moline for the night rodeo on their way home. Rather than run all the calf ropers at once, Wilbur would intersperse them among the other events, but always end with bull riding. Because it was his rodeo, Wilbur sometimes altered the rules to suit what he thought they should be. In professional rodeo, for instance, a calf has to be "daylighted;" i.e., if it is jerked down when the horse stops after the calf has been caught, the roper has to let it regain its feet or lift it into the air high enough so that daylight shows, then rethrow the calf before he can tie it. As a former calf roper himself, and one who raised good rope horses (he had often won the roping horse race at the Reed Pasture rodeos), Wilbur figured that if your horse was good enough to upset a calf and keep it on the ground until you got to it, you could "tie 'em like you find 'em," as he put it. You could almost see those well-mounted Okie ropers slavering at the thought. But rarely did anyone have a chance to tie a calf already on the ground at Countryman's. His Hereford calves, untouched since being worked in April or May, more often than not had jumped back up and were coming at the roper by the time he got to the ground. I've seen more than one shirt torn by those kicking little devils.

If the calves were trouble, their mothers were even worse. The wild cow milking (the demolition derby of rodeo) vied with bull riding as a crowd pleaser at Countryman's. Not only were shirts torn, they were ripped up by those snorty whitefaces. Rules will vary in this event, which is a staple of today's ranch rodeos but is not a standard rodeo event. At Countryman's two mounted men carrying ropes would take out after the cow when she left the chute. One man roped her and dallied his rope onto the saddle horn and the other man mugged her. Then the roper dismounted, stripped a few drops of milk into a pop bottle, and ran back afoot (or mounted his horse, if he could catch him) to the finish line, while the mugger got the rope off the cow. If the milker crossed the line before the rope was off, no time. Uncle Marshall was often in the money in this event, at least partly because for years Curly Davis was his mugger. Curly was a big, strong roper a couple of decades younger than Marshall, and he could handle a cow. The standard mugging technique is to go down the rope, get one arm around the cow's neck, then pinch her nostrils with a thumb and middle finger. I remember one year when the cow opened her mouth to beller just as Curly was putting his right arm around her neck. Instead of circling the neck, his arm went into her mouth, so he grabbed his right wrist with his left hand and pulled hard. He was bleeding from cuts on his lower arm made by the cow's teeth, but he said it was the easiest time he'd ever had in holding a cow. I think that the first money either I or my friend Jay Young ever won was the year we placed third in the cow milking at Countryman's. I roped the cow and Jay had to mug her, but he got his revenge twenty-some years later when we got in the wild cow milking at the 1984 Cassoday Centennial. I was expecting both of us to be mounted, as at Countryman's, but here the mugger had to be on foot, and since Jay had been the one who entered us, he listed himself as the roper. Unfortunately, he caught the cow.

I have many good memories of Wilbur Countryman and his rodeo. After the rodeo was over, some of the cowboys would run some roping calves into the chute and let us kids ride them with a pigging string borrowed from some calf roper. We got our first taste of rodeo (and of dirt) on those calves. One future world champion saddle bronc rider, Bob Berger, rode his first bronc at Countryman's, and another, John McBeth, competed there before joining the Association. Often in the summer several of us (Greg and Bob Watkins, Richard and Jay Young, Al Plummer, and I, among others) would go down to Wilbur's on a Sunday afternoon, and he'd let us run some broncs in to practice on. Richard got on his first saddle bronc there. He'd been riding bulls and barebacks, and when he bucked

The author and his sister, Rita, ready to go to Countryman's Rodeo, 1945.

off the saddle bronc he forgot to turn loose of the hack rein. Talk about getting thumped down on that hard sod!

Countryman's Rodeo was a true folk event, a community celebration that extended to people throughout Butler, Chase, and Greenwood counties and beyond. People would sometimes start arriving two or three days before the rodeo, camping along Durachen Creek, fishing, picnicking, and shooting off fireworks. There was a small set of bleachers on the west side of the arena near the concession stand and the outhouses, but most of the spectators parked their cars along the arena fence. The rows of cars were often four or five deep. Many would bring a car or truck in a day or two before the rodeo to park it in a favored spot, particularly on the west side in order to have that hot July sun at their backs. Jim Young always parked their ton-and-a-half truck, a tarp over the stockracks for shade, the night before in a certain place about three-fourths of the way up the west fence. We usually parked our one-ton truck just south of Young's. I remember one time when someone else was in that spot. A standoff in a B-Western movie couldn't compare with the confrontation that ensued, but when the dust settled, the Youngs watched the rodeo the next day from their usual vantage point.

Some of my favorite memories of Countryman's Rodeo are helping to gather the stock. Early on rodeo morning Wilbur and his hired hands (including at various times Ernie Love and Don Hebb) and anyone else who wanted to join in would ride out to the far side of the section and round up the stock, drive them into the arena pens, and sort out whatever horses, cows, calves, and bulls were needed for the show, then turn the others back out into the pasture. Dad had usually driven our truck down the night before and parked it along the west fence of the arena, then he and Mother would arrive early on the Fourth and set up the entry books at the porch before moving to the crow's nest an hour before the show. Rita and I would be up, chores done, and on our horses riding the seven or eight miles to Countryman's in the early morning light. We would ride past the stockyards at Aikman, then cross the railroad near Cornwell's, and enter Countryman's pasture through the high pole gate on the west side just in time to help gather. In 1967, the last year I went to the rodeo, Cathy and I rode from the home place to the arena, but there was no stock to help gather because by that time Wilbur and Virginia had divorced and he had sold his bulls and broncs.

I'm not sure if 1968 was the last rodeo, or if it continued a year or two after that, but after the last bull had been ridden in the last performance, Wilbur took the announcer's microphone and read the following words, which he had scribbled in pencil on the back of an envelope: "I am Wilbur Countryman and as bad as I hate to, I have to make this announcement. Due to circumstances beyond my control, I will not have any more Fourth of July rodeos at my ranch at Cassoday. I want to thank all of the cowboys and cowgirls that have contested and helped so much and all of the fine people who have attended for so many years. I guess that is about all I have to say and thanks to everyone who has been so good to help."

Now that might seem to be a good place to end this account of Countryman's Rodeo, but there's a postscript, one that brings in the Flint Hills Rodeo as well. Some twenty-five years after his rodeo had ended, Wilbur was attending the Flint Hills Rodeo (undoubtedly having leaked in). Following the grand entry, as the announcer was introducing the judges, the timekeepers, and various members of the rodeo committee, he also pointed out E.C. Roberts, who was sitting in the contestants' seating area. Someone in the crow's nest told the announcer that Wilbur Countryman, who used to have a big Fourth of July rodeo on his ranch, was sitting next to E.C. The announcer, misunderstanding, then introduced Wilbur: "Sitting next to Emmet Roberts is Wilbur Countryman, who is going to have a big rodeo on his ranch this Fourth of July."

For the next month Wilbur got dozens of phone calls and inquiries about the rodeo. It got so bad that he took out ads in several area newspapers saying that he was *not* having a rodeo. And when the Fourth came, he left home for the day so that he wouldn't have to explain to people who came there why there wasn't any rodeo. Even a quarter of a century after it had last been held, Countryman's Rodeo was still a powerful force in the folk memory of the Flint Hills.

Eighteen

The Burdick Field Day and Rodeo

Like many Flint Hills towns, Burdick has mostly gone. At its peak in the mid-teens, nearly two hundred residents patronized a variety of businesses: two banks, two mercantile stores, a drugstore, a hardware store, a harness shop, a blacksmith shop, a lumberyard, a hotel, a meat market, an ice house, and a restaurant. Farmers and ranchers from the surrounding area shipped their grain and cattle through the local elevator and stockyards. Today fewer than fifty people live in Burdick, and of the commercial establishments only a gasoline station, a custom butchering service, and a feed and fertilizer store remain. Even the elevator and the stockyards are gone, casualties of the increased use of trucks. Remaining are the same fertile farms and the same bluestem pastures that continue to provide the true economic base of this southwest Morris County town sitting on the western edge of the Flint Hills.

In 1910 the citizens of Burdick initiated an annual fair in order to pay homage to the corn and cattle that had created their prosperity. In many ways this fair was a harvest festival, a spontaneous overflowing of the universal celebratory spirit that accompanies the closing of the agricultural season in rural areas. This same spirit manifested itself within a twenty-mile radius of Burdick in at least six other communities during the teens: Council Grove, Delavan, Dwight, Elk, Lost Springs, and White City. Burdick, however, was the first of these fairs, and except for Elk, the only one to have a rodeo as part of the festivities.

The first Burdick fair, held October 8, was called a Farmers' Institute. People from a twenty-five-mile radius were invited to come view the agricultural exhibits and stock show in the forenoon, then to have a communal picnic before watching the afternoon events—horse races, a steer-roping contest, a bronc-riding contest, a steer-riding exhibition, and an evening speaker. By 1913 the celebration had been given the name it would bear until it ended in 1923—Field Day—although the *Council Grove Guard* in 1916 gave it the grandiose title of "Burdick Worlds' Fair Frontier Day and Agricultural Exhibit."

Crowds were large at Field Day. In 1913 some three thousand people turned out for the one-day fair. That year the newspaper reporter also counted 102 automobiles, not including "one [that] ran so fast we couldn't count it." In 1914 over thirty-five hundred people attended, some from well over a hundred miles away. Crowds were down in the rain of 1915, but 1916 marked the peak of Burdick's popularity. A town of some two hundred residents drew to its celebration over five thousand visitors. Among the throng were candidates for congress, attorney general, and governor, including Arthur Capper. (Then, as now, ready-made crowds are popular with politicians.) Moreover, twelve hundred automobiles, the most ever in a rural area of Kansas at the time, crowded Burdick's streets that year. More than six hundred of these cars, parked two and three deep, formed the open-oval contest arena, while fifteen hundred people had to stand to watch the roping and riding in the brisk north wind.

The admission charge for Field Day was modest—twenty-five cents for adults, children free—and because there were no gates, visitors were on their honor to pay the ticket collectors who wandered through the crowds. Here's what the newspaper had to say about spectators and participants in 1913:

> It was a typical Kansas farm crowd. Sturdy men, good looking, good natured, and hearty women, babies, with candy-smeared faces, young farmers with their sweethearts in the family auto, the disgraced dog which barked at every team until its voice became an asthmatic wheeze, the nervous old maid who kept secret the first appearance of her new dress so that everybody knew it at sight, the water tanks where Crumbine's drinking cup law was utterly busted, the mounted marshal whose sash made the small boy blink and resolve to make his life one long run of marshalships, the hearty welcome to visitors and the fellowship of Kansans. No mishaps, no roughness, no drunks. [Dr. Samuel Crumbine was the progressive Kansas State Health Officer and inventor of the fly-swatter who initiated a state law prohibiting the use of the common drinking cup.]

The agricultural exhibits were every bit as impressive as the marshal's sash. The front page of the 8 October 1915 newspaper, for example, shows a stalk of corn, grown by William Atkinson, fifteen feet five inches tall. The highest ear was ten feet from the ground. Visitors also saw seventy-pound squash and pumpkins, eight-pound sweet potatoes, eighteen-inch cucumbers, and four varieties of corn, as well as prize wheat, oats, kaffir corn, feterita, cane, millet, Sudan grass, Irish potatoes, cabbage, onions, apples, tomatoes, and pears. Even locally grown tobacco, both green and cured, was on display. Livestock exhibits included Holstein, Jersey, Angus, and Hereford cattle, while the horse show gave prizes in the following classes: farm team, driving team, single driver, saddle horse gaited, saddle horse ungaited, ladies' saddle horse, colts, and mule colts. The prize-winning draft colts in 1915 must have been one of the best matched pair of yearlings imaginable. Both were dappled gray horse colts sired by the same stud, and their dams were sisters. One colt weighed 1,115 pounds and the other was only fifteen pounds lighter.

There was a parade with prizes for the best-decorated vehicle, the funniest clowns, and the best Indian-boy and -girl costumes. In the afternoon there were horse races, pony races, relay races,

Burdick Field Day parade, 1913.

and a fifty-yard turning stake race between a man and a horse and rider. There was even a calf-riding contest for children, a contest K.T. Anderson remembers entering when he was eight years or nine years old. In that year (1917 or 1918), he recalls, only three or four boys attempted to ride the ready-to-be-weaned stock calves, and the calves easily won the contest—no one rode much farther than a couple of yards.

There were baseball games. Town-team baseball was very popular in rural areas of the plains region in the early twentieth century, and ball games were often associated with early-day rodeos. Burdick's team played in a six-team league with Delavan, Lincolnville, Lost Springs, Tampa, and Wilsey. Each year at Field Day, baseball games were part of the entertainment, the proceeds being used to help finance the steer-roping prizes. Usually the ball game, played on the diamond at the south end of town, was held one day and the rodeo, staged in the half-section Fred Owen pasture on the north end, was held the next. Sometimes, however, there would be a ball game both days, and, less often, there would be rodeo events both days.

Other diversions were available to Burdick fair-goers. In 1920, for example, a hot air balloon, the first to be seen in the area, gave rides. Perhaps the most spectacular occurrence at Field Day took place a year earlier when prominent Burdick cattleman E.T. Anderson chartered an airplane to fly him home in time for Field Day. The pilot, Steve Clevenger of Salina, stayed around to do some barnstorming and give rides. Toward evening he undertook his most spectacular stunt, a diving tailspin. Even if he hadn't billed it as his grand finale, it would have been his last stunt of the day. Toward the bottom of his power dive the engine failed to start until just a few yards above the ground, and Clevenger crashed just a hundred feet north of a crowded street. The plane was smashed down on its nose after ripping through twenty-four telephone wires and breaking off five telephone poles. The pilot was bloody-nosed, but walked away from the wreck. The wreckage was carried to the railroad tracks and hauled away a few days later, but by then souvenir seekers had stripped practically every bit of cloth from its frame. According to Mrs. Beth Fisher, some of those cloth bits can today be found in the scrapbooks of local residents (including her own).

Just as there was scarcely a town in the Flint Hills without a baseball team, so each town also had a band. At Burdick, as at Cassoday, it was called a cowboy band because all the musicians wore cowboy-style clothing. (I don't know about Burdick, but Dad said that real cowboys were pretty scarce in the Cassoday Cowboy Band.) Alfred W. Musgrave, a photographer and musician from White City, was responsible for organizing not only the Burdick Cowboy Band, but also bands at White City, Parkerville, Pearl, Delavan, Dwight, Lost Springs, and Dickinson. These bands, as well as the Council Grove Band and the Herington Ladies' Band, all played at Field Day at one time or another.

Add to all the above attractions a free medical examination for school children, a baby contest, a pie-baking contest, a wild animal show, a merry-go-round and other carnival concessions, and

Burdick Cowboy Band.

a rodeo, and it is little wonder that area schools were dismissed so that the students could accompany their parents as they traveled by buggy, by wagon, by horseback, by auto, and by foot to attend the Burdick Field Day.

I have not been able to find out just why the organizers of the first Burdick Field Day decided to include cowboy contests as part of the festivities, but it was probably the same impetus toward skilled competition and spectacle that led late-nineteenth-century cowboys to originate rodeo in the first place. Two of the families most active in organizing and producing Field Day were prominent Burdick bankers and ranchers—the Andersons and the Atkinsons. The Andersons were predisposed to beef breeds such as Herefords and Angus and to feeding them out on locally raised grain, whereas the Atkinsons preferred to graze long-horned Texas steers on blue-stem pastures in the summer, then ship them grass-fat to market.

Both families were skilled in horsemanship and interested in rodeo competition; the names of Mark and Frank Atkinson and E.T. and Wilburt Anderson turn up regularly in the steer-roping placings at Burdick.

The premier event at Burdick was steer roping, the rules for which were similar to the ones at professional rodeos today, but the circumstances were far different. Cattle were held in strongly built pens, and the steer to be roped was simply turned out into a half-oval (open to the north) formed by buggies and Model Ts in a half-section pasture running north and south. Contestants weren't limited to one or two tries, but could take several loops at the steer before it got out of the oval. During the first years of the fair only half a dozen or so entrants competed, but towards the end this number doubled and even tripled. There were no entry fees, at least during the early years, and contestants in 1910, all of whom were local cowboys, competed for a ten dollar prize.

The first recorded steer-roping winners are listed in the 26 September 1913 *Council Grove Guard*. Fred Lemay of nearby Diamond Springs roped his steer in fifty-five seconds and won the top prize of fifteen dollars. R.C. Meger won seven dollars and fifty cents for a second place time of one minute twenty-two seconds, and Wilburt Anderson was four seconds slower to win the five dollar third prize. In 1916 Cliff King from Garden City, a professional rodeo producer and competitor from Garden City who had been hired to provide bucking horses and roping steers for the first time (up until then local farmers and ranchers brought in the horses and the steers came from the surrounding pastures), won the steer roping with the fastest time ever recorded at Burdick, forty-six seconds. In 1917 local cowboy Buel Oberholser's fifty-three-second time won first place and fifty dollars, while Percy Oberholser (probably a brother or cousin) won ten dollars for a third place finish of three minutes twenty-five seconds.

These times will sound laughably slow to today's steer ropers, who can consistently rope and tie steers in less than ten or eleven seconds, but when you consider the generally slower, all-purpose horses used ninety years ago; the bigger, faster steers (nine-hundred- or one-thousand-pound three- and four-year-old longhorns, as opposed to five-hundred- to seven-hundred-pound Mexican corriente steers), and grass ropes that softened in the heat and hardened in the cold as they hung on saddle horns all day long (as opposed to con-temporary synthetic-fibered ropes), these are creditable times indeed.

Bronc riding was the second most important event at Burdick, but it was far overshadowed by the steer roping. I have, for exam-ple, been able to discover names of saddle bronc winners for only three of Burdick's fourteen years of rodeos. There were no bucking chutes at Burdick. Broncs were snubbed up to another horse in the middle of the arena, then saddled and mounted. Rides lasted as long as the horse bucked, not just eight or ten seconds, and the rider was judged, as today, partly on the ability of the bucking horse. Harry Person, who in 1916 had returned from Montana to compete in his hometown rodeo, was told by Bob Woods, a black cowboy from Strong City, that had his horse bucked harder he would have placed higher than the second place he had won.

In addition to being a good bronc rider, Harry was also a good baseball player, pitching the Burdick team to several wins at various Field Day games. Earlier in 1916 he had gone to Montana, where he took a job breaking horses for the U.S. Cavalry at Fort Keogh. The horses, he told me, were four- and five-year-old free-range ranch horses from Wyoming, shipped in by train. They weren't mustangs, but they had run loose since castration as weanling colts. They were big and they were wild. When the stock cars pulled in to the unloading pens near the fort, many of the horses had chewed holes through the boards and had stuck their heads out, long mops of unshed winter hair on their faces flapping in the wind. It was a scary sight, Harry said. The army got a halter on each horse as it came off the train, but once the lead rope was handed to the civil-ian horse breaker, he was responsible until the horse was tamed. Each breaker had eight horses at a time to work with, riding each one an hour or more a day. The company commander wanted the horses gentled, not broken, but, Harry said, there was small hope of that—the parade ground was as torn up by bucking horses as if by bombshells. For that work the breakers were paid forty-five dollars a month, in gold. One evening, the commander saw young Harry throwing a baseball, and soon thereafter he was the only civilian member of the post team, his horse-breaking duties, but not his pay, cut in half. The horses Harry tamed, by the way, were sent to Texas to be used in the campaign against Pancho Villa. After World War I broke out, Harry joined the army, arriving in Europe in 1917 and staying for several months with the occupation forces after the war. While there, he again played army baseball, this time with a young farm boy from Nebraska—Grover Cleveland Alexander, who in later years was named to the Baseball Hall of Fame. Quite a set of experiences for a youngster from the Flint Hills.

Burdick spectators probably prized steer roping over bronc riding because in those days almost everyone rode horses, and townspeople were used to seeing impromptu bronc rides almost every Saturday, if not more often, when an area farmer would bring in a wild horse for the local youths to try out. In other words, riding a bucking horse was no special accomplishment because this skill was possessed by many area residents. Consider, for example, Ernest Poff of Wilsey (whose name never figures in the rodeo results at Burdick) who in 1922 "called the Wild West's Bluff ... when they advertised they would pay $5 to any one who would ride one of their famous bucking horses and remain with it for five minutes. He won the money, and was paid without comment by the managers," or so states the Wilsey reporter in the *Council Grove Guard*. Obviously skilled riders abounded in the Burdick locale, and people could witness a bronc ride at almost any time. Not everyone was so skilled with the rope, however, nor were opportunities to observe ropers in action so numerous as were those of watching bronc riders. Apparently Burdick crowds had sophisticated tastes in cowboy contests, and they happened to prefer the finesse of roping to the spectacle of bronc riding.

Steer riding ("on a longhorn fresh from Texas") is mentioned as an exhibition in 1910, and a steer riding winner (Roy Bass) is listed for 1915, but it seems to have lagged far behind steer roping and bronc riding in popularity in Burdick. According to Frank Frey, who rode steers at Burdick in the late teens, four-year-old Mexican steers, big and tough, were used, and the rules were far different from modern bull riding. Steers were ridden with cinched-on circingles, not with loose ropes. Sometimes a bell was belted to the neck of the steer, and the rider had to attempt to unbuckle the strap holding the bell at the same time that he was riding the bucking steer (a difficult feat, according to Frey, who told me that he failed to accomplish it).

Field Day visitors in 1915 got a spectacular introduction to bulldogging by the inventor of the sport, Bill Pickett. Pickett, who worked for the Miller Brothers' 101 Ranch Wild West Show, would leap from his horse onto the back of a running steer then pull it to the ground by biting the nostrils or upper lip bulldog fashion. The next year Ed Lindsey, one of the best of the early bulldoggers (or, more accurately in this case, steer wrestlers), performed at Burdick, twisting a steer's horns and wrestling it to the ground in eleven seconds. In 1917, after two years of exhibition by outsiders, local cowboy Buel Oberholser bulldogged a steer with his teeth for the amusement of the hometown crowd.

In addition to the contests and exhibitions listed above (all of which have since turned into standard events at modern rodeos), Burdick also featured some rather spectacular stunts. In 1915, for instance, Fred Pickering rode a "large, vicious mule cleanly and consistently both ways." What the newspaper reporter meant by "both ways" is that, after riding the animal with the saddle placed in a normal position, Pickering placed the saddle backwards on the mule, then rode him facing the tail, apparently without holding onto anything with either hand if the reporter's observations are accurate. The next day, to the delight of the crowd, Pickering rode the mule both ways again.

Another wild and woolly exhibition took place in 1916 when Cliff King decided to put on a flamboyant show. King was part of a Garden City, Kansas, rodeo family responsible for producing Garden City's big rodeo in the teens. He was also a champion bronc rider and steer roper. He twice attempted to bulldog a steer from the running board of E.T. Anderson's open-topped Chalmers Six automobile, but failed. Next he tried to rope the steer from the car. Unfortunately, Frank Frey, who was hazing the steer, pushed it too close to the car and the steer fell under the wheels. The car was not heavy enough to cause any real damage except to the animal's pride, which was definitely ruffled. The steer ran between two cars as he was heading for open pasture, and as he went by he hooked at some kids who were sitting on the fenders and the hood of one of the cars. None of them was hit, but the steer's horn poked a hole in the radiator as he went past. The man who told me about it said that his uncle, whose car it was, gave him some chewing gum, then plugged the hole and drove on home when the rodeo was over.

For all the rough and tumble excitement at the Burdick rodeo, surprisingly few contestants were hurt. Francis Sill told me that he

recalled a bulldogger getting a horn stuck through his arm sometime around 1921, but only one person seems to have had an accident serious enough to merit space in the Council Grove newspaper, and that was Frank Pickering of Herington, most probably
a brother of the Fred Pickering who rode the mule backwards. In
1919 Pickering houlihaned a large, fast steer; i.e., he dropped onto
the steer's head at a full run, thus causing the steer to stick one of
its horns into the ground and flip over. Both Pickering and the steer
went rolling together for some distance, but the steer got up (with
a broken horn) and ran off—Pickering did not. Spectators thought
that he had been killed instantly, but he revived, somewhat slowly,
and after a little while was able to walk away under his own power.
Thus Field Day's one brush with injury had a happy ending.

In many ways the Burdick Field Day activities were typical of
those in many Flint Hills towns during that time period. I think of
the fair at Cassoday during the first decade of the twentieth century, which featured ball games, band concerts, roping and riding
exhibitions, and races of various kinds, both on foot and horse.
What I find particularly interesting about Burdick, however, is that
its rodeo so clearly demonstrates the transition from folk game
to professional sport (the topic of a talk I gave several years ago
at the University of London for the Folklore Society). Consider,
for instance, the way in which bucking horses were acquired for
use at Field Day. The 1910 announcement of the first Field Day
stated that the "broncho busting contest" would feature "real live
broncos procured for the event." As with many early-day rodeos,
however, the bucking horses were procured from area residents. In
1915, for instance, L.R. Wiley of Elmdale, Kansas, was listed in the
newspaper as the owner of the "best pitching horse," while Wilburt Anderson had brought in the "best bucking mule." Another
example of this type of local provision of stock was told to me by
Robert Ecklund, who lived at Burdick as a young boy. His father
had a harness horse named Dan that had only one bad habit: He
would not tolerate a rider. For several years Albert Ecklund drove
his family to Field Day in a buggy, then let contestants attempt to
ride Dan. None ever did.

Beginning in 1916, however, as mentioned earlier, professional
stock contractor Cliff King was hired to provide bucking horses
for the Field Day rodeo. Along with his broncs (which he trailed

overland nearly 250 miles from Garden City, using them also in rodeos at Hutchinson and Wichita), King brought in a troupe of contestants and performers, including Ed Lindsey (a world champion steer wrestler), Delbert "Blood" Bledsoe (who a few years later won the steer wrestling contest at New York's prestigious Madison Square Garden Rodeo), two trick ropers, and a lady bronc rider.

A change in the method of furnishing steers for the roping contests occurred at the same time. At first, the Atkinson family had provided roping steers from the long-horned Texas cattle they ran in their pastures. In later years, however, steers were purchased especially for use in the rodeo. After 1916, neither roping nor bucking stock was provided by local ranchers or farmers.

After 1916, the nature of the contestants changed also. In the early years, contestants were drawn entirely from the Burdick area: Local cowboys were roping and riding locally provided livestock in competition with other local cowboys. By 1915, however, the year that Bill Pickett put on his bulldogging exhibition, Burdick's celebration was beginning to attract professional cowboys from across the state and beyond. Although area residents continued to compete at their hometown rodeo throughout its existence, toward the end the winners of the contests were Cliff King, Si Perkins, Doc Hayes, and other professional rodeo cowboys, not local hands.

Interestingly, this movement toward professionalism is mirrored in the clothing worn by rodeo contestants at Field Day. Photographs from the early and middle years of the rodeo show local contestants dressed in clothing typical of farm and ranch workers of the day. Fred Lemay, for example, who won the steer roping in 1913, was dressed like a farmer in denim bib overalls and work shoes; Buel Oberholser, who won the steer roping in 1917, wore high-topped cowboy boots and a large-brimmed western hat. Photographs from later years show the professional competitors who came to Burdick wearing the striped turtleneck pullovers (similar to rugby or football jerseys) preferred by professional rodeo cowboys of the period.

The most striking example of the folk nature of Field Day as reflected in dress is found in a photograph that shows winning steer roper Dave Person dressed in a suit, necktie, Sunday-go-to-meeting hat, and dress shoes (with spurs strapped on). As I was collecting information from people who had attended some of the early Field

Day celebrations, I asked them about this unlikely apparel, different from anything else I have ever seen in photographs of early-day rodeos in other places. The answer I received was both logical and convincing. Person, and other contestants like him, were wearing dress clothing, I was told, because Field Day was a holiday. They wore cowboy clothing or farmer clothing when they worked with cattle in their daily lives, but they put on their Sunday best to attend Field Day, even if they intended to rope steers after they got there. This notion of special dress for a holiday occasion is emblematic of the regard with which Field Day was held by the sponsoring folk.

To indulge in some theoretical speculations, rodeo, beyond its folklife origins, has a mythic element: By asserting mastery over animals (i.e., a symbolic mastery over nature), rodeo presents a ritualistic re-enactment of the conquering of the West. All rodeos share this mythic quality, but few are as close to their roots as was Burdick in its early years, nor does any other rodeo I am aware of reveal so clearly the transition from cowboy folk game to professional sport.

Nineteen

Bill Pickett in the Flint Hills

or most spectators the most exciting event at the local rodeo is bull riding, the American incarnation, I suppose, of one of Western Civilization's oldest mythic struggles—the skill, cunning, and limited strength of a human being pitted against the anger and raw brute power of a bull, the most dangerous of domesticated animals. (Think of Theseus and the Minotaur in the Labyrinth of Crete.) Personally speaking, however, I would rather watch bulldogging than bull riding any day. Maybe that's because I can still feel the adrenalin rush of sliding down onto a steer at full run, trying to stick his left horn into your hip pocket as you slide him to a stop, slipping your right hand up onto the tip of the right horn, your left one under his chin as you twist him to the ground. My heart races just thinking of it.

Bull riding, on the other hand, brings to mind less pleasant memories. I lacked not only the strength and coordination for bulls but also the right mental attitude. To put it another way, fear and trembling are not the best attributes for an inchoate bull rider. Any burgeoning confidence I might have been gathering in my late teens was pretty well squelched by Ronnie "Cutter" Cole, an old traveling partner from Brookville and a good bareback bronc and bull rider. I don't remember the location of the rodeo, but it was at one of the few where I had gotten up enough nerve to try a bull. The chutes were loaded and I was sitting on the gate, my rope around the bull I had drawn, too nervous to watch the barrel racers, when Cutter crawled up beside me and said, "Jim, you ever had anything cold and wet stuck in your ear?" then spit on the tip of the bull's horn. He might have been trying to distract and relax me, but believe me, it had the opposite effect.

You can get hurt bulldogging, too, especially if the steer sets up and you go tumbling through the dirt and under the hooves of your hazer's horse, but at least the steers don't come back looking for you.

Bulldogging today is officially called steer wrestling and, exciting as it is, it's a far cry from the wild and woolly spectacle that Bill Pickett invented back around the turn of the century. Pickett, you see, did his bulldogging like a bulldog—with his teeth. He would jump onto the back of a running steer, pull it to a stop, then twist its head up so he could bite a lip and pull the animal over onto its side, a crowd-pleasing Wild-West-show act that Pickett performed more than five thousand times during his lifetime. (He died without any front teeth, according to his biographer, Bailey Hanes.) Go to the National Cowboy Museum (formerly the National Cowboy Hall of Fame) in Oklahoma City, and the picture you'll see of Bill Pickett in action is one taken at a little punkin-roller rodeo in the Flint Hills.

A lot of legend has grown up around Pickett, a black cowboy from Texas who spent most of his life working for the Miller Brothers on their 101 Ranch near Ponca City, Oklahoma, and performing his bulldogging act for their Wild West show. One reason that folklore has replaced fact in Pickett's story is that he was a black man competing—and winning—in what was by 1900 the virtually all-white subculture of the cowboy. Another has to do with the sheer spectacle of his invention. Pickett first learned about biting steers by watching cow dogs as a boy, particularly the Catahoula-type dog that latches onto a cow's lip or ear or tail and hangs tight until the animal quits struggling. At age six or seven Bill is said to have used this technique himself when he held a calf still while

Bill Pickett bulldogging at Burdick, 1915.

cowboys branded it, much to their amazement. Later on he would use the biting technique when he and his brothers formed a cattle-retrieving service near their Texas home. If they jumped a steer in country too brushy to swing a rope, Bill would jump onto the steer and bite its lip to hold it still until his brothers could get there to help out. The Miller Brothers learned of his feat and hired him for their show.

But this factual version is not nearly so exciting as a version I was told by a former 101 Ranch rider. According to this story one of the little Miller daughters was going fishing, not knowing that some wild Texas longhorn steers had been turned into the pasture containing the fishing hole. As she went merrily skipping along in her sunbonnet and pinafore, one of the longhorns charged. Pickett and two other hands were in the pasture. His companions started taking down their ropes, but Bill realized that there was no time for that so he ran his horse right into the enraged steer. Realizing that unless he stopped it, the animal would still be able to attack the frightened girl, Pickett leaped onto the steer and grabbed it by the horns. He was so angry that the animal would even think of attacking this sweet young innocent that he bit the steer's lip and pulled it over to the ground, holding it there until his companions could get the girl up on a horse and out of harm's way.

According to legend, that's how Bill Pickett invented bulldogging. It's a wonderful story, replete with implicit cultural baggage about lowly black servants faithful to white masters and filled with respect for young white womanhood—but it's totally false. The very reason that Pickett was working on the 101 in the first place was because the Miller Brothers had learned about his bulldogging stunt and had hired him to perform it in the arena. The only black cowboy in the troupe, Pickett became a headliner for the show, featured on billboards and posters as "The Dusky Demon," performing all over the world and starring in a film called, appropriately enough, *The Bulldogger*.

Bill Pickett was the kind of man about whom legends grew, such as some of the descriptions of how he performed his act. One of these eyewitness accounts I heard from E.V. Nelson, who saw Pickett perform his stunt at the Burdick Field Day rodeo in the fall of 1915. Nelson, then a small boy, remembers seeing two black men—the first he had ever seen—come into the town from the southeast. "They were riding Indian ponies from the 101 Ranch at Hymer. One was Bob Woods from Strong City, and his friend, Bill Pickett, was a performer for the 101 Wild West show. He had come up from Oklahoma to check cattle on their ranch and Woods had invited him to come on over for the rodeo." Like many in the Burdick area, Nelson had mistakenly conflated the 101 Ranch owned by the Western Land and Cattle Company, a British syndicate, with the famous Oklahoma Ranch. The two men rode up to a group of cowboys and Pickett told them that if he could borrow a fast horse he would show them something no one there had ever before seen. E.T. Anderson, a Burdick native who later became one of the most prominent cattlemen in the Southwest (he donated the fairgrounds in Emporia to Lyon County, where the main building is named after him), offered Pickett his steer roping horse. Pickett mounted, cut a long-horned steer out of the catch pen in the half-section pasture at the north end of town where the rodeo was held, and, without a hazer, chased it across the prairie. At this point the story begins to strain credulity. Nelson told me that he saw Pickett leap from his running horse onto the steer, catch the steer's lip in his teeth as he slid headfirst at full career between the steer's horns, then somersault (the steer's lip still clenched in his teeth) in order to land on his feet and thus flip the steer down with a thud, all without any use whatever of his hands.

Stop a minute and reread the previous sentence. Such a feat, it seems to me, is physically impossible. Even if Bill Pickett could have accomplished such a thing at a dead run just a single time during five thousand attempts, it would have been a miracle. The first of two photographs taken that day clearly shows the steer at a standstill, all four feet firmly planted on the ground, Pickett's teeth equally firmly planted into the steer's lip and his hands held high in the air. In the second picture the steer is flat on its side, and Pickett is flat on his back, his teeth still in the steer's lip and his arms still outstretched. But Nelson, who told me the story, was not lying. He was merely describing what he saw (i.e., what he thought he saw and what he remembered seeing) as a very small boy watching a very unusual man do a very strange and wonderful thing. I have read a later account in an Oklahoma newspaper describing the exact same sequence except that Pickett is said to have turned a somersault down the steer's back before diving between its horns, biting its lip, turning a flip, etc., etc. The newspaper article was written several years after Pickett had retired from bulldogging, however, so the reporter was not giving an eyewitness account but was quoting others who had seen Pickett in action. Obviously the boy at Burdick was not the only one who saw more than actually happened when Bill Pickett bulldogged a steer.

Pickett's bulldogging act was spectacle enough to inspire at least some imitators. In 1917 Buel Oberholser, for instance, bulldogged a steer with his teeth at Burdick for the amusement of the hometown crowd. Pickett's technique, however, did not catch on with rodeo cowboys and not just because of the dangers to dental work or the sliminess of bovine saliva. Rather, it was too slow. It is difficult, at best, to make a contest out of what is essentially a spectacle. Wrestling a steer to the ground, on the other hand, is easily converted to a test of speed.

Of the few photographs of Pickett's famous stunt that have survived, the two best are from Burdick (or from a rodeo at the Middle

Bill Pickett's gravestone: CSCPA (Cherokee Strip Cow Punchers Association).

Creek Fair a few miles south; this unresolved issue is still very much in dispute among some residents of southern Morris and northern Chase counties). Raleigh Sill of Burdick, who passed copies on to me, told me that he was visiting the Cowboy Hall of Fame a few years back and noticed that he had better action pictures of Bill Pickett than those hanging in Oklahoma City, so he sent them some copies, figuring (correctly) that it was one way to get his name in the Cowboy Hall of Fame.

A cowboy to the end, Bill Pickett died 2 April 1932. He was about sixty-two at the time, his death the result of injuries he had received from the kicking hooves of a wild horse he was helping to break. Some years back I visited his grave, which is in a pasture of the former 101 Ranch just north of Marland, Oklahoma. The marker, nearly hidden beneath the tall bluestem, is unimposing—a small, plain stone slab bearing only his name and the initials, CSCPA. They stand for Cherokee Strip Cow Punchers Association, of which, as far as I have been able to learn, Pickett was the only black member. Bill Pickett's resting place may be no half-acre tomb, but his legacy lives on each time a rodeo announcer calls for the bulldoggers to start getting nervous.

Twenty

Baseball and Boxing

own-team baseball, by the time I got to high school, was on its way out in Cassoday, but when I was in the early grades it was going strong. Town-team ball has long been a thing of the past, replaced by T-ball and Little League baseball for the kids and slow-pitch church-league softball for the adults. Town-team ball, by contrast, was hardball, played for blood by grown men; men in their twenties, thirties, and even forties; men who were old enough to know better. Town-team players gave no quarter. They played all out for the love of the game, for the glory of their hometown, and, sometimes, for money. Ringers were not unknown.

In fact, one of the most famous baseball men of all time once played town-team ball in the Flint Hills, a ringer for an oil-boom town in Butler County. Oil Hill and Midian, just northwest and west of El Dorado, respectively, and something like half a dozen miles apart, were fierce rivals. One of them, I'm not sure which,

Kenneth and Marshall Hoy.

brought in a young professional ball player named Charles Dillon Stengel for a game. He was playing for a minor league team in Kansas City at the time, which is where he picked up the nickname by which he is better known: Casey. I don't know if Old Case's team won or lost, but the man who would later go on to become one of the most successful baseball managers of all time, taking the Yankees to seven World Series titles, played part of his early career in the Flint Hills.

My father and uncle, both better doing anything on a horse than on foot, used to play some ball, but that was in high school. Seems to me that the names I remember from the Cassoday town team were mainly Schulers and Hurshes and Millers and Hindes. All the little towns around Cassoday had ball teams—Burns, Rosalia, Matfield Green. The rivalry with Matfield, just across the line in Chase County, was particularly intense. I'm told that games between Cassoday and Matfield, no matter which town they were played in, rarely went a full nine innings without at least one fight, if not on the field then in the crowd.

The fun thing about town-team baseball in the Flint Hills was that instead of a seventh inning stretch, there would often be a between-innings bronc ride. Someone would bring to the game a horse that would buck, and some young fellow was always ready to show off in front of the crowd. Nowadays a coach would scream bloody murder if you led a Shetland pony across even the outfield, but in cowboy country folks admire a good bronc ride no matter how much it might chop up the infield. Besides, both teams worked under the same disadvantage and it made the fielding trickier and more fun to watch when the ball took unexpected hops.

My favorite baseball story from the Flint Hills involves the town teams of Maple Hill and Emmett from up in the northern part of the Hills. These two towns seem to have had the same sort of intense rivalry that marked the Cassoday–Matfield Green contests. Back around the turn of the century (nineteenth to twentieth), Emmett came down to Maple Hill for a game early one summer, and Maple Hill beat the visitors handily, in no small part because the umpiring was discernibly favorable to the home team. Now one thing about town-team baseball, the umpires were usually from the town where the game was being played, at least in most of the informal leagues that permeated the Hills. The home field advantage, even in contemporary professional sports that use nothing but highly trained and certified officials, is a major factor, so you can imagine what hometown umpires would have been like in rural Kansas a hundred years ago. Even if they tried to be fair, the local bias would usually come through, and from what I've been told, the Maple Hill umps didn't bother to try very hard. Which wasn't a smart way to win the game, especially since Maple Hill had to play a return game at Emmett later in the summer.

When the Maple Hill nine trekked up to Emmett, they found the umpiring to be blatantly slanted toward the home team. A pitch would sail over your head, and the plate umpire would call it a strike. Your throw would beat the runner by two steps, and the field umpire would call him safe. After only a couple of innings with the score zero to well into double figures and going higher, the Maple Hill team had had enough. Why put up with the charade of a contest and suffer the humiliation of a lopsided defeat? Forfeit, and be done with it. We see what you're doing, the visitors said, you can have your little revenge, we quit—and headed off the field. At the edge of the diamond, a tall, strapping young man stepped off the bleachers to confront the team: "You fellows can fight me one at a time, or you can fight me all at once, but you're going to play nine innings."

The Maple Hill team, I'm told, turned as a man and headed back onto the field. The young man who had stopped them was a local boy named Jess Willard. The same Jess Willard who, in 1915, would defeat Jack Johnson for the heavyweight boxing championship of the world, a title he held until 1919 when he, in turn, was defeated by Jack Dempsey. Even as a rawboned young cowboy, Willard's reputation as a fighter was enough to face down an entire baseball team.

Jess Willard's hometown was actually St. Clere, a few miles north of Emmett. His father had died a few months before Jess, youngest of four brothers, was born on 29 December 1881. Ten years later his mother married Elisha Stalker, who ranched between St. Clere and Emmett. Young Jess grew up cowboying on his stepfather's ranch, but he found that his unusually large size (six feet six inches and 245 pounds, while his brothers were all of average size) was better suited to breaking horses than ordinary cowboy work. As a fighter he was variously nicknamed the "Kansas Giant" or the "Pottawotamie Giant," but whether this latter sobriquet came from the county he lived in or from the Pottawatomie with whom he traded horses on the reservation in neighboring Jackson County I don't know.

In 1908 Jess married Harriet "Hattie" Evans in Leavenworth, Kansas. Willard had taken up livery-stable work, and he and his new wife found themselves moving to various towns in Kansas, Oklahoma, and Texas. His appearance may have been formidable (he had a reach of eighty-three inches from one big outstretched fist to the other), but Willard was gentle and easygoing by nature. How he got into the brutal sport of boxing, no one knows for sure, for he had never even seen a professional bout until 1910. His own

Jess Willard. (Kansas State Historical Society)

professional career started the following year when he was twenty-nine years old.

Three years later he was champion of the world, lauded as "The Great White Hope" who had defeated Jack Johnson, the first black champion, in the twenty-sixth round of an outdoor fight held in 100-degree-plus heat in Havana, Cuba. During those three years he had fought around thirty bouts, winning all but four. One of his victories was a haunting one, for in 1913 John "Bull" Young died a day after being knocked out by Willard's uppercut.

As was typical of the times, Willard made more money as champion with exhibition bouts, vaudeville, and personal appearances than with title defenses. He rode with both the Buffalo Bill Wild West and the 101 Ranch Wild West shows, earning up to $2,500 per day. He also made some movies, including a feature film, *The Challenge of Chance*.

During his four years as champion, he defended his title only twice, a successful one against Frank Moran in 1916, and an unsuccessful one against Jack Dempsey on the Fourth of July in 1919. Despite his size, his strength, his agility, and his reach, and despite that fact that he scored several knockdowns in the first round, Willard was knocked out by Dempsey in the third round. Some boxing fans still have suspicions that one of Dempsey's gloves was loaded, for Willard had bruises on only one side of his body. He was nothing if not game in defeat, suffering a broken jaw, cheekbone, nose, and ribs. In 1923 Willard attempted a comeback, defeating Floyd Johnson but losing to Luis Firpo, thus ending his boxing career.

The Willards moved to California in the 1920s, where Jess earned a living in the supermarket business, in addition to occasionally refereeing wrestling matches (and exposing their fakery). During World War II he toured with the USO. He and Hattie had two sons and three daughters. He died in Los Angeles in 1968, two weeks shy of his eighty-seventh birthday.

Twenty-One

Cowboy Polo

side from rodeo cowboys, Jess Willard is the only world champion athlete to have come from the Flint Hills. I don't know of any baseball, basketball, or football stars from this region who have achieved anywhere near his fame, and no self-respecting ranch-reared Flint Hills youth would ever take up golf or tennis. Rodeo, now, that's another matter. And so is polo. Of the ten PRCA world champion rodeo cowboys from Kansas, five (Ken and Gerald Roberts, Joel Edmondson, Sonny Worrell, and John McBeth) have lived in the Bluestem Grazing Region. No world-class polo player, to my knowledge, emerged from the Flint Hills, but cowboy polo has been a popular pastime in the region at various times. I've heard that the Kimball brothers, Richard and Louis, who ran lots of country near Virgil and Yates Center, fielded a polo team from among their cowhands back in the twenties and thirties. Dad and Uncle Marshall used to play pasture polo at about that time. In fact,

I have Dad's old mallet and a couple of the polo balls that they used when they would get together with friends, often on the Watkins Ranch east of Cassoday, and play polo, alternated with bronc riding, on Sunday afternoons.

The most interesting polo game at Cassoday occurred in 1923 when the Santa Fe railroad was completing its tracks through town. Cassoday, founded as Sycamore Springs some fifty years earlier, had waited a long time for a railroad. Rumors of railroads were always popping up, and the Orient line even went so far as to grade a right-of-way through town before going bankrupt. Apparently the Santa Fe couldn't get clear title to the Orient right-of-way, so they graded up their own a few yards to the west and extended the line from Bazaar, which the railroad had reached in 1887, on down through Matfield Green to Cassoday, Aikman, Chelsea, El Dorado, and beyond, all the way into Oklahoma.

Matfield Green held a rodeo to celebrate the new line, and Cassoday, in typical competitive response, topped that by holding a two-day rodeo, dance, barbeque, and polo match. Glen Watkins, son of pioneer Cassoday cattleman Tom Watkins, whose ranch east of Cassoday was, as noted above, the favored practice grounds for the local cowboys who wanted to ride broncs and play polo, was the promoter of the event.

To stray a bit: Tom Watkins got his start loose-herding cattle in the Flint Hills east of Cassoday. I'm told that he would camp out with cattle over the summer grazing season, keeping them from straying too far in any one direction and coming into town every couple of weeks for supplies before heading back out to the range. This seems to have been standard practice in the days before the Hills were fenced. Wayne Rogler told me stories about Arthur Crocker loose-herding cattle between Matfield Green and Madison, and my own grandfather, Frank Hoy, as a boy used to look after cattle owned by farmers from Newton, following them north of Cassoday across unfenced prairie toward Jack Springs during the day, driving them back home at night.

Back to Glen Watkins: Now, from here on I'm reporting legend, not fact, for this is the story oft repeated around Cassoday as I was growing up a quarter of a century after this famed celebration. How much, if any, is actually true and how much is gossip I don't know, but I think it's a good tale, so here it is. Glen took out a bank

Cassoday polo team, 1923. From left: Jewell Million, Ward Watkins, Fisk Watkins, and Glen Watkins.

loan to fence in a rodeo arena in the Oliver Pasture on the west side of the new tracks and just north of the stockyards that would soon become the busiest on the entire Santa Fe line. He also financed the construction of a dance platform and hired a cook to provide the barbeque. He collected admissions for the polo games, the dances, the barbeques, and the rodeos, and he also, as was the custom at the time, collected entry fees from the rodeo contestants, offering set amounts of prize money for the winners (instead of adding a purse to the combined entry fees, as is required today). On the third morning after the two-day blowout, I'm told that when Cassoday awoke, Glen, and all the money, was in eastern Colorado, where he became the proprietor of a ranch financed by the gross, the *entire* gross, proceeds of the Cassoday celebration. Nobody—not the cook, not the bankers, not the dance band, not the event winners in the rodeo—collected a dime. Now, I don't know if that's what really happened or not, because I have been told that Glen would occasionally come back to Cassoday to visit, and it seems to me

Wichita polo team, Cassoday, 1923.

that he wouldn't have done that if he had really stiffed everybody the way he is said to have done.

One winter day back in the later 1980s, after he had lost his right arm at age eighty-one to an Allis Roto-baler, my father and I, out driving around some of the country he and I had both ridden over in earlier days, stopped in to see Fisk Watkins, then around ninety years old but still plenty sharp enough to be complaining about the deviousness of various elected officials on both the state and national levels. I asked Fisk about what had happened at the 1923 celebration, if it was true that his brother Glen had absconded with the receipts. His clipped response precluded further inquiries into the matter: "Enough people have already talked about that."

But to the polo match, which is where I was headed earlier. When Glen came up with the idea of a polo game as part of his big gala, he wanted a match that would draw a crowd. (After all, more gate receipts translated into more Colorado acres.) People around Cassoday could see local players any Sunday, but what if he brought in the real thing, a polo team that wore jodhpurs and helmets, that rode English hunt saddles (what Dad referred to as a "postage-stamp saddle") and controlled their horses with double-bitted, four-reined Pelham bridles, a team that rode trained polo ponies and knew a chukker from a prairie chicken? What if he invited a team from Wichita, a town that had produced a number of successful polo players (and that only since the 1980s has allowed developers to turn its long-time polo field into houses and offices)? So he invited them, and they accepted.

The only problem with Glen's plan was that the Wichita players were good. They knew the rules, they knew the techniques, and their horses knew how to follow the ball. The Wichita team won the first match easily, and the Cassoday team—comprised of Glen himself, his teenaged son Ward, his brother Fisk, and Jewell Million—was more than a little embarrassed to have been beaten by the city slickers. That evening, replaying the match among themselves, they figured out why they lost and they planned a strategy for the next day's game. Polo ponies are trained to follow a polo ball like a calf-roping horse follows a calf; ranch horses know enough to dodge a charging bull or get out of the way of an aggressive horse. So earlier in the day when a Wichita player had cut in for the ball, the cow ponies had veered off. But ranch horses are also trained to do whatever the hell you ask them to do, whether they like it or not. So the Cassoday players determined that the next day they would hold their horses on the ball, not let them pull away when another horse came charging in on them.

In the second match when Wichita players rode to the ball they found cowboys coming right at it, too, not veering off as they had the day before. Remember, now, that the Cassoday players were not only riding their pasture horses with their high-backed, wide-swelled pasture saddles, but they were excellent riders as well. Ward Watkins, as would his brother Tommy, later became a professional rodeo bronc rider, competing successfully at Madison Square Garden and other top rodeos around the country. So when the inevitable collisions occurred and polo players went flying through the air, none of the unseated riders were wearing Stetsons or cowboy boots. The Cassoday team won the second match going away. And Jewell Million told me that the Wichita team without hesitation declined an offer of a third match to play off the tie.

A few years back my son decided to revive Cassoday polo and put together a match between some of the local guys (including me) and a team from Matfield Green. We played it on the old alfalfa field on our home place, on Labor Day if I remember correctly, and we drew a pretty good crowd. The field size was reasonably close to regulation, but other than that I doubt if a real polo player could have recognized the game. Not only were we all riding regular stock saddles, but we used a soccer ball and the stated rule for a mallet was that it had to have begun its life as some kind of broom. The originality that people displayed in their creation of mallets was impressive. Some used a regular broom, unaltered; some had attached a small push-broom head onto a regular broomstick; some had attached a push-broom head onto handles made of a whip-like metal; and one player had rigged up a brace on the end of his handle that ran up to his elbow, thus increasing his hitting power. And also, I thought, the likelihood of a broken arm. Fortunately, although there were several collisions and at least two horses running free after dislodging their riders, no one was hurt. We got Dick Keller, one of my English professing colleagues at Emporia State University who referees college soccer games, to officiate, we got a couple of other people to watch the sidelines for out-of-bounds balls, and we played three chukkers to a match. The weather was muggy, and the field was on bottom ground next to the creek with what breeze there was blocked by the timber, so the chukkers were only five minutes long.

Matfield won the game something like four to three, helped to that score by a traitorous Cassoday horse whose leg hit the ball and knocked it across the goal line. All in all the spectacle was more than a bit ragged. I'm sure that the Cassoday players of seventy years ago would have thought we were as feckless as the Wichita team at first thought them. But with practice I'll bet that the contemporary cowboy polo team could have held its own with that of the 1920s. Certainly neither team would have had an advantage when it came to rough and tumble riding.

Twenty-Two

Bud Gillette, World's Fastest Runner

It was Helen Bradford who first told me about Bud Gillette. Helen's a pretty remarkable woman herself. Born in 1907 and a direct descendant of William Bradford, Helen is a native of Greenwood County. She was teaching at Kansas State Teachers College (now Emporia State University) when I first joined the faculty there in 1970 and she retired the following year, ending at the college level a career in teaching that had begun in a one-room school. After her retirement she became a tireless worker in the Greenwood County Historical Society. She, among many others, helped to compile the two-volume history of the county that, in my opinion, stands as a model of local history books, and she also pointed me toward the stories of many interesting Greenwood County residents. One of the most remarkable was Bud Gillette, the world's fastest man.

At least that's what the people down around Quincy in eastern Greenwood County think. At the time Helen first told me about Bud Gillette, back in the early 1980s, I was writing a regular column for the brief-lived, and sorely missed, *KS. Magazine*. Helen had read one of these pieces and called to tell me I might be interested in Bud's story. So the next time I was near Eureka, I went into the museum and took a look at the photocopied account of Bud's life. I also got the name of a woman, Nettie Slough, who lived at Quincy. Mrs. Slough, in her eighties at the time, lived in one of only three occupied houses in the once-bustling community of Quincy. At its peak, during the first few decades of the twentieth century, Quincy's three hundred or so residents were served by two grocery stores, two churches, two schools (elementary and secondary), a bank, a hotel, a restaurant, a drugstore, a hardware store, a filling station, a Ford dealership and garage, a blacksmith shop, a lumberyard, a dry goods store, a furniture store, a barbershop, and a millinery. It even boasted its own newspaper. Quincy was, in other words, as active as most of the other small towns of the Flint Hills. And today, also like most of the rest of them, it is nearly deserted, as is the countryside.

At any rate, a couple of days later I telephoned Mrs. Slough, identified myself, and asked her if she might be able to tell me something about Bud Gillette. Her immediate response was, "Oh, yes, he was the world's fastest man, you know." She herself had not seen Bud run, but her late husband had, and she was pleased to tell me the story, which corresponded in its particulars with the account I had read in Eureka.

Later I made a trip or two to the Kansas State Historical Society library, which houses one of the nation's most thorough collections of state newspapers, and looked at microfilms of back issues of Greenwood County papers. There I discovered that Gillette was indeed renowned for his speed, and I also discovered the truth behind the legend of Bud Gillette. As legends are generally more colorful than truth, we'll start with that.

Although the immensely popular nineteenth-century sport of pedestrianism was beginning to wane elsewhere in the country, it was still popular in the Midwest through the end of the century. Pedestrianism is a fancy word for foot racing—running races, walking races, distance races, dashes. Every time a community came together for some sort of holiday or celebration, foot races, organized or impromptu, would be held. (I have in my possession a couple of photographs from my hometown, taken during a celebration in 1905 or 1906, that show a race being run right down the middle of the main street. I also have a copy of the festival program that lists, among other things, separate races for boys, races for girls, and one called a "fat man's race." No indication as to how old or how fat one had to be to participate.) And every time a number of communities came together, say for a band picnic or a county fair, the fastest runners from each town would be set against one another, vying for both individual honor and community bragging rights.

Foot races can generate quite a bit of excitement, and they're a whole lot cheaper and easier to put on than horse races. No feed to buy, no stable help or farriers to hire, no jockeys or trainers to pay, no mile-long race track to maintain—just find a level stretch of ground a couple of hundred yards long, a man with a pistol to start the race, and a couple of others to judge the finish. Most important, the opportunities for wagering are just as available with humans as with horses.

Bet people did. Communities were proud of their runners and would back them with their wallets. And wherever someone is putting money on the line, someone else is more than willing to try to take it. Promoters would travel the countryside, hauling with them professional runners to match against the hometown favorites.

That's what happened in Quincy. One day a promoter, from somewhere in southwest Missouri or southeast Kansas, drove into town in his buggy, his "rabbit" sitting beside him. The two men pulled up in front of the hotel, and the promoter asked the loungers if they had anybody around who might give his man a contest in a foot race.

Oh, yes, was the reply. We've got a mighty fast man in Quincy, Bud Gillette.

Well, said the promoter, I don't think he's as fast as my man here.

How much you willing to put up on that? they asked. And before long, they had a match. They set a day and a time for the race, to be run on the community track in downtown Quincy.

Now Bud Gillette was indeed a fast man. He lived with his parents out east of town, near his brother Frank's ranch. When Bud's

Foot race at Cassoday Fair, circa 1905.

father and brother would lope their horses into town, Bud would run along between them, hanging onto their saddle straps and easily striding in rhythm with the horses. Bud would often practice on the track in Quincy, a straightaway a couple of hundred yards long, from what I gather. When the schoolkids would come by to watch his sprints, he would sometimes spot them a third to half of the track, then beat them to the finish line. Bud's speed was amazing. According to most sources, his usual mode of racing was to let his opponent get the jump at the starting gun, watch him run for a way to check out his style, then blow past him in a cloud of dust at the finish line. But occasionally he would explode at the starting line, building up a huge lead and then turning his head to watch his opponent strive to keep him in sight.

Yes, the promoter had no trouble whatever filling his carpetbag with bets. Quincyites and their neighbors from the surrounding countryside couldn't get their money out fast enough. Every one wanted to bet on Bud Gillette. According to one newspaper account, the bank at Virgil, ten miles to the north of Quincy, had to wire

Kansas City for more cash to cover the run caused by its customers drawing their accounts dry to get money to put on Bud. Another newspaper reported that after the race there was only one timepiece left in that corner of the county, an old grandfather's clock that hadn't run since the Civil War. Men were hocking watches, clocks, milk cows, saddles—anything they could to get cash to bet on Bud. There were two churches in Quincy, both Protestant and both decidedly opposed to sin. The preachers in both churches, however, are said to have told their congregants that it was all right to bet on Bud. Gambling might well be an abomination in the sight of the Lord, but Bud was no gamble.

When the day of the race arrived, a beautiful fall day in 1894, the town filled with people. Everyone from Quincy was there, along with many from across the line in Woodson County and others from Eureka and other towns in Greenwood County. After the usual preliminaries and last-minute betting, the two runners took their places at the starting line. At the gun, Bud stumbled a bit and was a step behind the challenger. No one was the slightest bit concerned; remember, Bud almost invariably ran behind in the early stages of a race.

But when the two men sped past the finish line, Bud was still behind. Jaws dropped all over Quincy. Their hometown hero, the world's fastest man, had been beaten! And then a funny thing happened. Neither Bud nor the other man stopped running! If anything, they sprinted even faster, dashing through a hole in the hedgerow that bordered the park and both jumping into the buggy where the promoter had parked during the prerace excitement. The promoter cracked his whip and the three men disappeared in a cloud of dust. Quincy jaws dropped even farther. The race had been fixed! Finally someone regained enough presence of mind to yell something about catching them, but by then the three were far away. Besides, most of the men had hocked their saddles, and a posse riding bareback isn't all that effective.

People in Quincy were shocked and then angry, but they didn't stay mad long. For one thing, they didn't blame Bud for fixing the race; they blamed his brother Frank. And they were probably right. Frank had a reputation. He could go into western Missouri and buy fifty cows and by the time he got them home, the herd would marvelously have multiplied to a hundred and fifty. If you bought cattle from him, it was hard to pen the wild, unruly animals in his ramshackle pens and invariably it was nighttime before the cattle were corralled, too late to leave that day. Next morning would find the pens broken down and a number of the cattle, already paid for, escaped and irrecoverable. Then there was Frank's hired man, a shifty looking character who would duck into the barn or run out among the blackjack oaks whenever anyone rode onto the place. If anyone had gotten close enough to see it, they could probably have matched his face with a picture in the post office. No, there wasn't much doubt among Quincy citizens that Frank had colluded with the promoter.

The people of Quincy were still proud of the ability of their illustrious runner, however, even if he had hoodwinked them. Besides, stories of Bud's exploits as a professional racer began to funnel back into town. My favorite of these stories is about a race in Texas where a wealthy rancher approached Bud before the race and told him, "I hope you're feeling good today. I've got $25,000 riding on you."

Now I rather doubt the size of that bet, for $25,000 back in the 1890s seems astronomical to me. Nonetheless, whatever the sum, it was such an ungodly large amount that Bud stammered, coughed, and sputtered, "But, but I'm supposed to lose this race."

"Lose this race," smiled the rancher, patting his six-gun, "and you'll never lose another."

The race started and Bud, as usual, was behind. About halfway down the track Bud was still behind. Gunshots rang out, the dust spurted up around Bud's feet, Bud spurted up, and he won going away. The promoter was mad as hell, for he had lost a bundle, but the rancher was there in his buggy, one hand on his six-gun, collecting his winnings and hauling Bud off to safety.

Runners last only so long before the legs start to go. Eventually Bud's racing days ended, his ability so attenuated that he couldn't even be used to fix races. It's at this time that he finally returned to Quincy, where he spent his last days. The story of how and why he returned to Quincy, however, takes one of three variants. According to one version, he had been at first afraid, then embarrassed to go back home, even when his father died, but when he learned a couple of years later that his mother was ill, he swallowed his pride and returned, but too late. His mother passed on shortly before he got there, and he spent his own final, sad days in the house where she had died.

In another version Bud returned home because he had nowhere else to go. His running days were over; he had been used up by unscrupulous promoters, drained of his youth, his talent, and his honor. He came home a penniless alcoholic, broken in health and in spirit. He became the moral object lesson of the community, hanging around town and doing odd jobs for nickels and dimes—beer and cigarette money—and buttonholing the schoolkids on their way home, shaking his finger in their faces and telling them: "You study hard and make something of yourselves; don't turn into a worthless wretch like me."

The third version, my favorite, has Bud returning home wealthy and in style. He was driving an automobile, one of the first in that part of the county, and sitting beside him was a fancy lady. So fancy, they say, that she had pierced ears, which, I guess, meant something different back about 1905 than it does today. He lived the rest of his life in relative comfort, and when he died he was buried in one of the two Quincy cemeteries, which one I'm not sure. No one seems to know the location of his grave. His headstone was apparently a limestone rock that has been chipped away over the years, a victim of careless lawn mowers.

Thus ends the legend of Bud Gillette; however, the truth of the story runs a little different. What really did happen that fateful day in Quincy? As I was reading through Greenwood County newspapers at the Kansas History Center, I found many articles about races Bud had won. He was indeed a fast man, and he did indeed become a professional runner, winning races throughout the Midwest.

Then I came across a brief article in the county seat newspaper, a narrow column maybe six inches long, headlined "Gillette Loses." The gist of this brief account, which the editor composed from information called in by an eyewitness who had been in Quincy the day Bud Gillette was finally defeated, was not only that Bud had lost, but that the rest of the county was elated. The folks at Quincy were paying for their arrogance, finally getting their comeuppance after years of boasting and strutting. Nothing at all was said in the article about the race being fixed, nothing at all about the two racers continuing to speed on beyond the finish line, nothing at all about them leaping into a buggy and disappearing in a cloud of dust. Nope, just that Bud Gillette had been beaten, fair and square. Finally, said the correspondent, Quincyites knew the feeling of defeat, just like the folks in Eureka and Severy and Madison and Tonovay and Hamilton had for years. And the man who had sent the report in to the *Eureka Herald*? He was the county sheriff. I think he might have noticed if something crooked had been going on.

So the question is, how did such a story get started in the first place? How, in the space of only twenty or thirty years, did the legend supplant the truth? I think I have it figured out. Remember, now, that even a hundred years after the big race, people in the Quincy community were still thinking of Bud Gillette as a great runner, the fastest in the world, in fact. Remember, too, that there's not much left of Quincy. Since Mrs. Slough's death, only two houses are now lived in. The bank, the hotel, the cafe, the filling station, the schools, the post office—every business in Quincy is long, long gone. Bud Gillette was the biggest thing ever to hit Quincy, and his legend began to grow at about the same time that Quincy began to decline. People there honestly thought that Bud was the world's fastest man. There's no way he could ever have been beaten, unless he threw the race. Even if the newspaper account said he had just plain lost, people at Quincy knew better. They'd rather be hoodwinked and cheated than lose their champion. So in order to make the story of a fix seem more plausible, they ended the race not at the finish line but in a sprint to a waiting buggy and an escape in a cloud of dust.

And the dust has yet to settle on the story of Bud Gillette.

Part five

A Rough Country

A mock holdup, Greenwood County. (Greenwood County Historical Society)

Twenty-three

Death in the Hills

Stories of violence and death form a solid core of legend in most geographical regions—gunfighters in the cattle towns of the Great Plains, vigilante justice in the gold camps of the high Sierra, revenuers and moonshiners in the Ozarks, blood feuds in the Appalachians. A wealth of this material for the Oklahoma and southern Kansas portion of the Bluestem Grazing Region was published some seventy years ago by Arthur H. Lamb, who called himself the Sage of the Osage. Just about the time I began to suspect that the movies had greatly exaggerated the bloodshed of the Old West, I ran across *Tragedies of the Osage Hills* (published in 1935) and found out that not only was the violence real, but that it had continued well into the twentieth century. Lamb told fascinating tales, from old American Indian legends to contemporary (late 1920s) accounts of all sorts of murders and bloody accidents. But finally the mind numbs as one gory incident piles onto the next; Chaucer's Monk and Arthur Lamb were twins when it came to telling depressing stories.

Take world champion steer roper Henry Grammer, who must have been as quick on the trigger as he was with a pigging string. "Henry Grammer Kills Jim Berry" is the title of a chapter that tells how, in 1920, at least one dispute over pasture rent was settled in the Osage Hills. A little later in the book we learn that "Grammer Shoots Again," with an account of a 1923 scrape in which Grammer literally shot to pieces the clothes of his victim before putting a bullet into him. The next day, after the wounded man realized that he wasn't going to die, he recanted his accusation against his assailant, obviously more afraid of what Grammer would do to him than what the law would do to Grammer. A little later that year Grammer was killed in an automobile wreck, although testimony in a murder trial a few years afterwards suggests that the accident may not have been so accidental.

Oh, it was rough country down there in the Osage Hills, but the Kansas Flint Hills have their own legends of death and stories of violence, only spread out over a larger territory and a longer period of time.

Several years ago Emile Soyez (pronounced A-mul SOY-yer) told me about a lone grave out in the middle of a pasture. Local tradition has it that this was the grave of the first cowboy in the Flint Hills. Naturally, I was interested in the story, and he said he'd take me to see it sometime. I've known Emile ever since Dad traded him a big dorsal-striped dun horse we called Jack. The Soyezs have lived in the Cedar Point country in western Chase County ever since Emile's great-grandfather escaped from Elba (where, as an officer in the French army, he had been exiled with Napoleon) and sent his sons to America. Emile's grandfather and a couple of his great-uncles homesteaded in dugouts north of the Cottonwood River, helping to establish a colony of French settlers in the Florence–Cedar Point area.

One bright, cold February day I drove out to Emile's ranch, which is south of the Cottonwood in sparsely occupied country. The grave is not in one of his pastures, but he had found the location many years earlier while helping a neighbor work cattle. As we drove to the site, he told me some of the stories he had heard about it over the years. No one knows who the cowboy was, the year of his death, or how he died, although one version has him a member of a trail-driving crew standing night guard. Another says he was loose-herding cattle that were being pastured on the open range. Local lore agrees in placing his death in the days before barbed wire had become common and Texas cattle were still being grazed before being driven on to the big shipping centers in Abilene or Newton or Wichita. So it was probably sometime in the 1870s when the body was discovered, perhaps by some other cowboys, perhaps by the cattle owner taking out supplies, perhaps by homesteaders in the area. Whoever it was buried him there in a narrow grave on the lone prairie, just like in the folksong.

The grave, according to stories Emile had heard before he actually saw it, was supposed to lie along the top of a ridge. That might have been where the body was discovered, he said, but the grave was actually in the flat bottom area of a draw a few hundred yards below a spring. That made sense, I agreed, because who in his right mind would try to dig a grave on a rocky Flint Hills ridge when there was rock-free dirt just down the slope in the bottom of a draw? The grave site, Emile said, might well have been the cowboy's campsite, too, for the fresh spring water flowing close by would have made it a good place to build a cooking fire and pitch a tent.

Emile parked the pickup by the spring and we walked along the trickling water down to the marker. The grave itself was covered with a dozen or so small limestone rocks, each about two inches thick and lying flat on the ground, thus suggesting a shallow grave with the stones placed on it to deter coyotes from digging up the body. A similar small piece of limestone placed upright in the ground served as a headstone, unmarked on front or back. Along the middle of the top edge, however, someone had carved what looked a brand. It could be read several ways, but if you stood behind the stone and faced the grave, the marks formed an HI. Seen from the foot of the grave looking toward the stone, they would be read IH. For what it's worth, two IH brands were recorded in early-day Chase County, one by Isaac Hammer in 1881 and one by Ira Hamilton the following year. Pioneer Cedar Point rancher John Sauble called it a Bar H, reading the bar vertically instead of horizontally, as is the usual method. On the other hand, the marks could as easily be initials as a brand.

Is it a brand, or are these the initials of the name of the man buried there? Who was this IH cowboy? Who found his body? Was his saddle horse standing beside him, as some have said? How and when did he die? And from what? A fall from a horse? Gored by a steer on the prod? A bullet from a rustler's gun? The strike of a rattlesnake? Lightning from a fierce prairie thunderstorm? Or was the cause of death something much more prosaic—flu or pneumonia? Or something ironic, like food poisoning from his own cooking?

On one question—was this the grave of the first cowboy in the Flint Hills?—I did get an answer. "Oh, I don't know about that," Emile Soyez told me, practical Flint Hills rancher that he is, "but it was the first grave in this part of the country."

The dead cowboy buried in this grave might have been a Texas drover, part of a trail crew, but I'd rather think of him as someone who already lived in the Hills, someone who was earning his wages by looking after somebody else's cattle, just as have thousands of other Flint Hills cowboys down the many years since. The way I see it, somebody had to be the first cowboy to die in the Flint Hills, and if we don't know just who or exactly where it was, then why not give this dead herder the honor? Let his be the Grave of the Unknown Cowboy, a tribute to all the early-day drovers and herders who helped create the cowboy image of the Flint Hills.

Just after the turn of the twentieth century, when there weren't yet many fences, Turk Harsh and other men from Cassoday would ride to Clements in the fall of the year, stay all night, drink beer, and generally have fun. Early the next morning they would mount up and head back to Cassoday, gathering their cattle, which had spent the summer grazing on unfenced ranges, as they rode. It was probably about this time, or maybe a few years earlier, that the body of a dead cowboy was found at Jack Springs, about halfway between Cassoday and Matfield Green, just after a summer rainstorm; the man was apparently struck by lightning, his saddled horse standing at a drinking trough nearby. Whoever found the body failed to mention the pair of fancy spurs, their steel shanks decorated with silver-embossed American Indian designs, that he took from the dead cowboy's boots before he reported his discovery. Those spurs, passed down through the years, are in the possession of Ed Smith, reared at Cassoday and now living in Texas. Ed got them in the mid-1980s from the late Lloyd Yoakem, who was given them by his brother Charlie (also deceased). Ed doesn't know anything about the man who gave them to Charlie except that he was old—perhaps the very man who had unbuckled them from the boots of the dead cowboy.

Another death at Jack Springs occurred during a bad winter when one of the men working for the Crocker Ranch froze to death there. He had been feeding cattle, and the mules returned to the ranch alone, unhitched from the feed wagon. The man was found frozen in a sitting position, still holding the reins of his saddle horse. This might have been the same winter Turk Harsh tells about, one so cold that scores of cattle froze to death in the Farrington Pasture, where Jack Springs is located. Many of the cattle were standing when the norther blew in and were frozen upright.

We lived about a mile from Sycamore Springs, the original settlement of what later became Cassoday. All I ever heard about Sycamore Springs was that it was a watering hole on the various trails that ran through the area. Nothing was ever said about any frontier justice having been dispensed on the branches of the towering trees that gave the springs their name. Dave Pinkston of Cedar Point, however, told me that half a dozen horse thieves were lynched at Sycamore Springs back in the 1860s, before many pioneers had moved into the area. He said that the thieves were apprehended in Chase County, but that Sycamore Springs was the only place for miles around that had trees big enough to handle the job. Did it really happen? I can't find any evidence in the old newspapers. I even asked a dozen octogenarians and two nonagenarians at the 1989 Old Settlers' Picnic at Cassoday about it, and none of them had ever heard of the story.

I grew up about half a dozen miles from Dead Man's Hollow, a low spot marked by a pair of gigantic cottonwoods in a draw down on the old Ellis place. Only later did I learn that there were Dead Men's and Women's Hollows (and Canyons and Gulches) scattered throughout the Flint Hills. Let's see, now—there's another Dead Man's Hollow near Matfield Green; a Dead Man's Holler on the Greenwood–Lyon county line; a Dead Man's Gulch along McDowell Creek in southern Riley County; a Dead Man's Canyon down near Beaumont where Elk, Greenwood, and Butler counties come together; and a Dead Woman's Canyon in Greenwood County. I've heard stories for many of these places, some in greater detail than others.

Unfortunately, one place whose story seems to have faded beyond the mists of memory is Dead Woman's Canyon. Did a pioneer mother die there, defending her dugout against American Indians—or perhaps against border ruffians during the struggles of Bleeding Kansas, those pre–Civil War years that pitted abolitionists against pro-slavery settlers in bloody conflict over whether Kansas would enter the Union as a free or as a slave state? Did some soiled dove, an outcast from polite society, meet a miserable end wandering the prairies? Or perhaps a midwife venturing out on her errand of mercy on a wintry night perished in a sudden blizzard. More likely some farm wife might simply have died from pneumonia or influenza or some other mundane affliction, but the name suggests a tragic, romantic end.

Nor do I know much about the Dead Man's Canyon down by Beaumont, except that it supposedly got its name from some acrimony between sheepmen and cowmen, as did Dead Man's Gulch on the Aye Ranch in eastern Geary County. There a man was killed and buried, and buried again, and yet again, back in the open-range days of the 1870s. I don't know the full story, but according to Skip Pickering, whose family in this area goes back to the late 1800s, this was the site of an episode in that classic confrontation of the grazing frontier, cattleman versus sheepherder. Pickering heard the story years ago at a sale barn from an eighty-year-old man named Clark, whose father had been one of three young men to find the body.

As Pickering relates the tale, the sheepherder, infringing on cattle range, had been warned to get out of the country, but he didn't go. The official cause of death was never established, but the circumstances, as recalled over a century later, were certainly peculiar. It seems that the sheepherder built his campfire too close to the base of a big cottonwood tree one evening. During the night the campfire burned through the trunk of the tree (big, green cottonwood trees are just like tinder, as any cattle-respecting cowboy on a coroner's jury would know), the tree blew over, and of the 360 degrees available to it just happened to fall on the sheepherder. No need for the coroner to look for a gunshot wound. That's how Mr. Clark's father and his friends found the body—crushed by the tree and partially burnt, his faithful shepherd dog at his side. Whatever happened to the sheep Clark didn't say and Pickering doesn't know.

The spot where the body was found and buried, on the upper reaches of one of the branches of McDowell Creek, was given the name Dead Man's Gulch. After the first burial a heavy rain the next spring washed out the body, so it was carried higher up the hillside and reburied. A few years later, after a bigger flood had again exposed the remains, his bones were removed to their present resting place, an unmarked grave in Welcome Cemetery. Ironically, this rural graveyard near Alta Vista seems to have been the only place in the Flint Hills the poor shepherd was welcome, even in death.

Neither the occupation nor the name of the dead man of the Dead Man's Holler in Lyon County is known, but his death was grisly. It happened in 1873, according to the way I heard it from Fred Burnham of rural Madison, whose father, eighteen years old at the time, witnessed the aftermath of the killing. A neighbor named Burns, on his way home from Emporia to his farm in northern Greenwood County, had found the body while investigating a foul odor near the trail just north of the county line. When word reached the Burnham household, Fred's father, uncle, and grandfather hitched up a wagon and drove to the site. The body was lying in the middle of a big patch of tall bluestem all trampled down, "like there had been a hell of a fight," as Fred put it. The head was crushed and there were three bullet holes in the chest. The apparent motive was robbery. A few days earlier this man, when paying for his supper at an inn along the Eureka-to-Emporia trail, had conspicuously, and foolishly, pulled out a big wad of bills. As to the assailants, local suspicion settled on three men who had been in the inn at the same time, but there was no evidence and no arrests were ever made, Fred said. But he wouldn't tell me their names, not wanting to upset descendants who still live in the area.

Once when I was talking with Wayne Rogler, he told me that there was a Dead Man's Hollow near the old Cities Service booster station at Matfield Green. Not too surprising, considering the reputation Chase County had with us Butler Countians. Chase-'em County, my Aunt Lilly used to call it. Mason Blackmore (who was a deputy sheriff and our neighbor the year my wife and I lived in Strong City) once told me that he was driving his uncle, George Golden, down to the old Brandley place (George had once worked for Captain Brandley back in gun-toting days) and as they neared the Matfield Green cemetery George reeled off the names of seven men killed in the immediate vicinity. Mason doesn't remember the names, but one of them could well have been the man in Dead Man's Hollow.

All Wayne Rogler knew was that a body had been found there; he didn't know who the man was or the cause of death. He said that in the early years of the twentieth century, when he was growing up, kids were afraid to ride through the hollow, especially at night. Not because of suspicious sounds or Sleepy Hollow specters, just the general spookiness that afflicts suggestible kids.

To my mind, the real Dead Man's Hollow in the Flint Hills is the one I grew up with in Butler County. It lies about six miles southwest of Cassoday, about a mile south of the Degraff Road near where Pauly Cooper used to live. When I worked on the turnpike maintenance crew for a few months back in 1961, Toad Griffin and Jay Hoy (no relation) pointed out the two cottonwood trees that marked the spot where the body was found. The more romantic version of the story went something like this:

Two men and a woman, traveling by covered wagon through the countryside near Old Number One School, camped for the night under some trees in a small draw. That night the husband slipped off and went to a nearby farmhouse and asked to be taken in. He said that he was afraid of what would happen to him if he went back to the wagon. The farmer, either not believing him or not wanting to get involved or perhaps just apprehensive, refused his request. The farm family watched the man walk back toward his camp in the draw, and the next morning they saw the wagon moving on southwest toward El Dorado.

The disquieting visit soon passed from the farmer's mind, but a few weeks later he was out hunting when his dog started barking between two large cottonwood trees where the wagon had stopped. As he neared the spot, the farmer saw a hand sticking up through the dirt. Uncovering a shallow grave, he discovered the body of the man who had asked for asylum. He, as was later determined, had been murdered by his wife and her lover, neither of whom were ever seen again. In later years, the two cottonwoods grew into giants, monuments to the murdered man and the unfaithful love that had led to his death. When I worked on the turnpike maintenance crew for a couple of months after graduating from college, the trees had both died and lost their bark, but they stood, stark, ghostly silhouettes marking the site of the murder. Sometime later one of the trees blew over and for several years it rested against the other, creating an even more eerie silhouette on a frosty moonlit night. Today both trees have fallen, their trunks rotted away (cottonwood doesn't last long once it's on the ground), leaving only a legend to carry on the memory of Dead Man's Hollow.

A less romantic version of the story was recalled by John Ramsey, whose farm was in the same section as Number One School. Sam Ramsey, John's uncle, was out hunting one day, and his dog dug up a body buried along the small stream near his house. The grave was under some oak trees (not cottonwoods) near the trail where, indeed, some travelers (two men, a woman, and a little girl) in a wagon had been seen camping a few weeks earlier. Someone notified the law, but the people in the wagon were never caught, although the girl was thought to have been the same one who had been abandoned at the Newton depot at roughly the same time as the murder.

What really happened at Dead Man's Hollow? Well, a murder was committed and a man was buried, victim of his scheming wife and her lover, and a child was abandoned at the Santa Fe train station in Newton, but the truth is far different from the legend, even the more prosaic version.

The 14 May 1886 edition of the *Walnut Valley Times*, published in El Dorado, gives a good summary of the trial of Orlin Larriway for the murder of Oscar C. Krusen. "On the discovery of the body," the article relates, "it was believed that nothing would ever bring to light the horrible crime that had been committed or that the murderer would ever be caught. Still less was it anticipated that the future would reveal a conspiracy of a wife and her paramour to murder her husband." That much of the legend, at least, is accurate. But at the time of the murder Hattie Krusen was not with her husband and her lover in the wagon but in their old home at Elk Point, Dakota Territory; the child left at the Newton depot was not a girl but the couple's five-year-old son, Johnnie; and the body was discovered not by a local farmer but by another "mover" camped on the site, whose dog dug up the shallow grave.

Larriway and Hattie were cousins as well as lovers, and he had apparently been living with the Krusens for some time in Dakota before they all moved to Osage City, Kansas, in March 1885. The move itself may have been part of the conspiracy, to get Oscar far from Dakota Territory so that the two lovers could return and be together there. Murder may well not have been part of the original plan, at least as far as Hattie was concerned. The stated reason for leaving Dakota was to take up homesteads in Kansas, but that seems to have been a ruse cooked up by the lovers. After a couple of months in Osage City, Hattie returned to Dakota around the first of May, ten days or so before the two men and young Johnnie headed southwest in a covered wagon, ostensibly to look for land. The stated plan, as understood by Krusen, was that he and Larriway would take up adjoining homesteads somewhere beyond Wichita, then send for Hattie. Hattie's understanding was that after the two had settled onto their homesteads, Larriway would return to Dakota, leaving young Johnnie in the care of his father. Just what Larriway had in mind is not clear. He told one person that he was going to seek work as a carpenter in Wichita, while he told another that he and Krusen and Johnnie were going three hundred miles north, which would put them (or Larriway at least) back in Dakota with Hattie.

The murder must have taken place in mid-May, shortly after the men left Osage City on 14 May 1885; the body, or what was left of it, was discovered in August. Identification was made on the basis of clothing remnants and some tools, including a spade with the initials O.C.K. carved into the handle. The spade, which Sam Ramsey had found some weeks before the body was discovered, played an emotional role in the trial. Young Johnnie, allowed to roam the courtroom, had come upon the spade among the exhibits of evidence and cried out, "Why, this is papa's spade!" That helped to establish that the victim was Krusen, which Larriway had tried to obscure by removing any identifying labels from Krusen's clothing. The Butler County sheriff did some fine detective work in figuring out who the victim was and in tracking the perpetrator from Kansas to Dakota Territory to Iowa.

The spade may also have been one of the weapons used by the murderer. Four physicians testified at the trial that the cause of death was a bullet to the brain, and that the heavy blow to the head that broke Krusen's cheek bone was probably delivered after the gunshot. Dr. J.A. McKenzie said that the bullet would have caused instant death and that the "blow to the head afterwards would hasten death." (Just how one hastens instant death, I'm not sure.) I think the blow with the spade was an act either of sheer brutality or more likely great anger and frustration, perhaps a kind of revenge, on Larriway's part. It fits the cold-bloodedness of the crime: The unsuspecting Krusen was shot while at rest, according to the doctors.

Did Johnnie awaken at the sound of the shot? Apparently not. Testimony indicated that he was puzzled by his father's disappearance. After the murder Larriway drove to Newton where he told the boy "he would never see his pa any more" and left him at the depot with instructions to tell people that his name was Tommy Jones. Next Larriway went to Wichita to sell Krusen's wagon and team of horses before returning to Dakota in late May to run off with Hattie.

It was a union the lovers seem long to have planned, according to the testimony of a Mrs. Gray, whose husband had bought Krusen's Dakota farm in March. Both families (the Grays and the Krusens) had lived in the same two-room farmhouse before the Krusens went to Kansas, and Hattie's behavior was scandalous in Mrs. Gray's prim and proper eyes. Oscar Krusen left for Kansas with a team of horses a few days after the Grays had moved in, but Hattie refused to go "unless she could go on the cars [i.e., the train] with Larriway." After Krusen was gone, Larriway and Hattie would, according to the watchful Mrs. Gray, "go off somewhere and come back very late at night." One time Hattie went into the bedroom and Larriway followed her, remaining half an hour, but Hattie didn't emerge for another three hours, very suspicious behavior in Mrs. Gray's eyes. She also said that she had seen the two "together on the bed before others of the house were up." Whether sitting or supine was not specified. Another witness, who had been on the train to Kansas with them, testified that Larriway and Hattie shared the same seat, slept leaning together, and were quite loving and attentive to each other.

In Hattie's favor was testimony indicating that Oscar was less than a loving husband, that indeed he may have mistreated her. One witness said that he had heard that Krusen did not treat his wife right, that Larriway had stated that he would kill Krusen if he abused Hattie. It could well be that Larriway had not planned the murder and that he killed Krusen in a fit of anger when the latter related some cruelty he had inflicted on his wife. This scenario might also explain the blow with the shovel.

Some of the most damaging testimony was contained in the letters Larriway wrote to Hattie and her sister, Ida Batchelder. Writing from Kansas to Dakota, he told Ida twice that he "had won his bet," but would not be in Dakota for "some months yet." He went on to say, enigmatically, that "I bought the wedding dress last night and it will be used in Dakota, I guess. It will be made there if nothing happens and I guess there won't." He affirms his happiness several times, then signs off "soon to be your brother-in-law."

A letter from Larriway to Hattie dated 26 May from Osage City is even more enigmatic and casts doubt as to whether she was aware that Oscar was to be killed.

> I send a few lines hoping they will find you in Dakota and feeling better than I do.
>
> I feel very lonesome and I know you feel the same, but it won't be long before we are together again and we won't part any more, will we, my pet? You need not be surprised to see me inside of a month but you must not worry if I don't come until the last of June. Then I will surely come.... Well, dearest, I must close for I have got to set the table for supper and go to bed. I don't know whether I will sleep or not. I went home Tuesday morning and cried all Tuesday night. It woke Krusen up and he said that I must feel awful bad—a d–n sight worse than he did, but I did not say anything. Well, good-bye and write often. This is from
> Your Intended Husband,
> Orlin E. Larriway.

Not only was this letter dated one day after another witness reported having talked to Larriway in Hawarden, Iowa, where he and Hattie were living after leaving Dakota, but it is twelve days after he and Oscar and Johnnie Krusen had left Osage City. Perhaps the letter had actually been mailed in Iowa, where Larriway had gone to look for a house. Certainly it had been mailed at least a week after Krusen was already dead. Was Larriway's conscience bothering him, causing him sleepless nights with sobs loud enough to wake the dead? Was he hallucinating? Or was he merely trying to shield Hattie from knowledge of what he had done?

Perhaps the original plan had been for Oscar to believe that she would return to Kansas after he had found land to homestead, whereas she, unbeknownst to him, intended to stay in Dakota and wait for Larriway, who would return to marry her after he had helped Oscar and Johnnie get established on a claim. I am not at all convinced that Hattie knew that Larriway meant to kill Oscar and abandon Johnnie. It seems to me that Hattie might have been willing to desert her husband and even her child for her lover, might even have hated an abusive Oscar enough to wish him dead, but it's hard to believe that any mother would be callous enough to acquiesce in having her five-year-old child abandoned with a made-up name at a railroad depot in a strange country, hundreds of miles from home. (Johnnie, by the way, was taken in by relatives soon after being found at Newton.) Perhaps when Larriway came back to Dakota, he told Hattie that all was fine with Oscar and Johnnie down in Kansas and she lived happily with that belief and with her new husband during their time in Iowa.

Larriway's guilts—murder, deception, betrayal—must have weighed heavily on him. Perhaps that is why he put up no defense at this trial; he deserved punishment and he knew it. So did the jury and so did the crowds that flocked into the courthouse. The jury began deliberations at 4:00 p.m., 11 May 1886, only a few days short of a year from the time the murder was committed. Less than half an hour later they were back in the courtroom, having decided in twenty-two minutes and one ballot that Larriway was guilty.

According to the account in the *Walnut Valley Times*, "The prisoner sat upright and quiet, making no show of emotion whatever. The verdict in Larriway's case meets with universal commendation. While the evidence is circumstantial purely, it has all the force that eye witnesses could give had the murder been seen. The case is most remarkable."

Remarkable enough that residents of Sycamore and Chelsea townships, even though time has clouded facts and details, have, in the legend of Dead Man's Hollow, preserved the story and commemorated the site.

A postscript: El Dorado's other newspaper at the time, the *Daily Republican*, was much less objective in its coverage of Larriway's trial. In fact, the reporter seems early on to have decided that the defendant was guilty, and his biased dispatches from the courthouse were written in florid prose. Upon being led from the courtroom after sentence had been pronounced, Larriway turned and pointed at the reporter, saying "You're the reason they found me guilty." That young journalist was a cub reporter on his first job. A few years later William Allen White, as editor of the *Emporia Gazette*, had become the most celebrated journalist in America, and that early purple prose had matured into a style that was rewarded with two Pulitzer Prizes.

Twenty-four

The Brandley-Rinard Murder Case

O ne of the tales I remember hearing from my father when I was growing up was about the Brandley house near Matfield Green and the bloodstains on the porch that could never be washed off or painted over—they always showed through, no matter how much scrubbing or how many coats of paint. The blood was from a young cowhand who had been shot, supposedly because of his relationship with one of the Brandley daughters. The house of Captain Henry Brandley was actually a mansion, especially considered so in the Cassoday–Matfield Green area, where a two-story house, much less one with a tower on top, was a rare display of conspicuous opulence. The story of the bloodstained porch is well known at Cassoday, but when I go ten miles farther north and ask people at Matfield Green about it, I get either blank stares or disapproving looks. It seems that the story, if it is known there, is not given credence, just as the story about horse thieves being lynched at

Sycamore Springs is brushed off by Cassoday residents. Maybe that's because the Brandley mansion was not built until a couple of years after the killing took place. But what are a few facts to get in the way of a good legend? Here are the facts:

On a Sunday night in July 1898, Frank Rinard was murdered on the Brandley Ranch, about three miles south of Matfield Green. Two trials failed to convict Harry Brandley, the man accused of the killing; the first, held in Cottonwood Falls, ended in a hung jury, while the second, conducted in Emporia following a successful motion for a change of venue to Lyon County, resulted in acquittal. To this day the murder is unsolved. Unsolved murders were certainly not without precedent in early-day Chase County (down here in Butler County we were always told that if you wanted to kill someone, do it in Chase County because you'd never go to jail; Chase Countians say that the reason no one ever gets convicted of murder up there is because they only kill people who need killing), but the Rinard case is one of the more sensational, in no small part because of the prominence of the family involved. It is also one of the more memorable because of its recounting in William Least Heat-Moon's *PrairyErth*. Now, over a century later, a recently discovered 1899 document adds one more twist to this already tangled tale. First, here's a little background on the family, then I'll give a summary of the murder and the trial, and finally I will discuss the document (a report from a private detective hired to infiltrate a cattle-theft ring) and comment on its relevance to the case.

Before going on, maybe I should point out that, as a shirttail relative (a very tattered shirt with a very long tail) of the Brandleys, I claim some right to discuss the case without appearing to be a gawking outsider. Here's the Brandley-Hoy relationship, such as it is: My great-grandfather, William Hoy, had a sister who married a Diller. They had a daughter who married Uncle Phil Parsons (so called by everyone in Cassoday), and they in turn had a daughter, Roberta, who married Bud Brandley. Bud was the son of Bob Brandley, who himself was the younger brother of Harry Brandley, the man who twice stood trial for the murder of Frank Rinard.

Captain Henry Brandley, Harry's father and Frank Rinard's employer, was one of the largest landholders in the central section of the Flint Hills. A Swiss immigrant, he had settled in Chase County in 1859, then joined the Ninth Kansas Cavalry during the Civil

Captain Henry Brandley. (Chase County Historical
Society).

War, which involved service in Kansas, Missouri, Arkansas, Colorado, and Wyoming. His duty in the West included escorting the
newly appointed governor of Utah to his post and guarding various forts and trails. In 1863 he was wounded in the left arm and
side in a skirmish with Utes near Fort Halleck, Wyoming. He was
mustered out in 1866 and the next year married Katherine Patterson, who died in 1869. A year later he married Elizabeth Romigh,
a union that produced eight children. Brandley's land claim, taken
along the Southfork River a couple of miles southeast of Matfield
Green, was fertile ground, and his farming and ranching enterprise

prospered, as did his ventures into real estate and the lumber business. One of the wealthiest men in the county, he was a founder of the Chase County National Bank, and he served as both a representative and a senator in the Kansas Legislature. Brandley died at age seventy-two in 1910, three years before Elizabeth. Both are buried in a small family cemetery not much more than a hundred yards from where Frank Rinard was shot.

Heat-Moon notes in his account that Brandley carried his prosperity openly, which undoubtedly contributed to feelings of resentment among some community members. Ruth Meyer, perhaps exaggerating slightly for effect, once told me that whereas Cassoday society seemed relatively democratic (among cattlemen there, only Fred Burk lived in a two-story house), Matfield Green, in keeping with its English name, had three baronial families with the rest of the population filling the roles of peasants. To be fair, she said, the Roglers and the Crockers didn't put on any airs, but with the Brandleys it was a different matter, which helps to explain Heat-Moon's conclusion. At the time of the shooting, the eldest Brandley child, Clara, lived in Oklahoma Territory with her husband, E.A. Hildebrand, a financially venturesome man who, having made and lost one fortune, secured a homestead in the Cherokee Outlet land run of 1893 (a year after he and Clara were married). He then leased out his farm and indulged his entrepreneurial inclinations by successfully developing local telephone exchanges in northern Oklahoma and southern Kansas, eventually selling out to Bell Telephone. The second Brandley child, Maud, was married to Ed Crocker at the time of the shooting, and Daisy, the fourth, would later marry his brother Arthur, young men well on their way to becoming two of the most prominent cattlemen in Kansas and the nation. In future years the Crocker Brothers would run large ranches in Texas and Arizona, in addition to their sizeable Flint Hills holdings in Chase, Butler, and Greenwood counties.

Thus family members, both parents and siblings, were not pleased when the fifth child and fourth daughter, Pearl, became enamored of Frank Rinard, one of the hired men. Brandley girls were meant to be the wives of ranchers, not of mere cowhands. This displeasure was made explicit, according to trial testimony, but young lovers are not easily deterred, and Rinard's attentions, if unwanted by the family, were welcomed by Pearl. It was reported at the trial that she

Elizabeth (Mrs. Henry) Brandley. (Chase County Historical Society).

was observed going for walks with Rinard, dancing with him at community dances, and looking at photographs while seated beside him on his bed in the ranch hands' quarters.

On the night of the shooting, 24 July 1898, the Brandleys' first son (and third child), Harry, then twenty-four and living on the Farrington Ranch near Jack Springs some three or four miles west of his parents' home, had been visiting his mother and picking up his laundry. Captain Brandley, having earlier in the day checked on the progress of the wheat threshing underway on his farmland, was apparently at his land and loan office in Matfield Green. After dark,

Pearl Brandley. (Chase County Historical Society)

and about an hour after Harry was said to have left about 9:00 p.m. to return to Jack Springs, Frank Rinard trotted into the barn-yard, his day's work complete, and began to unsaddle his horse. Inside the Brandley house Elizabeth Brandley was putting away some fresh milk, brought into the house by another hired hand, Cecil Richards, while she and Harry had been talking. Bob Brandley, Harry's only brother, had ridden in from Matfield Green, eaten some supper, and was sitting on the porch. Over at the site where the Brandley's new, two-story mansion was to be built, and west of the barn where Rinard was unsaddling, Daisy Brandley was talking to Arthur Crocker, who had come to pay court.

A single shot, a loud roar from the direction of the barn, broke the stillness of the evening. From this point on, confusion reigned. Shortly after the shot Mrs. Brandley's voice was heard screaming, "Someone's been shot! Is it Bob?" Her younger son reassured her of his safety, then joined Arthur and Daisy in rushing to the barn where they discovered Frank Rinard, bleeding from a head wound. Bob and Arthur carried the body to the porch, where Rinard presently died without ever regaining consciousness. A hired hand was sent into Matfield Green for a doctor, who arrived at approximately 10:30, about half an hour after the shooting and at about the same time as Captain Brandley, who was returning home from his office in town. About two hours later, a little after midnight, the creaking sound of a gate being opened and the hoofbeats of a running horse were heard and the captain and one of his employees, John Knowles, went to investigate. Knowles suggested pursuit, but the elder Brandley pointed out that by the time they had caught and saddled a horse, the rider would be long out of earshot.

The next day at the inquest the doctor testified that Rinard's assailant had been slightly above him, perhaps on horseback while Rinard was standing on the ground, and had fired from a distance of between a half yard to a yard. Or the killer could have been in the loft of the small barn where Rinard was unsaddling. That same morning, 25 July, the south gate out of the Brandley yard, the one nearest the Farrington Ranch (where Harry Brandley was living), had been found open, but later testimony would establish that this particular gate was often left unclosed. Bob Handy, one of the Brandleys' hired hands, said that when he arrived at the Farrington at one in the morning to tell Harry of the shooting, he had found him asleep in bed. At the inquest Harry was asked to produce his pistol, a Colt .44, which proved to have been recently fired, with one shiny cartridge and five dull ones in the cylinder—he said that he had shot at a wolf (i.e., a coyote) the previous Thursday. There was also the suggestion that Harry was angry with Rinard because of his attentions to Pearl. Although all the evidence produced at the inquest was circumstantial, nevertheless Harry Brandley was arrested for the murder of Frank Rinard and was bound over for trial.

At the end of that trial, held in Cottonwood Falls, the county seat, in March, 1899, the jury was deadlocked. One newspaper reported that the first ballot was six to six, although by the time of the final vote only one juror stood between Harry Brandley and a rope. When prosecutors attempted to mount a second trial in Chase County, they were unable to seat an impartial jury. Thus Brandley's request for a change of venue to Lyon County was granted, and his second trial was convened on 14 May 1900. (Because court records of both trials are missing, information comes from newspaper accounts in the *Chase County Leader-News* and the *Emporia Gazette*.)

The circumstantial evidence that formed the state's case was greatly damaged by the judge's ruling to exclude all references to any unfriendliness that may have existed between Brandley and Rinard because of the latter's perceived courtship of Pearl. That left prosecutors the difficult task of proving a murder case without a motive. One witness, W.H. Dosier, testified about a conversation he had held with Harry Brandley wherein he, Dosier, asserted that if Captain Brandley had offered a reward for the killer, as he had done for two other recent murders near Matfield Green, neither of them involving his ranch, an employee, or his son, then suspicion would not have settled on Harry. Further, Dosier reported that Harry had replied that if his father had done what he should have done, then "the damned dog would have been left lying in the hog lot where they found him." Another witness, Cecil Richards, the hired hand who had brought the fresh milk into the house while Harry was talking with his mother, claimed to have heard Harry say "I'll fix him," but did not know who was being talked about. Perhaps the most serious remaining bit of prosecutorial evidence, and that not very solid, was the one shiny cartridge found among the five tarnished ones in the cylinder of Brandley's recently fired revolver.

The defense, for its part, put up a number of witnesses who said that many men in the Matfield Green community carried sidearms and that many of those weapons were .44 caliber. Other witnesses testified to hearing Harry's mare, Roxy, which had a distinctive running-walk gait, leaving the Brandley Ranch about 9:00 p.m. Bob Handy told of going to the Farrington Ranch and rousing Harry from sleep about 1:00 a.m. to tell him of the murder. He also stated that Harry had fired a single shot at a coyote the previous Thursday. When Mrs. Brandley took the stand, she spoke of her conversation with Harry, of mending some clothing for him while they talked, then of hearing a shot about an hour after her elder son had left.

She heard, she said, a gurgling sound and called out in fear that her younger son, recently returned from Matfield Green, might have been shot. Once reassured of his safety, and learning that Rinard was the wounded man, she instructed Bob and Arthur Crocker to carry him to the porch. There she felt for a pulse and found none. She also sent Frank Calvert, another hired hand, for the doctor. Defense lawyers then called a number of witnesses who questioned the credibility of W.H. Dosier. Next they recalled Cecil Richards and questioned him as to why his testimony had changed from that which he had given at the preliminary hearing, thus calling his veracity into serious question. Captain Brandley took the stand and averred, as had others, to the amiability that existed between his son and Frank Rinard. He spoke of the hoofbeats that had been heard about 12:30 and stated that he had then gone to the barn to check on the horses, including Bender, Rinard's horse. None was missing.

The final witness for the defense was the defendant himself, who, according to the newspapers, "made an excellent witness and created a favorable impression on the jury." He gave an account of his activities on the day of the murder and repeated his feelings of friendship for the victim. He left on Roxy, he said, about 9:00 p.m., going down the south lane and closing the gate, then riding southwest across the prairie to his home, arriving there a little before 10:00 p.m. He told of being informed of the murder by Bob Handy, of going to Ed Crocker's house the next day, then of testifying at the inquest and, at the request of the magistrate, going back to Crocker's to get his pistol for the jury to examine. He told of buying cartridges in Cottonwood Falls and of shooting at a coyote the previous Thursday (as previously reported by Bob Handy). He carried the gun, either on his belt and or in a saddle scabbard, to kill dogs and coyotes that sometimes troubled the three thousand cattle in his charge. In refuting the testimony of W.H. Dosier, Brandley claimed that he was responding to malicious gossip that his father, in leaving the body of Rinard on the porch, had been less than humane. Harry said that a lot of "dirty dogs" were impugning his family for a perceived lack of respect in their treatment of the body, whereas by law Rinard should have been left in the barnyard until the coroner arrived, but that instead they had carried him to the porch to try to care for him. Concerning the murder, Harry's final words of testimony were: "I was not on Father's place when Frank was killed. I was at home in bed—and I did not shoot him."

On 21 May, a week after the trial began, Chase County Attorney J.T. Butler made his closing argument, followed by three attorneys for the defense (I.E. Lambert, T.P. Cochran, and John Madden), with the final appeal for the state made by A.L. Redden. At 5:15 the case was sent to the jury, which took only forty minutes to return an acquittal. Upon hearing the verdict, Harry Brandley, according to the *Emporia Gazette* reporter, put his head on the table and cried, then stood with "tears streaming down his face, shook hands with each juryman and thanked him for his decision."

Acquittal meant that Harry Brandley could never again be tried for the murder of Frank Rinard, and no one else was ever arrested for the crime. Someone got away with murder—but who? Wayne Rogler, whose grandfather had come to Chase County in the later 1850s at the same time as Captain Brandley, once told me that people around Matfield Green were sure that the killer was in the courtroom when the verdict was delivered, but was it Harry? His father? Or his mother?

In 1994, while doing research for *Riding Point: A Centennial History of the Kansas Livestock Association*, I found in the files of the Kansas Livestock Association office in Topeka an intriguing document that, although not conclusive, nevertheless casts even further suspicion on Harry Brandley as the killer of Frank Rinard.

Sometime during the summer of 1899 the KLA, officially organized in Emporia five years earlier for the purposes of combating cattle theft and protesting the high freight charges levied by the railroads for hauling cattle, engaged the services of a St. Louis detective agency, Furlong's Secret Service, which sent an undercover agent to Kansas on 13 August. Two months later, in a document dated 16 October, the agent submitted a report of his activities to the "Cattlemen's Protective Association," as he called it. When he arrived in Chase County, the agent circulated the story that he was an out-of-work cowboy who had temporarily left his home area because of some unspecified trouble. The plan was for him to hang around Bazaar (the major cattle-shipping point in the central Flint Hills at this time), find work (late summer being the height of shipping season), and attempt to win the confidence of (and get evidence against) the rustlers. In his role as agent provocateur he urged various suspected thieves to steal livestock, but he was, to say the least, remarkably unsuccessful; the only animal stolen during his two months on the job were a couple of calves he himself had helped to spirit away from the Bazaar stockyards, and the money from their sale was ultimately given to the rightful owner.

On 14 October, his cover blown, the detective met in Florence with a committee from the livestock association and two days later submitted a final written report from St. Louis. Although no evidence was produced against the supposed gang of rustlers, the report does contain a paragraph that Chase County Attorney J.T. Butler might well have found useful the following spring in the second trial against Harry Brandley. The paragraph, toward the end of the report, is essentially an aside. One of the Brandley hired hands had approached the agent in Matfield Green, saying that he had heard from Ed Crocker that the supposed cowhand was really a "protector" from the livestock association. When Crocker was asked about this incident, he said that he had been joking with the Brandley employee.

Soon thereafter this exchange occurred between the agent and Harry Brandley himself, which is quoted in full from the report:

One day Harry Bramley [sic] came to me on the street of Matfield Green and asked me if I wanted a cigar, and I said I didn't care, and we had cigars and talked about different things, and he asked me what kind of six shooter I had. I told him that it was only a common one. He said, "Let me see it." I said, "It is over at the house where I am stopping." He said, "Let us go over and see it." I said, "Come on," and we went over and looked at it. He stayed quite a while and we talked about one thing and another. Finally he said, "I was told that you were a detective." I said, "People are liable to say anything." I told him I had a little trouble at home and had to get away, until my friends fixed it up. He said, "I was told you were working up some evidence in my case, but I was never afraid of you." I said, "You never heard of my asking any one a word concerning your case did you?" He said, "No." I told him that I never thought or cared anything about it, and that if he did kill that man he had a good cause for doing it. He said, "*You or I or any other man could be placed in a position where you would kill a man*" [italics added]. He said he did not have it in for any one particular, but the lawyer who prosecuted him. He said that this lawyer had made him out in his talk to the jury lower down than any one could be. He said that if he was convicted he was going out of the court house right there as he had a six shooter and would use it to go away; that he had made up his mind not to go to the penitentiary; and that if he was acquitted he would wear the six shooter out over the lawyer's head there in the court room.

Granted, Harry Brandley's statement to the detective is not an unqualified confession of guilt, but on the other hand it is certainly no ringing protestation of innocence. I find it interesting that the tone of his response to the assertion from a relative stranger that he had good cause to have killed Rinard is not that of an indignant categorical denial, but instead is dispassionate and philosophical, almost acquiescent. Furthermore, he makes explicitly clear that he, or anyone else, is in fact quite capable of killing another man. Moreover, he establishes beyond doubt his proclivity toward violence against those he believes to have threatened his honor and reputation. He is willing to face death (from the return gunfire with which law enforcement officials would certainly have met his own, had he attempted to shoot his way out of the courtroom) or the miserable life of a fugitive rather than accept the punishment that would have resulted from a guilty verdict. Finally, he openly threatens revenge, in the form of a pistol-whipping, against the prosecutor who he thinks has maligned his reputation. Consider that the impugning of the honor of the Brandley family name, as represented by the perceived courtship of his sister by a hired hand, was exactly the provocation that the prosecution had advanced as the motive for the killing of Frank Rinard, whose very death seems itself to have tragically embodied the feelings of retributive violence that Brandley obviously harbored. Admittedly, even in the hands of a skillful prosecutor this quasi-confession might not have been enough to have gotten a verdict of guilty, particularly considering the circumstantial nature of the evidence, but it certainly would have made the task of the defense attorneys much more difficult.

Toward the end of his account of the Brandley-Rinard affair, Heat-Moon states that, "looking at all the evidence, it's difficult to believe that Frank Rinard's murderer was not in the courtroom when the clerk read the verdict, but to conclude that the killer was the man acquitted is much harder." It seems to me that the Furlong report makes it a lot easier, although not conclusive, to think that it was Harry Brandley who pulled the trigger.

Back to the bloodstained porch. Even though those stains were on the small house the Brandleys lived in before their big house was completed, still my father's belief that the mansion was somehow cursed was reinforced in his mind by the fact that a few years after the death of Captain and Mrs. Brandley, when financial reversals had resulted in the loss of much of the family's holdings, the mansion, for no discernible reason, burned to the ground one day while the occupying family was away. Even more eerily coincidental, on the day that Harry Brandley, having died at a relatively young age (officially from heart failure, but many thought from self-ingested poison), was buried in the family plot mentioned earlier, the small house where he was living at the time of his death also burned to the ground, again for no discernible reason.

Whether guilty or not, Harry Brandley led an uneasy life after the death of Frank Rinard. Dad said that on Saturday nights when Harry would come down to Cassoday to play cards or dominoes at Al Gennet's barbershop, he always sat with his back to the wall.

Twenty-five

The Murder of Robert Clark

Here in the cowboy country of the Flint Hills we've had our share of Old West violence. When I was growing up in Butler County, we used to look northward with awe at all the stories of gunplay coming out of Chase County. Later on I learned that people up there thought that Butler County was a pretty wild place. But our neighbors to the east in Greenwood County had their share of frontier excitement as well. One of the legendary crimes over there was the murder of Robert Clark, said to be the first man to bring a family to settle in what is now Greenwood County.

I first heard the story of Robert and Mary Ann Clark back in the early 1980s, from Becky Lindamood, if I remember correctly. A few years later her mother, Zenith, who is a repository of Greenwood County history, wrote an article about them for *Kanhistique*. The tale of Clark's death, reputedly the first murder in the county, and the subsequent fate of his killer is ultimately a lesson in true humanitarianism; Mary Ann's religious impulses were obviously those of New Testament forgiveness, not Old Testament retribution.

Mary Ann Connor, the first white woman to live in Greenwood County, had married Robert Clark in Illinois in 1847, seven years before they moved to Kansas. They settled first in Leavenworth and came to Greenwood County four years later. Three of their seven children were born in Illinois, the rest in Kansas. As natives of Massachusetts (Robert) and New York (Mary Ann), the Clarks were active abolitionists, and, although their Flint Hills homestead was far from John Brown country, Greenwood County, with both free-state and pro-slavery settlers, was not immune from the factional strife of Bleeding Kansas. In fact, one of the leaders of the southern sympathizers, Washington Petty, lived just south of the Clarks. Petty was captain of the company of home guards that had been established for protection against American Indians, and Clark was one of the lieutenants. Tension arose over whether or not to hoist the American flag at a Fourth of July celebration (Clark won the argument and it was flown), and the ill will intensified when Clark accused Petty of planning to commandeer the home guard unit for the southern cause.

Then South Carolina seceded and the Civil War began. Clark immediately joined the Union Army, while Wash Petty aligned himself with Border Ruffians from Missouri. As far as I know, he did not ride with Quantrill or Bloody Bill Anderson, but he nevertheless became acquainted with some pretty nefarious characters. He also harassed Mary Ann Clark by filing a claim for the Clark property on which she was living in Robert's absence. Clark was discharged in 1864 and immediately filed suit against Petty, successfully winning back title to his land. Petty's grudge against Clark was exacerbated a year or so later when he thought, wrongly though sincerely, that Clark had smashed the gravestone of Petty's wife, who had died during the war. (I have also heard that it was the tombstone of his parents that Petty accused Clark of defiling.)

Soon after the grave-marker episode, Petty departed Kansas for Texas, where he became reacquainted with some of his fellow border guerillas. Distance did not ameliorate his grudge against Clark, however. Accounts vary in the details, but in May of 1866 Petty rode some eight hundred miles north with from one to three of his wartime companions. Petty hid at the side of the Clark house

Pioneer house in Greenwood County. (Greenwood County Historical Society)

while his friends called out from the front, asking directions to a neighboring farm. Robert and Mary Ann had each been holding one of their one-year-old twin sons when the query came, and as Robert stepped out onto his porch to point the way, baby still in his arms, Wash Petty shot him in the back and killed him. Mary Ann saw Petty as she ran out onto the porch and cried out: "For God's sake, Wash Petty, you have killed my husband. Don't kill me and my children." Without saying a word, Petty turned and rode off, heading back to Texas.

Mary Ann was devastated, widowed by an act of violence that left her with seven children to rear all by herself. But she was strong and a woman of faith, blessed with compassion and a capacity for forgiveness worthy of sainthood. John, the eldest son, was sixteen when his father was murdered, and Mary Ann made him swear on the Bible, as she did with each of her other four sons as they reached that age, that he would not seek to avenge Robert's death by committing murder on Wash Petty.

Despite a five-hundred-dollar bounty on his head, Wash Petty made his escape, and nothing was heard of him for six years; he was thought to have died. But in late 1872 a Greenwood County rancher, William Brazel, just returned from buying cattle in Texas, told John Clark that he had seen Petty near Waco. Early the next year John headed for the Brazos, but Petty was gone, reportedly in Mexico. John stayed in Texas, working on farms and ranches, all the while remaining alert for information about the whereabouts of his father's murderer. Two years later John happened by chance to meet one of Petty's sons, who told him that his father had a farm near Austin. John worked his way south, located the farm, and actually spoke with Petty, without, of course, identifying himself. True to the vow he had made to his mother, young John Clark made no attempt to harm or apprehend Petty, returning instead to Greenwood County and notifying the sheriff, who started legal proceedings to bring Petty back to Kansas for trial. Then John returned to Texas so that he could keep an eye on the fugitive.

Twelve years after Robert Clark's murder, the Greenwood County Sheriff arrested Wash Petty and brought him back to Kansas to stand trial. The trial itself was sensational, with Petty's old pro-slavery friends loudly asserting his innocence. One even went so far as to declare (to a newspaper reporter, not under oath on the witness stand) that Petty had been captain of a Union military company, apparently referring to Petty's command of the home guards before the outbreak of the war, and denied that Petty had been a bushwhacker during the hostilities. Where the money came from is unclear, but Petty's attorney is said to have received fifteen thousand dollars for his work, a very large sum for the times. It was money wasted, however, for on 18 May 1878, Petty was convicted and sentenced to be hanged.

Petty's attorney, T.L. Davis, working hard for his client, appealed the case and won a new trial. But to no avail—almost exactly a year later Wash Petty was again found guilty of first-degree murder. After another futile appeal, which went all the way to the Kansas Supreme Court, Petty was sent to Leavenworth to await his fate.

That fate, however, was to be a natural death many years later, not one at the end of a hangman's rope. But for the merciful intervention of Mary Ann Clark herself, Wash Petty would have been executed. Mary Ann learned that after his flight from Kansas, Petty had reformed. He had remarried and his new wife in Texas was struggling under the burden of trying to raise four young children, much as Mary Ann had had to struggle to raise her children alone after Robert's death. The thought of the suffering of this innocent woman and her children troubled Mary Ann so much that she went to Topeka to plead with the governor to pardon Wash Petty. His response was that it was her own eyewitness testimony that had damned Petty in both trials. If she had herself identified the murderer, how could she expect the governor to pardon him? Mary Ann searched her memory and her soul and found a way out of this dilemma. At both trials she had indeed identified Petty as the killer, but in neither had she been directly asked by the prosecutor if she personally saw Petty pull the trigger. Thus she could claim, without being accused of perjury, that she had not actually seen Petty shoot her husband. She drafted a petition of clemency for Petty and carried it throughout the county, getting, as Governor George Glick noted in his pardon, issued 22 February 1883, the signatures of "nearly every citizen in Greenwood County."

The wording of the pardon stated that the accused was found to be "not guilty of the offense." But Wash Petty knew better, and he knew that Mary Ann Clark knew also. Her suffering, and his, had made a different and better man of him. Upon his release he immediately set out for his home and his new family, but instead of going directly to Texas, he swung by the Clark farmstead on his way. As he approached the house, he saw Mary Ann sitting in the doorway in nearly the same place as her husband had stood when Petty had shot him seventeen years earlier. Petty stopped at the gate, took off his hat, and said in words to this effect: "Mrs. Clark, I would not be bold enough to come closer to you, but I want you to know that

I am truly sorry for the grievous wrong I have committed against you."

"Yes, Wash Petty, you are guilty," she said.

He continued: "I am unworthy of your forgiveness, and I am humbled by and grateful for what you have done. I have come to thank you for my wife and children."

Mary Ann replied: "You may indeed thank them, and not me, for your pardon by the governor. Wash Petty, go your way to your innocent family, and may God help you to be a good husband and father. Go in peace."

The mercy shown by Mary Ann Clark is a lesson from which we all could learn.

Twenty-six

Dave Rudebaugh, Outlaw

lthough not as notorious as such Old West outlaws as Jesse James or Sam Bass, "Dirty" Dave Rudebaugh was no slouch as a bad man. Born in Illinois in 1854, Dave at age sixteen moved with his family to Eureka, Kansas, which was the address he gave authorities in 1878 when he was arrested for train robbery. According to some sources Dave began his outlaw career in 1873, ranging out from his home base in the Flint Hills to steal horses and cattle in Arkansas, but it was in New Mexico that his prowess as a bad man was fully realized.

I first ran across a reference to Rudebaugh while working with the memoirs of Frank Maynard, who in the summer of 1873 helped a man named Jim Graham move a small herd of good-quality cattle from Missouri to the ranch Graham was starting near Granada, Colorado. When Graham's herd passed near Maynard's home in Towanda on the western edge of the Flint Hills, Frank hired on,

Frank Maynard.

joining John Sullivan as a cowboy with the outfit. The cook and driver of the supply wagon was, according to Maynard, "a smooth faced young fellow" named Dave Rudebaugh, then nineteen years old and setting off from his widowed mother's farm in Spring Creek Township near Eureka in Greenwood County. On July fourth, perhaps after a little too much Independence Day celebrating, Rudebaugh and Graham got into a scuffle that soon turned into a serious fight. When young Dave grabbed an ax, his employer pulled a gun, and only the intervention of Maynard and Sullivan prevented some serious bloodshed.

The drive continued to Granada where, their differences apparently patched up, Rudebaugh stayed on to work for Graham while the other two members of the crew headed back to Dodge City. By the mid-1870s Rudebaugh was back in Kansas and tangling up with bad company. After a few cattle rustling ventures, Rudebaugh and five companions planned to rob the eastbound Santa Fe train between Dodge City and Kinsley on New Year's day of 1878, but a blizzard stopped them. Three weeks later they tried again, not all that successfully.

About two or three miles west of Kinsley was a water tank where the gang tied their horses to a trestle and waited for the train to stop to take on water. But it didn't stop. Instead of seeing this as a bad omen and aborting the plot, the gang decided to go into Kinsley and rob the Pueblo Express when it stopped on its way west. One man was left to watch the horses while the rest of the gang walked to the town. The plan was for two of them to board the engine and cover the engineer and fireman while Rudebaugh and two others would hold up the express car. When they had the loot, they would fire two shots to signal the engine to move on west.

As soon as they reached the depot, three of the robbers held up the brave (one might say foolhardy) night clerk. In response to their demand for money, he told his assailants that it had all been sent out on the eastbound train, the very one they had originally intended to rob. When they demanded he open the safe, the clerk told them that he didn't have the key. He then tried to draw a derringer, but was disarmed.

About that time the train pulled in, but it overshot the platform. The door on the express car was open, but too high for the outlaws to jump into. The baggageman, instead of throwing out the express box as ordered, grabbed his pistol and started shooting. No one was hit in the exchange of about a dozen shots, but the volley caused the two outlaws in the engine, who were expecting only the two signal shots, to jump off, at which point the engineer pulled out of town.

An impromptu posse of townsmen set out on a handcar, not realizing that the would-be robbers were not on the train but instead were hoofing it back to their horses, where they mounted up and headed southwest. When the two local posses (another had set out horseback) failed to catch up, they sent word to Ford County where sheriff Bat Masterson mustered his own posse and moved to intercept the outlaws. He captured Rudebaugh and one other gang member at a cow camp on the Cimarron River southwest of Dodge, the others a few months later.

All the gang served time in prison for the caper, all except Rudebaugh. He escaped punishment by turning state's evidence and testifying against his erstwhile companions. Dave had managed, however, to steal the only loot in the botched robbery attempt, a canvas coat with brass buttons. It was pure poetic justice, then, that the express company sued for the coat's return and Dave, in jail at the time the papers were served, was forced to give it up.

After that, Dave made a brief attempt to go straight and headed for New Mexico Territory. At Las Vegas, which was much more lawless than Dodge City had ever been, Rudebaugh worked for a time as a policeman before reverting to train and stagecoach robbery. The head of the outlaw gang he joined was John Webb, a Las Vegas lawman who had earlier been part of the Kansas posse that had captured Rudebaugh after the Kinsley robbery. (Interesting, isn't it, how many of those Old West toughs seemed equally comfortable on either side of a badge?) When Webb was arrested for murder because, as marshal of Las Vegas, he had (not exactly in the line of duty) killed a man he disliked, it was Dave Rudebaugh and his gang who held off the mob intent on lynching Webb. Shortly after that, Dave and a friend killed a jailer while attempting to break Webb out of jail.

To escape the murder warrant at Las Vegas, Rudebaugh went to Fort Sumner, where he joined up with Billy the Kid's gang. Pat Garrett captured him, along with other members of the gang, in December 1880, and Rudebaugh was tried and found guilty of stagecoach robbery and murder. In late 1881, however, he and four others, including Webb, dug their way out of the Las Vegas jail.

There is some evidence that Rudebaugh then went to Arizona Territory before escaping into Old Mexico. According to one version, he met his death south of the border in 1886. After being accused of cheating at poker, Rudebaugh killed two of his accusers and wounded another, but was himself ambushed and killed when he left the saloon. As a warning to other gringos who might think that they could bully the local citizenry, his attackers chopped off his head and stuck it on a pole at the entrance to town.

Another version of his demise is that Rudebaugh escaped, hid out on a Chihuahua ranch, went straight, took a job trailing cattle north to Montana, married, had three daughters, lost his wife, turned to drink, and drifted into Oregon where, in 1928, he died in poverty of alcoholism.

Whatever his mode of departure from this world, this former youth from the Flint Hills was the only man of whom Billy the Kid was afraid. Not a bad epitaph for an outlaw.

Coda: Coincidentally, two other former residents of the Flint Hills figure, albeit tangentially, in the saga of Billy the Kid. Attorney Alexander McSween practiced law in Eureka before moving to Lincoln, New Mexico, where he soon became associated with John Tunstall. Billy the Kid was one of the supporters of (and hired guns for) the McSween/Tunstall faction in the infamous Lincoln County War. Wayne Brazel, the son of southern sympathizers who moved to the Flint Hills in 1856, was born and reared in Greenwood County, although he later worked as a cowboy on a New Mexico ranch. It was there, in 1908, that Brazel shot and killed Pat Garrett, the killer of Billy the Kid.

Twenty-seven

Bank Robbers

s far as I'm aware, neither Jesse James, the Dalton Gang, Pretty Boy Floyd, nor any other outlaw celebrated in Western legend ever robbed a Flint Hills bank, but that doesn't mean that the banks here were immune from stickups. I'm sure there must have been dozens of attempts in the century and a half since the Hills first began to be settled when Kansas Territory was opened up in 1854, but I'll tell about just a few. As is often the case with matters concerning Greenwood County history, I got my first word about the robberies there from Helen Bradford and later learned more from Zenith Lindamood's articles in *Kanhistique*.

Quincy, the hometown of the fastest runner in the world, was a bustling little community back when the nineteenth century turned into the early years of the twentieth. Among its many businesses was a bank, which got robbed twice. The first robbery was a break-in, not a stickup. In the early morning hours of 24 March 1903, a mighty blast resounded throughout the town, the result of nitro-glycerin blowing the safe apart. Although many people were awakened, no one rushed out to see what had happened. The town's physician, Dr. Pusey, who roomed in a building next to the bank, suspected like everyone else in town that the bank had been hit, but, again like everyone else, as the doctor said afterward, he was not about to take the chance of running outside and meeting armed and desperate thieves. This inaction was undoubtedly prudent, as would become evident when the bank at nearby Virgil was robbed some twenty years later. The Quincy robbers most likely had hiked into town, for they made their escape by rail on a handcar appropriated from the Santa Fe depot. The take amounted to around fifteen hundred dollars and two gold watches. Two suspects in possession of four hundred dollars and a safe-cracking kit but no gold watches were detained in Independence, but without an eyewitness or the physical evidence of the watches, there were no credible grounds on which to charge them. The crime was never solved.

The blast at the Quincy bank destroyed not only the safe but ruined the wooden building as well. Taking a cue from the third little pig in the fairy tale, the owners rebuilt their bank out of brick, and this time they enclosed the safe within a steel vault. The safe was also protected by a jar of "burglar acid," a precaution that prevented a substantial loss of funds when the bank was again broken into during the middle of the night on 29 October 1921. An explosion at 2:00 a.m. woke several Quincyites, including Jess Knowles, who lived directly across from the bank building. When he looked outside to see what had happened, he saw an armed man standing lookout, which made it unwise for Jess to leave his house to seek help. Nor could he telephone the law because the crooks had first cut all the telephone and telegraph lines before breaking into the bank building.

The blast Knowles heard occurred when the safe door was blown off, but the fumes from the burglar acid were so strong that the robbers were unable to get at the contents. A couple of hours later there was another explosion as the thieves tried the safe again, but once more the fumes did their job. The thieves were able only to empty several lock boxes, which contained mainly government bonds and other securities. They made their getaway in a stolen car (stolen from Arkansas City); no one was ever arrested for the robbery. The

Quincy bank, like many others during the Great Depression, failed in 1932 and was never reopened.

The heist at Virgil, which occurred a couple of years after the second bank job in Quincy, was a stickup, and it had serious physical consequences for two local men. About midmorning on 11 January 1923, a large automobile (likely a Paige, although some witnesses said it was a Case) carrying three men stopped in front of the bank. While two remained outside on lookout, the third went inside, pulled a gun, and demanded money—all of it. There were no customers at the time, only two employees, R.J. Atkinson and Lela Dalton. After handing over several bags containing forty-eight hundred dollars in currency, Atkinson, the cashier, and Dalton, a teller, were locked inside the vault. Foreshadowing their later actions, the robbers forced a bystander, Charles Wegley, to help carry the heavy sacks of cash to the car (later determined to have been stolen), one bag of which was inadvertently dropped, thus immediately recouping some fifteen hundred dollars for the bank.

Tossing the money sacks into the car and shoving Wegley aside, the robbers roared out of town and headed south towards Quincy, eight miles away. Atkinson, having opened the vault door from the inside with a screwdriver that was kept hidden there, notified law officers, who at once set up a roadblock in Quincy. Two miles north of town, however, the speeding driver wrecked the getaway car, forcing the three thieves, loaded down with the bags of cash, to take off on foot. They soon heard the sound of a buzz saw in the woods along the Verdigris River and surprised Bundy Johnson and Pike Ditty cutting firewood. Adding kidnapping to their tally sheet, the robbers commandeered the two men and Johnson's open-topped Dodge touring car. Ordering Johnson to drive, the outlaws again headed toward Quincy on a route that took them right past the Johnson home. After the ordeal was over and Johnson was safely home, Nellie Johnson said that her reaction when she heard their Dodge car go roaring by was "He knew I wanted some groceries. Why didn't he stop? What's his big hurry, anyway?" Unbeknownst to her at the time, of course, the big hurry was that pistol digging into his back.

As the car entered Quincy, Johnson saw the roadblock but was ordered to put his foot to the gas and smash through. Someone manning the barricade recognized Bundy and Pike, but too late to stop posse members from shooting. Pike Ditty was hit by a shotgun blast and slumped in his seat, apparently dead. Sixth-grader Howard Johnson, Bundy's son, saw his father driving fast past the school and ran down to the roadblock to find out what was happening. Running back to the school he shouted out to Edna Ditty, "My dad's been kidnapped by bank robbers and yours has, too!"

A few miles east of Toronto one of the wheels on the Dodge broke down and the fugitives abandoned the car with the apparently dead Pike Ditty still slumped in the seat. Johnson was coerced into service as a pack horse, lugging the heavy money sacks on his back through the rugged blackjack oak country. The rope holding the bags together cut into his shoulders, causing them to bleed as the bandits viciously urged him on with kicks and curses.

Meanwhile, once the robbers were completely out of sight and earshot, the severely wounded but still alive Ditty dragged himself out of the car and to a nearby house. The farmer took him to a doctor, who was able to remove the shotgun pellets from his arm and leg but could not get all of them out of his neck. By 9:00 that evening Pike was home, but Bundy was holed up in a cave with his abductors, who were attempting to avoid the posse out searching for them. A day or so later they had moved south through the thick scrub timber nearly to Fredonia. On Highway 96 they stopped a Buick car with four men in it. All four of the fugitive party crowded in and headed west toward Fall River. There they met some accomplices in a Ford, so the three robbers transferred their loot and themselves, leaving Johnson with the men in the Buick and telling the driver to turn around and head to Fredonia without stopping or looking back.

It was two days before Bundy Johnson finally got home after his abduction, bruised and bloody from the chafing ropes and heavy money bags. Two men were apprehended in connection with the robbery and kidnapping, one in Bartlesville, Oklahoma, and the other in Parsons, but neither one was identified by either Johnson or Ditty. Many people think that the two suspects were recognized by their victims, but that fear of retribution from the third member of the gang prevented Johnson and Ditty from identifying their tormentors.

Both men carried mementos of their adventure for the rest of their lives, Johnson with scars on his back and Ditty with a shotgun pellet in his neck.

Early-day Elmdale.

I'll end these bank-robbing stories on a lighter note. The attractive native-stone bank building in Elmdale, half a dozen or so miles west of Cottonwood Falls in Chase County, still stands and, in fact, was in use as a bank until the early 1990s. I'm not sure how long before that the robbery occurred or to what extent the details of the story have been altered for humorous effect, but I like the tale. To really appreciate the story, you need to know something about Elmdale. Like Quincy, it was once a vital community, but whereas Quincy today has only a couple of occupied houses and no businesses, Elmdale still has a post office, a church, a grain elevator (open only during harvest season), and Bummie's Grocery Store and Locker Plant. According to the last census some eighty-two inhabitants constitute the citizenry of Elmdale. Many houses are abandoned, as is the old high school building on the south edge of town, and many have been razed, which gives the town an open, airy look. The main street, which is also the northernmost, runs from the Santa Fe tracks on the west to the east edge of town, about four blocks away. North to south the town is about three blocks wide. There are, in other words, some four streets running north and south and three, maybe four, going east and west. If the entire town takes up ten acres I'd be surprised.

It is into this metropolis that our lone intrepid Robin Hood drives his car, parks it (but because, unlike the Virgil robbers, he does not have a lookout, he does not park in front of the bank), walks to the bank, enters the door, demands money, warns the employees not to do anything rash or stupid, grabs the sack of cash, then leaves. The employees wait long enough to be sure he is not coming back, then call the sheriff's office in Cottonwood Falls. By the time a deputy gets to Elmdale, at least fifteen minutes have passed since the bank was robbed, plenty long enough for a thief with a heavy foot to have reached Marion, Morris, Lyon, or Butler county, take your pick, on a paved highway. Or he could be well out onto the back roads of the surrounding Flint Hills pastures in a car that can't be identified because no one at the bank saw him drive it into town.

But then, no one saw him drive it out of town, either, because this bewildered bank robber was still wandering the streets of Elmdale when the sheriff arrived and arrested him: He couldn't remember where he had parked his car.

Twenty-eight
Bootleg Whiskey

liff Cannon once told me about his grandfather, Willis Naylor, and Arthur Crocker sitting on Arthur's front porch north of Matfield Green in 1917, drinking some of the whiskey one or the other of them had made and lamenting the fact that Kansas had recently gone bone dry. Willis was nonplused when his drinking companion mentioned that he had voted for prohibition. Why? he wanted to know. Because, said Arthur in all seriousness, some people, like me, can drink and handle it, but others, like you, can drink but not handle it. Willis cussed Arthur a little, then in the ensuing silence both men continued to sip quietly from their glasses as they watched the evening shadows gather on the Southfork River to the east. Cliff didn't say how the logic of Crocker's reply sat with his grandfather, but the two men remained friends and they, like the rest of Kansas and the Flint Hills, drank illegal whiskey for years to come.

What they were like in their younger days I don't know, but based on some of the stories they told, I have a feeling that my father and my uncle were not always the near-teetotalers they were when I knew them. I don't recall ever seeing Uncle Marshall take a drink, not even a beer, and about the only time Dad ever had a beer was on the Fourth of July after Countryman's rodeo. At the end of the day when the winners were all paid off and most of the crowd had dispersed, a dozen or so people (chute help and some of Countryman's friends) would gather under the elm trees in Wilbur and Virginia's front yard. There would be a tub full of beer on ice, Budweiser and Blue Ribbon, usually, and even my sister and I would be allowed a swallow and, once we were a little older, our own bottles. (The taste of that Bud, by the way, which is as fresh on my tongue today as it was in the 1950s, is still my benchmark for beer; the closest anything comes these days is an icy Carta Blanca.)

Dad did keep a little snakebite medicine (his term) in a cabinet above the refrigerator. I remember once after he had been to the Kansas City stockyards a new bottle got added to the stash, although I never knew of a single drink that was ever poured in our house when I was growing up. I remember finding a couple of half-filled pint bottles, one in a manger and another in a shed, at my grandparents' place a quarter of a mile north of where we lived, but when I got old enough to understand something of the prostate cancer that killed Dad Hoy, I realized that he had been most likely keeping his painkiller hidden from Grandmother. (He also smoked, rolling his own or packing a pipe with Prince Albert or sometimes Velvet, a vice that neither my father nor uncle acquired. Uncle Marshall, unlike Dad, did pick up the coffee habit, but he drank his from a cup instead of saucering it with cream like Dad Hoy.)

Kansas was dry, so Dad Hoy must have gotten his whiskey, if it was store-bought, from someone who had been to Kansas City, or maybe from my uncle in Oklahoma, who flew pipelines and occasionally set his Piper Cub down in the Big Pasture in the middle of our section. The bottles I found had no labels, the brown whiskey in them most likely having been decanted from a fifth. White lightning is clear, at least as far as I know from my limited experience (the only drink of bootleg I ever had was at the Chicago rodeo, brought up by some bull rider from Arkansas or Alabama or one of those southern states who either didn't like store-bought or else thought there would be no bars in Chicago). The nearest my young crowd came to illegal alcohol at Cassoday was trying, unsuccessfully, to get Bill Young to open up her beer joint after hours to sell us a six-pack. But from some of the tales I have heard, there must have been quite a few drinkers around town back when Dad and his brother were in their youthful prime.

Cassoday itself never had a population of more than three hundred, with probably about two hundred more living on farms and ranches in the surrounding countryside. The town supported at least ten bootleggers during Prohibition. Assuming the average family had a husband, wife, and three kids, that means that there were a hundred heads-of-household in the Cassoday community. Further assuming that it was the men who did most of the drinking and all of the buying, that means that there was one bootlegger for every ten customers. Obviously the market was good.

As far as I know, most of the local bootleggers were retailers of booze, not makers. Some seem to have bought bootleg whiskey in bulk, then redistributed it into smaller bottles for resale. I have heard of one enterprising wholesaler in Greenwood County who made several trips each month to Missouri and southeast Kansas to buy whiskey. In order to elude the law, which he did successfully, this dealer enlisted the aid of a horse, hauling him thousands of miles back and forth in a trailer with a false bottom. He was never stopped.

Like my father did, many Cassoday stockmen who had been to the St. Joe or Kansas City stockyards would bring back a couple of bottles for themselves or their friends. Bob Vestring recalled that one time in his younger years when he was at the yards, another cattle owner from El Dorado asked if he could fill up the empty space in Bob's suitcase. Fill it up he did, so full that young Bob could hardly carry it. When the two men transferred onto the Doodlebug (officially called the Little Ranger, a self-contained Santa Fe engine-freight-and-passenger car that made daily runs from Winfield to Kansas City), the older man, also staggering under the load, had to lift Bob's suitcase onto the overhead luggage rack. I'm told that one Cassoday cattleman, Dewey Harsh, used his regular cattle-selling trips to the stockyards to supplement his income by bringing back good-quality legal Missouri whiskey to resell at Cassoday and at El Dorado, the county seat, where the clientele was somewhat more elite than at Cassoday. Although not legal, bringing bottles back from the stockyards was unquestionably better than the practice of a Chase County cattleman who, Pat Sauble told me, would often "drink a whole load of cattle" before he got back to the Flint Hills.

At Cassoday, Hattie Palmer, whose Palmer House was the local hotel and boarding facility, successfully made and sold her own liquor. It seems to have been consumed more for the power of its punch than for the subtlety of its flavor, being known locally as "sheep dip." Frank Cannon was less successful as a distiller of spirits. When I was a freshman in high school, a couple of the seniors crawled back into the cave at Jack Springs in the Farrington Pasture four or five miles north of town. In the first chamber of the cave they found some pieces of rotting board and several glass bottles, apparently left there decades earlier by a bootlegger. No doubt the pure spring water flowing out of the cave had seemed right for the enterprise. Years later, talking to Cliff Cannon about the old days around Cassoday, I learned that his father, Frank, was probably the one who had left that paraphernalia at Jack Springs. Frank knew the area well, having cowboyed all over Chase, Greenwood, and Butler counties, and he figured that the remote area of southern Chase County would be a pretty good place to set up a still. But before he went into production, he heard that the revenuers were onto him so he busted up his own still, throwing the boiler over the side of a rocky canyon and hiding the bottles in the cave. Cliff also told me that there was a woman who lived on the old Cross place south of town who made bootleg, but he couldn't recall her name.

I'm not sure what the situation was in other Flint Hills towns, but I'd be surprised if the per capita consumption of alcohol at Cassoday was much if any higher than that of the rest of the Hills. I've heard that Al Gennet's barbershop was the place to go on Saturday nights if you wanted to play cards, shoot pool, or have a game of dominoes. Al also sold illicit beer and spirits on the side. I think that most Flint Hills towns probably had their own version of Al Gennet's, but what undoubtedly enhanced the wild reputation of Cassoday back then was the lake a mile east of town. Built by the Santa Fe Railroad in 1923 to supply water for steam engines and named after a Santa Fe official, Fox Lake had both weekend cabins, mostly owned by people from Wichita, and a clubhouse, open to both lakers and locals, for dances and parties. The dances, I've been told, were lively affairs. Mix the exuberance and touchiness of youth with the natural antagonism of town and country, add a little alcohol, top it off with more males wanting to dance than female dancing partners, and you can usually expect a little excitement.

Fights were common, some of them degenerating into general brawls, like the time Turk and Marie Harsh had gone out to a dance. They liked to dance, and before they had children they would ride horseback cross country from Cassoday to Cedar Point, twenty-five miles one way, to go to a barn dance, stay until the fiddler was too tired to lift his bow, then ride back, reaching home just in time for Marie to change clothes and go teach school (in later years she was my third and fourth grade teacher) and for Turk to change horses and go ride pastures. This particular melee at Fox Lake occurred when their daughter Mary Frances was just a baby and slept in a baby basket during the dance. When the fight broke out, Turk told Marie to get outside and he'd get the baby. Her basket was sitting on a table on the far side of the room, and Turk got knocked down four times before he got there. In order to get outside with the basket and the baby in it, he had to crawl on the floor through the combatants, pulling the baby basket behind him. Just a typical Saturday night dance at Fox Lake.

Then there was the time Dad told me about when a big tough from Wichita jumped up on a table and challenged the room: "I can whip the toughest son-of-a-bitch around!" The band stopped playing, and a circle opened around the table as the crowd melted back to make room for an opponent, should one be brave enough to appear. Into the circle waddled Deke Young on his bandy bow-legs. Deke, eldest (and shortest) of the Young brothers, was, like all of them, a cowboy, but his appearance, slim not muscular, did not much impress the man from Wichita: "Are you the toughest man here?" he asked.

"I don't know," said Deke, looking around the room, "but I'll keep you busy 'til he gets here." Before the man could jump down from the table, Deke reached out and grabbed the calf of his leg, squeezing so hard that, like a twitch on a horse's nose, it immobilized him, bringing tears to his eyes and a quick end to hostilities.

Should the would-be Wichita fighter have depleted his bottle before issuing his ill-conceived challenge, and should he have needed more whiskey to numb the pain in his leg, he could have replenished his supply by calling on Blackie Coffelt. I never knew him, but I've heard my dad tell stories about Blackie, as he did about many of the characters who populated my hometown. Blackie was born Clarence, one of the six children of Thomas and Mary Louise Coffelt, on their farm southeast of Cassoday, located just about where the flats break into the hills. One of his brothers, Ches (short for Chester), was the janitor at the grade school when I was growing up, an easygoing man who chewed Redman and always dressed in khakis, even when he was cowboying, as he regularly did for Karl Harsh. Another brother, Clyde, had the great nickname of Plunk, but I don't know how he got it.

Blackie, however, was so called from his fondness for wearing black. When Ace Lanning (a cousin of some sort of ours from Ohio) first visited Cassoday, the first resident he saw when he got off the train was Blackie Coffelt, dressed in black from his big cowboy hat to his black boots, black pants tucked into the high tops. With his spurs jingling as he walked up to the depot window, probably to check on the arrival of a cattle train, he looked like a Western-movie villain, a formidable figure who caused Ace to duck around behind the depot and cross the street to avoid meeting him head on. When he later became acquainted with Blackie, however, he found him to be easygoing, not at all rough and tough. That's how I remember Ches, too. Friendliness seems to have been a Coffelt trait.

The Coffelts lived southeast of Cassoday on a road that eventually came out at Lapland in Greenwood County, whereas Fox Lake was on the Teterville road, which wound up at Madison, itself an oil-boom town of no little reputation in those days. As I understand it, Blackie bought his bootleg wholesale in gallon-sized containers, placed them in the bottom of post holes in his corral, then gently put posts in the holes and poured in a little loose dirt around them. When Saturday night came, he would lift out a post and the jug, fill several pint and half-pint bottles, replace the jug and the post, then head to Fox Lake. Along the way he would occasionally slow down and toss out one of the filled bottles beside a fence post. By the time he got to the dance, the only whiskey he carried was in his stomach and in his back pocket. But if your own bottle ran dry, you could hop in with Blackie and he would drive back toward the ranch. Dad said that no matter how dark the night, Blackie would stop at a fence post, kick around in the grass a little until he felt boot leather on glass, then stoop down and pick up the bottle he had tossed out several hours earlier.

Let's see, now, at an average of one post every five yards, that would be roughly 352 posts per mile of fence. The Coffelt place is about eight miles from town, and with fence on both sides of the road, there would have been some 5,632 posts with which to mark the locations of bottles. How Blackie knew which post to stop at no one knew; he must have had an unerring radar for whiskey bottles.

Saturday night dances were one thing, but for the other days of the week Cassodayites had some other choices. One was Kate Cannon's cafe. Kate, the sister-in-law of Frank, was married to Pud Cannon, who was killed when he was run over by a steer in the Wichita stockyards. The cafe, located on the southwest corner of the main intersection in town, was a small one, I'm told (I don't remember it), with no tables, just a lunch counter. More bar than counter, most of the "lunches" that Kate served on it came in shot glasses and beer mugs.

Ott and Ruth Meyer ran a filling station and cafe in Cassoday. I don't remember Ott, but Ruth was later a journalist with a keen eye for the human condition. (Their son, Bill, won a solid reputation in the profession as editor of the *Marion County Record*. Recently retired, he is, in my opinion, the last of the old-time country editors in the honored Kansas tradition of E.W. Howe, William Allen White, and Rolla Clymer.) When I interviewed Ruth back in the 1980s, she told me that even though her family had moved to the Flint Hills from western Oklahoma, she didn't realize what a cowboy was until they arrived at Cassoday in the 1920s. The oil boom east of town was in full swing, she said, and the town was a bustling, noisy place. Texas steers were being unloaded in the stockyards all night long, filling the air with their bawling. At daylight the cowboys would start driving the steers to pasture, their bawling replaced by the constant clanking of well casing being rolled off flatcars to be hauled by team east to the Teterville and Scott oil fields. In her first days in town Ruth vividly recalled a be-hatted, be-chapped, be-spurred cowboy galloping up to the blacksmith shop, sliding to a stop, and hailing another cowboy there with a stream of profanity that could be heard all over town. She braced herself for a fight if not a killing, but it turned out to be just one friend greeting another.

Ruth and Ott Meyer.

Ott Meyer's father was a physician. Doc Meyer, according to my father, administered some sort of foul-smelling concoction that saved the lives of most of his Cassoday patients during the killer flu epidemic of 1918–1919. During the anti-German fervor that accompanied World War I, one local man who referred to Doc Meyer as Kaiser Bill found himself first thoroughly pummeled by the patriotic physician (who always insisted that English be spoken in his home), then led to the good doctor's office where his injuries were treated by his erstwhile assailant free of charge. Ott himself had a brilliant mind. I have read some of the letters on current events that he published in the El Dorado newspaper, letters that reveal him to have been a master of wit, logic, and style. But he was content to run a filling station. I remember vividly Ruth's comment about her late husband: "If we had lived anywhere else but Cassoday, he would have amounted to something. But it was just too easy there." Her ambiguous observation was simultaneously praise and blame. Life was good at Cassoday, so good that if one weren't possessed of innate ambition, one would be satisfied with life there and would not strive for temporal acclaim or worldly riches. Ah, the evil of natural abundance, of a time and place congenial to ease and satisfaction, conditions that have caused moralists everywhere to lament the want of want because want necessitates a life of industry, thrift, and piety. (Slaughter the bison and those free-spirited, free-ranging Plains Indians will acquire character and humility by being forced to take up the hard work of farming, made even harder by the arid, acrid soils of their reservations.) Not that Ruth was puritanical and Ott impious. But they did run a good cafe and filling station, and Ott was happy doing just that.

Bill Meyer told me, to my mother's irritation, that when my dad and mother were courting, Dad would pull into the filling station in the car he and Uncle Marshall owned jointly and holler out to Ott, "Fill 'er up!" (Whichever of the brothers used the car was supposed to make sure it had plenty of gasoline for the next driver.) Then, Bill remembers, Dad would hang his left arm out the window and hold out one or two fingers, a signal for one or two dollars' worth. That way he came across as a jaunty big spender, but was simultaneously being both frugal and careful not to leave too much fuel in the tank for Marshall. Mother, who of course couldn't see his left hand, indignantly denied that Dad ever did this, but that just shows how successful his ruse was.

To the bootlegging: Dad said that Ruth sold near-beer in the cafe (she also sold bootleg cigarettes under the counter; loose tobacco and rolling papers were legal in Kansas at the time, but ready-mades were not), but if you wanted the kick of beer, not just the taste, then you could go back into the garage where Ott tuned cars and fixed tires and for fifty cents buy a squirt from one of the oil cans on the workbench. A particular oil can. One filled with straight alcohol. A squirt or two took the near right out of the beer.

Down the street a ways from Meyer's garage was the site of the Green and Kitzelman livery stable. Harry Kitzelman, who was another of the bootleggers in Cassoday, lived about a mile southwest of town on property that was being bisected by a new highway (K-13, now K-177). Out one morning to look over the progress of the road builders, he noticed that one member of the fencing crew, which was made up of inmates of the county jail, was a local, Lessie Cannon (Frank's brother, I think, or maybe an uncle).

In his younger days Lessie had left the Flint Hills to cowboy in the north country. Like all the Cannons, he was a tough hand, and he had spent years riding the rough string on various Montana ranches. Between bad horses, worse winters, and a collection of broken bones, Lessie had to give up the steady cowboy life up north, and he had returned to his home country, getting by with day work on ranches, odd jobs around town, and a little bootlegging on the side. Like Blackie Coffelt, Lessie buried his whiskey in a corral, but he was too much of an old-time cowboy to overdo things in the digging department. Instead of putting his whiskey in big jugs at the bottom of post holes, Lessie just buried individual bottles. And instead of burying them vertically, he dug shallow holes and laid the bottles in lengthwise. Blackie never got caught, but not so Lessie. It seems that a revenuer, walking across Lessie's corral, stepped on the neck of a bottle, tipping the back end out of the ground. I've also heard that Lessie himself, accompanying the agent as he searched the grounds, stepped on the bottle neck that led to his arrest. Whatever the case, a little more walking across the corral unearthed several more bottles, enough to convict Lessie as a dealer, not just a consumer. Without a defensible case, Lessie pled guilty and got sixty days in jail.

Rather than sit inside a small cell all day at a nice time of year, Lessie volunteered for the work detail, which, ironically, involved building fence along the new highway running through Cassoday. That is where Harry Kitzelman found him and engaged him in conversation. Discovering that his fellow townsman had been convicted of bootlegging, and motivated perhaps by professional courtesy, Kitzelman asked Lessie if he'd like to have a little whiskey to help ease the pain of incarceration. Sure enough, was Lessie's response. Then, said Harry, why don't you at the end of the day dig a post hole and leave a post in it, but don't tamp it. I'll come along in the evening and put a pint in the bottom of the hole. Then next morning you can pull the post and get the bottle.

Which is just what happened every working day over the next few weeks. It was, I understand, the happiest two months anybody ever spent in the Butler County jail.

Coda: One time during shipping season Lessie and Blackie Coffelt were left to watch a herd of cattle while the rest of the hands went into the ranch house to eat a typical shipping-day dinner—tomatoes and sweet corn from the garden, home-raised roast beef or fried chicken, potatoes and gravy, and homemade pie. When the other hands had finished and it was Blackie and Lessie's turn to eat, only two pieces of pie were left, one noticeably larger than the other.

Blackie wolfed his dinner down, reached for the pie pan, and took the larger piece.

"What the hell do you think you're doing?" Lessie demanded.

"Getting ready to eat pie," Blackie said.

"Don't you know that it's ill mannered to hog the biggest piece?"

"Well, what would you have done if you were me?"

"Why, I'd have taken the smaller piece," Lessie said.

"Well there you are, you son-of-a-bitch," was Blackie's response. "Help yourself."

Twenty-nine

The Saga of Greenwood City

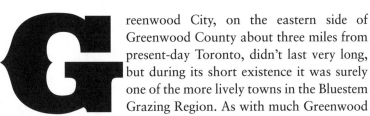reenwood City, on the eastern side of Greenwood County about three miles from present-day Toronto, didn't last very long, but during its short existence it was surely one of the more lively towns in the Bluestem Grazing Region. As with much Greenwood County lore, it was Helen Bradford who first alerted me to Greenwood City and its characters.

During its heyday, from the time it was founded in 1869 by John P. Mitchell, a one-time U.S. marshal, until its demise amid a flurry of lawsuits and legal wrangling five years later, Greenwood City had a population of nine hundred, second only to Eureka, the county seat. The majority of that population was composed of law-abiding, hardworking, God-fearing citizens, and at first Greenwood City was a peaceful town. But about midway through its existence, four residents plunged into the booming cattle market that followed the Civil War and bought three thousand head of longhorns as a speculative venture. With the longhorns came cowboys, and with the cowboys came guns and whiskey and hell raising.

Not that the young Civil War veteran Edwin Walters, who had been sent down to Texas to help bring the herd north, didn't try to civilize his fellow drovers. Walters, a teetotaling school teacher, had taken a portable blackboard along on the trail and would spend the evenings around the campfire giving lessons to the cowhands. You have to wonder how much of the music, language, geography, penmanship, botany, and geology stuck with them, but Walters seemed to think his efforts a success: Later in life he opined that "there is much real manhood in even ignorant cowboys." Based on the account of his life that I read in the second volume of *The History of Greenwood County*, Walters must have been an interesting fellow to be around. Born in 1849 into a slave-holding Missouri family, he became a committed abolitionist after being punished for teaching a slave how to read. At only thirteen he joined the Union army and served until the end of the conflict. He came to Greenwood County in 1870 and held a variety of jobs, at the same time reading deeply in various scientific disciplines. Thus self-educated, he was appointed a U.S. surveyor in 1883 to help determine the boundaries of the Ute Reservation. He later worked as a civil engineer, a geologist, a hydrologist, a mineralogist, and a writer. He owned copper and gold mines in New Mexico and invented a type of plaster that would set and dry in one hour. Now that I think about it, I don't believe that this fellow would have much trouble at all in entertaining a bunch of trail drivers with his portable blackboard.

Civilizing them, on the other hand, was a different matter. Many of the cowboys who had delivered the cattle to Greenwood City were outlaws and desperadoes. These were men with prices on their heads: ten thousand dollars for Kinch West (who is reputed to have buried over five thousand dollars in gold coins somewhere near Greenwood City), four thousand for Jack Tedford, fifteen hundred for Vid Farr, and five hundred for Bill Holliman, who had two aliases—Leather Bill and William the Innocent. I guess that, having committed crimes worth only five hundred dollars for his capture, Holliman would have seemed relatively innocent in this crowd.

Greenwood City became an early focal point for the grazing business that would later characterize the Flint Hills: Texas cattle growing fat on Kansas grass. It became a cow town, although not

Unidentified cowboys at a chuck wagon.

a shipping center such as the more famous cow towns of this era—Abilene, Wichita, Dodge City—but instead a place where cattlemen and cowboys could rendezvous. As a gathering point for cowboys, especially ones on the dodge from the law, it tended to be a bit on the rough side. There were five saloons in town, a number of gambling establishments, a brewery at one edge of town, and a distillery on the other. As one proud citizen remarked, "We are mighty civilized in this here town."

Edwin Walters's efforts on the trail were not entirely wasted, however, for on their return to Greenwood City Bill Holliman asked Walters why there wasn't a Sunday school in town. Because, Walters told him, he was afraid that the cowboys would come there drunk and cause trouble. No problem, was Bill's response, "I'll stay sober in the forenoon of every Sunday, and ask for all the other fellers to do the same. You start it," he said, "and I'll come and Kinch West will come and we'll shoot the first man that misbehaves." But,

Walters protested, you can't have guns at Sunday school. Holliman protested in turn that many of the cowboys were on the lookout for sheriffs and marshals. In the spirit of compromise, Holliman promised that they would keep their guns hidden. In that same spirit 2:00 p.m. was compromised upon as the starting time. Walters had suggested 3:00, but Holliman wanted a morning service because "the boys will want to get drunk in the afternoon." So Sunday school began, attended only by cowboys for the first two or three weeks until the local housewives and farm families realized that there would be no trouble. From then on until the town expired, the Sunday school was a huge success.

One of the most colorful characters of old Greenwood City was Andrew Parks, a young Texas cattleman who would drive longhorns from the family ranch to Kansas for fattening before sending them on to market. As did many Texans in later years, Parks held a sort of dual citizenship, making something of a second home for himself in the Flint Hills, particularly during grazing season. Following one successful selling trip to the Chicago stockyards Parks stopped in at a tailor shop and ordered a new suit made of blue velvet, topping it off with a brightly beaded buckskin cap. To put it mildly, Andrew was not the retiring sort, as was made quite clear when soon thereafter he presided at the trial of John Taylor in Greenwood City.

Now Taylor was a tough hombre. He had been involved in a legally questionable episode a few years earlier when he was appointed one of three guards who were supposed to protect two brothers accused of stealing horses, William and Jacob Bledsoe. While taking the prisoners from one location to another in Wilson County, the group was attacked, supposedly by American Indians who were avenging stolen horses of their own, and the two brothers were killed. Most likely the attackers were white men dressed like Indians, and the three guards were charged with homicide. One was convicted, although the verdict was set aside on appeal. Taylor evaded capture until 1879, fourteen years after the killings, but had the charges dismissed.

At the time that Andrew Parks returned from Chicago attired in blue velvet, John Taylor was one of his cowhands. Parks was twenty-three at the time, Taylor nearly three times that. As soon as Parks hit town, Taylor collected his back wages and, despite his age, got drunk and shot up the town. One of his pistol shots went through the wall of a house, narrowly missing a woman and her baby inside. In fact, the bullet came so close that it passed through her rolled-up blouse sleeve (leaving six holes when she unrolled it), went right through the cradle, and hit a chunk of stove wood. Taylor hightailed it out of Greenwood City, but an impromptu posse chased him west to the Whitlock Ranch where Bill Holliman, perhaps feeling righteous from his Sunday school lessons despite the price on his own head, roped Taylor and brought him back to town.

The trial was held the next day in Sam Sparks's general store. Sparks was justice of the peace, but just as the trial began Andrew Parks strode in, undoubtedly turning all heads, being bedecked in his Chicago finery, and literally pulled Sparks over the counter of the store, which in this instance was serving double duty as the bar of justice. Sparks, apparently knowing his Shakespeare, thought it best to show his valor by muttering something discretionary about court being adjourned until the next morning.

Andrew Parks, after threatening Sparks with a fine for contempt because of his muttering, called the case, swore in the witnesses, and conducted the trial. After hearing the evidence, he commanded Taylor to rise and pronounced sentence: "John Taylor, this court finds you guilty. You deserve a long term in the penitentiary for shooting into a home where there was a woman and a baby. I did not believe there was a true Texan in the world who would endanger the life of a mother or baby. But, owing to your extreme youth, this court places your fine at one hundred and fifty dollars and costs."

Taylor, of course, had already spent all his money on liquor and cards the day before, so Parks loaned him the cash to pay the fine and the court costs. Then he called the real magistrate back to the bench and said: "Squire Sparks, come around here and sign this verdict. You haven't the backbone to fine a cowboy more than ten dollars, but these damned cowboys have got to learn to obey the law in this man's town." Sam Sparks, reassuming his judicial mantle, accepted the money, signed the paper, and dismissed the court. Thus Andrew Parks, with flair and money, defused a potentially difficult situation as well as old Solomon himself might have done.

The demise of Greenwood City was as sudden as its growth. One day in 1874 a homeowner went to mortgage his house to get money for some improvements, and he discovered that he didn't legally own a single square inch of the lot where his house stood. It seems that the town promoter, John Mitchell, hadn't actually had title to the land that he had sold for building lots—it was all officially the property of his young son, David, who had inherited it from his uncle, William Mitchell. The irate citizenry rode John Mitchell out of town on a rail and dumped him on the other side of the Verdigris River. There he camped, claimed the land they dumped him on, built a house, and lived in it until his death many years later.

Within weeks the residents of Greenwood City had disbanded and dispersed. People jacked up their little houses and moved them to some of the other towns in the area: Toronto, Fall River, Eureka. Today nothing at all remains of this colorful frontier cow town of the Flint Hills. Nothing physical, that is, but the town lives on in the memories of Greenwood Countians.

Thirty

A Hunting Tale

Back in the later 1800s, Otis Satchell came to Kansas from Illinois. When he arrived there were no fences, no trees, no roads, no houses. He sat in the wagon and his father rode a horse, but he could hardly see his father because the grass was so tall.

Later on in life Otis moved to Oklahoma where he was the first mail carrier to use a motorized vehicle. But before he did, he experienced one of the most unusual waterfowl hunts you can imagine. Upon arriving in Kansas, the Satchells had camped on a rise between two streams in what is now Butler County. One stream was the Walnut River and the second was in later years called Satchell Creek, named after Otis's family.

One morning young Otis got up at dawn, before anyone else in camp had stirred. It was the fall of the year, the weather still temperate, but cool enough so that the ducks and geese were beginning their southward migrations. As he emerged through the

A.G. "Jim" Young hunting with his dog.

tent flap, Otis saw a big V of geese descending and splashing into the Walnut. Tired of the family's steady diet of rabbit and squirrel, Otis slipped back into the tent and unwrapped his father's double-barreled, muzzle-loading, ten-gauge shotgun. Checking the loads and the priming, Otis hunched down into the tall grass and began to ease his way down the slope to the river, thoughts of roast goose fluttering through his head.

He slowed as he neared the junction of the two streams. The grass was so tall that he didn't have to worry about the geese seeing him, but it was so thick that he could hardly walk through it, certainly not without making so much noise that he was afraid the geese might fly.

Wending his way through the grass, he felt almost like a mole burrowing through the earth and making a tunnel as he went. As he stopped to press the grass down with his left arm so he could see how close he was to the geese, he saw out of the corner of his eye a flock of ducks settling onto Satchell Creek. The two bunches of birds were just a little way upstream from where their respective waterways met. Now he had a dilemma—which was he hungrier for, roast goose or roast duck?

At just that moment, right in front of him, not three feet away, Otis simultaneously heard and saw the most dreaded sound and sight he could imagine. He had disturbed a huge timber rattler, and the snake was mad. Its tail was vibrating a mile a minute and it was poised to strike. All thoughts of a waterfowl dinner instantaneously left Otis's head as he let fly at the snake with both barrels.

But unbeknownst to Otis, the barrels of the gun had gotten plugged with grass seed as he had poked his way through the big and little bluestem, and the blast of gunpowder and birdshot split and shattered the barrels, one flying off to the left, the other to the right.

When the smoke cleared, young Otis saw ducks and geese flying away, but on the surface of Satchell Creek were half a dozen dead ducks and an equal number of geese floating on the Walnut.

I know this story is true, because Grogan Ebberts, Otis's grandson, told it to me, just as he had heard it told at his grandfather's knee. I'll admit I had my doubts at first. How could Otis have lived to tell this tale when there was no way he could have escaped being bitten by the rattlesnake? I asked. He had wondered the same thing, Grogan told me. But his grandfather had allayed his skepticism: "The snake? Oh, he got speared by the ramrod."

Afterword

A couple of miles northwest of Strong City, highway K-177 bisects the old Spring Hill Ranch, more recently known as the Z Bar. Only a few hundred of its nearly eleven thousand acres are visible from the highway, but the spectacular three-story barn and Second Empire–style house on the west side of the road, both constructed from bright limestone quarried nearby, catch the eye. If you slow down to get a better look, you might notice at the end of the driveway an attractive wooden sign proclaiming this property the Tallgrass Prairie National Preserve, since 1996 part of the U.S. National Park system.

Back in the 1970s my feelings about establishing a prairie national park were ambivalent, although a little heavier on the pro-park side. On one hand, I could sympathize with the arguments of the anti-park faction (my parents, after all, were members of the Kansas Grassroots Association), and I would have been upset to have lost the home place to eminent domain. On the other hand, it seemed to me that the eminent-domain threat was pretty remote, and I knew from observation that not all landowners were good stewards. Besides, the idea of a national park in the Flint Hills appealed to my pride of place.

Thanks in no small part to a meeting of ranchers and environmentalists convened by Senator Nancy Kassebaum (R-KS), the park is now a reality. The National Park Service owns about a hundred acres of the Z-Bar, while the remainder (still on the tax rolls) is owned by the Nature Conservancy, which also holds title to another fifteen thousand or so acres of Flint Hills pastureland, including the Konza Prairie Research Natural Area south of Manhattan, one of the world's premier grassland research facilities. Alan Pollom, head of the Kansas chapter of the Nature Conservancy, has noted that only 3 percent remains of the tallgrass prairie that once stretched from Indiana and Kentucky in the east to the midgrass prairie of the central plains, from Texas into Canada, and that two-thirds of that tiny remnant is found in the Flint Hills. Tallgrass prairie, in fact, is one of the most severely threatened ecosystems in the world, more so, even, than rainforest. We should do all we can to preserve and protect the national treasure that is the Flint Hills.

The native prairie is a wondrous thing, so ordinary and yet so exquisite, so tough and yet so fragile, so forgiving and yet so susceptible to human greed. The pastures of the Flint Hills are an infinitely renewable resource. Their bounty of grass and beef can be harvested annually into perpetuity if they are not overstocked and if they are occasionally burned in the spring. But they can be destroyed easily and permanently by those who would ravage them for housing developments or industrial wind factories.

Sadly, the Flint Hills that I and many others know and love may well be coming to an end. The eleven thousand acres of the Tallgrass Prairie National Preserve make up only about one-four-hundredth of the four million acres of native grass in the Flint Hills, and that is not enough, not nearly enough to preserve the beauty and the heritage of the Hills, for those four million acres are under threat. As I write these words in the summer of 2005, bulldozers and backhoes are ripping into thousands and thousands of acres of native prairie grass near Beaumont in Butler County, building scores of miles of roads, digging miles and miles of trenches, and erecting over a hundred giant wind turbines, each of them over four hundred feet tall with propeller blades bigger than the fuselage of a 747 jet airplane. A dozen energy companies are looking at other sites in Cowley, in

Chase, in Wabaunsee, in Morris, in Marion, in Riley—in nearly every Flint Hills county, from south to north. If indeed all or even part of these projects come to fruition, then the Flint Hills will no longer be cattle country, no longer be a haven for those seeking wide open spaces and serenity, but instead will become a giant industrial complex, a scene from a bad science-fiction movie.

The late editor of the *El Dorado Times,* Rolla Clymer, known as the Poet of the Flint Hills for his evocative editorials about the beauty and the bounty of the Hills, once wrote: "The Flint Hills are changeless and unchanging—and have so stood since their limestone ridges first broke from beneath the surface of prehistoric seas. All modern development, the growing complexity of civilization's advance, have surrounded and hemmed them in but have failed to alter their essential character."

Hundreds, perhaps thousands, of these giant wind turbines, however, *will* change the essential character of the Flint Hills, change it beyond recognition. No longer will those of us native to the Hills be able to drive down into them for the restoration of our souls. No longer will visitors from afar, who often arrive in Kansas expecting to see nothing but a flat, monotonous landscape, experience delight in the serene beauty of a vast, unspoiled prairie. The Flint Hills are as near to a sacred landscape as we have. Unlike towering mountains, the Hills do not startle the senses with wild grandeur. Rather, they inspire a contemplative awe, an appreciation of Nature's bounty and goodness, not its harsh spectacle. Theirs is a quiet and subtle beauty, one that allows you to catch your breath, to gather your thoughts, to feel the calmness of, the oneness with, Nature. Perhaps not everyone is immediately capable of appreciating this beauty, but those with eyes to see love the quiet majesty of the Hills with a joy that is almost visceral. Would that those who would exploit the Hills for ephemeral gain had such eyes.

My hope, my prayer, is that this book will not be a valediction.

Index

Wichita, Kans., 8, 123, 226–27, 241, 248, 249, 286–87, 296

Wiggins, Harold, 173–74

Wilcox, Doc, 183–84

Wiley, L.R., 206

Wiley Ranch, 16

Willard, Harriet Evans, 219, 221

Willard, Jess, 219–21, 222

Williamsburg rodeo, 73

Wills, Al, 162

Wilsey, Kans., 199, 204

Wilson, Annie Browning, 16

Wilson County, 297

Wilson, John, 16

Wind factories, 304–305

Winfield, Kans., 44, 129, 190

Wonsevu, Kans., 53, 76

Woods, Bob, 30, 203, 212

Worrell, Sonny, 222

Wright, Jerry, 20

XIT Ranch, 135

Yates Center, Kans., 94, 222

Yoakem, Charlie, 242

Yoakem, Lloyd, 242

Young, Wilma "Bill," 285

Young, Buss, 86, 188

Young, Deke, 86, 188, 287

Young, Frank, 86, 188

Young, Jay, 68, 74, 192

Young, Jim, 86, 188, 194, 301

Young, John, 221

Young, Richard, 192